Patrick Caulfield

The Complete Prints 1964-1999

Alan Cristea Gallery

Patrick Caulfield

The Complete Prints 1964-1999

Foreword by
Alan Cristea

Essay by
Mel Gooding

Compiled by
Kathleen Dempsey

ALAN CRISTEA GALLERY 31 CORK STREET LONDON W1X 2NU
Telephone 0171 439 1866 Facsimile 0171 734 1549

Published by Alan Cristea Gallery, London
to coincide with an exhibition of Patrick Caulfield's prints
opening at the Alan Cristea Gallery on 9 February 1999

All prints photographed by Rodney Todd-White & Son, London
except for 'The Hermit', 'Coloured Still Life', 'Vase on Display',
and 'Wine Glasses' where photographs were provided and are
reproduced courtesy of Tate Gallery, London 1998

Designed by Tim Harvey, London
Printed by BAS Printers, Hampshire

ISBN 0-9534839-0-8

Jacket illustration: 46. **Evening Menu** 1975

Foreword

I have been involved with the publishing of Patrick Caulfield's prints for the past twenty-six years, firstly as an employee and then as a director of Waddington Galleries, and subsequently, since 1995, under the aegis of the Alan Cristea Gallery. My first experiences of his work date however from the early to mid sixties when, as a student, I visited the ground-breaking 'New Generation' exhibitions, mounted by Bryan Robertson at the Whitechapel Art Gallery. Indeed Bryan, who has always admired and championed Patrick's work, wrote the eloquent introduction to the previous Caulfield print catalogue, which documented all his editioned prints from 1964 to 1981. Even before joining Waddington Galleries in the autumn of 1972, I had saved up to buy a copy of *Café Sign*, which I was only able to afford due to Leslie Waddington's generosity in reducing the price from £24 to £16.

My arrival at Waddington's immediately preceded the publication and exhibition of Patrick's illustrations to poems by the late nineteenth century poet, Jules Laforgue. To my mind this book of twenty-two screenprints ranks as one of the most successful and felicitous marriages of text and image in the twentieth century. Laforgue's witty, ironical and melancholy insights into the significance of mundane, everyday objects, as he moves easily back and forth between reality and reverie, find an almost uncanny parallel in Caulfield's attitude to life and art a century later. Patrick regards printmaking as an essentially simple and direct medium and the concision which he achieved in his illustrations to Laforgue captured the tone of the verse perfectly. This body of work represents the quintessential example of his approach to printmaking.

Whereas in his paintings Patrick often works on a grand scale, his prints for the most part do not need to be large, because he is evoking a mood through the depiction of a single object or of a strictly focused domestic scene. Even when he occasionally strays outside the interior setting of the studio, the home, the restaurant or the bar, his subject matter remains domestic and his compositions remain undisturbed by human presence. The traces of human involvement – the discarded napkin, the empty wine bottle – are present but unstated. All is treated as *still* life, but the still-life conjures up the most subtle inflections of mood and emotion. The means of expression is disarmingly and deceptively simple and the chosen technique to achieve his artistic ambitions is always the same. Screenprinting is often disparaged as a bland medium, but this very blandness suits Caulfield to perfection. I once tried to tempt Patrick into trying his hand at linocuts, which Picasso used to create images of comparable immediacy, but he was not to be deflected, and it is a tribute to master craftsmen such as Chris Prater at the now defunct Kelpra Studios and to Chris Betambeau and Bob Saich at Advanced Graphics that they have been able so successfully to convey the subtleties of line and colour which underpin Patrick's desire to entice the spectator into his world of contemplative irony.

Having published his prints for over a quarter of a century I am now excited by the challenge of publishing a book which illustrates and documents all the prints which he has ever made. The launch of this book will coincide both with a selected retrospective exhibition of his prints at our gallery in February 1999 and with a simultaneous retrospective exhibition of his paintings at the Hayward Gallery in London, an exhibition which will also be accompanied by an extensive catalogue.

In an age when networking and self promotion are as important to the advancement of an artist's reputation as innovation and sheer talent, Patrick remains an unwilling participant in the politicking of our all too esoteric 'art world'. Although his work has been collected and exhibited internationally, he has always shunned attention. He continues to make all his paintings and designs for prints in his studio in London, and will never show a new painting or print to even his closest acquaintances before he is totally satisfied that the work in question has been completed. These exhibitions and publications should serve to force him, albeit unwillingly, into the limelight which both he and his art so richly deserve.

Alan Cristea, November 1998

Patrick Caulfield: The Prints

The intelligence is part of the comedy of life Wallace Stevens

Patrick Caulfield's career as printmaker begins in 1964, with *Ruins*, his contribution to a portfolio of screenprints by twenty-four artists commissioned by the ICA, and printed at Chris Prater's Kelpra Studio. Richard Hamilton, whose idea the portfolio was, and who selected the artists, had been one of the first artists to work at Kelpra, in 1962. Having no inhibitions about the use of mechanical techniques or commercial media, he had quickly recognised the wide-ranging creative possibilities of silkscreen printing, and his ICA project dramatically extended its use by artists in this country. The portfolio was exhibited at the ICA rooms in Dover Street in November 1964. *Ruins* was one of six prints subsequently chosen by the British Council to represent Britain at the 4th Paris Biennale in the following year, where it won the unofficial Prix des Jeunes Artistes. Although he made no more prints until 1967, Caulfield had discovered the perfect graphic medium for his work. In conversation with Pat Gilmour in 1975 he said 'I couldn't do a screenprint of my own if I was given a chance. I don't see why it's necessary really.' What he could do, however, was to exploit particular qualities of the medium, and collaborate with master technicians like Prater, and later, Chris Betambeau and Bob Saich, to create images that on a smaller scale matched the conceptual subtlety, the pictorial wit and the visual intensity of his paintings.

Characteristically, it was its capacity to assimilate photography and *collage* effects, precisely those aspects of the new screenprinting processes that so excited Hamilton, Kitaj, Paolozzi, Self and others of the Pop generation, that Caulfield refused to exploit. A note in the 1964 portfolio catalogue had set out the advantages of the medium, among them that 'it lays down a heavier deposit of pigment,' and makes possible a 'richness of colour and body'. These aspects of the medium perfectly suited Caulfield's predilection for linear exactitude and invariability, for immaculately flat surfaces of pure undifferentiated colour, and for uniform densities of hue and tone. It also allowed him to prepare the complete image in his own studio, using acrylic on board or paper, and to develop the subtleties and deviations that the screenprint medium makes possible after that initial, private, creative phase. Above all, for a painter who works slowly, and often on a large scale, the medium was a means to the wider dissemination and exhibition of his imagery: for Caulfield the primary concern has always been to create an impeccable image, a visual proposition lacking the distraction of 'expressive' gesture.

Ruins is a perfect essay in Caulfield's typical reductive early manner. A scatter of grey masonry blocks, cracked and damaged, on a yellow ground that may suggest the desert, with spiky, cactus-like fleshy plants growing round them: a metonym of dereliction that recalls with an extreme economy the Victorian vogue for romantic watercolour images of the ruins of ancient classical or Levantine civilisations, of the kind associated with David Roberts and Edward Lear. Architectural grandeur is reduced to its most basic modular components, cut stones like bricks, whose disposition itself resembles an ensemble of ruined buildings. There is a touch of Shelley's Ozymandius about this image – 'round the decay . . . boundless and bare / The lone and level sands stretch far away' – but it's a light touch: *Ruins* is low burlesque; a mock-heroic tableau.

It introduces, at the outset of his work as a printmaker, what might be called a characteristic *tone*: an anti-heroic take on subject matter that has a history of *gravitas*, or a po-faced presentation of low material, common-place subject-matter, that seems to have pretensions to significance beyond its station, and yet remains resolutely banal. This ironic stance shifts in later work, though the essential subject matter of the prints has remained constant. Behind much of this imagery lies the complicated history of the still-life, with the underlying significances of the genre, its symbolic burdens, its reference to the vanity of human wishes, its inherent melancholia. In his earliest prints Caulfield seems intent upon a radical simplification of the key themes of his painting at that time, a paring down to essentials, an isolation of motif that demands of the viewer contemplation without distraction, what in the practice of meditation is called 'composition of subject' (the discipline of the lone hermit perhaps!). In each case the baldness of presentation begs a question: *what is the meaning* of these jugs, this window, this coal-fire, etc.? Our response may begin in the eye's delight at the brilliance of colour, the magical realisation of space, the immediate readability of image; it quickly complicates, as the mind engages with associations and allusions, with visual ironies, with references to life and to art, and whatever may lie between.

The candle and the half-peeled lemon, the prodigal array of fruit and game, vegetables and flowers, the goblet and decanter, the mandolin, those things painted in a thousand Dutch genre and still-life paintings with such wonderful precision and truth to appearance are more than what they seem: they are emblems and reminders. In Caulfield's early still-lifes, the prints of 1967-71, certain of these classical motifs – wine and water jugs, bowls, glasses of wine – are laconically isolated, appropriated to modernist flatness, reduced to descriptive outline and decorative colour (the only plenitude – sweets in a bowl – is ironic). Sometimes subjects with rich associations in other art histories, other genres, are presented with the same deadpan flatness: the letter, the house in the landscape, the meditative figure, the mirror, the window. We are reminded here of Vermeer (*The Letter/Earthenware*); here of Caspar David Friedrich (*The Hermit*); here of Mondrian (*Bathroom Mirror/Café Sign*/the 1971 *Interiors*); here of Duchamp (*Found Objects/Small Window*); the *vanitas* candle is re-interpreted as an electric light, the musical instrument as a loudspeaker, the cross a necklace crucifix with its beads scattered and lost. In every case the presentation is of an absolute simplicity, the comic-book black line drawing, the uniform planes of colour.

When the Cubists turned to still-life, the lowest in the hierarchy of genres, minimising the importance of their subject matter the better to emphasise the centrality to their concerns of the relation of perception to conception, of seeing and knowing, they unwittingly discovered new and complex destinies of signification and significance for their humble 'pretexts', the bottle, carafe and glass, the pipe, the guitar. Twentieth century art has since continuously utilised these simple recognisable motifs as key devices in formal programmes that emphasised the objectivity of the work, and/or as counters in epistemological play (this latter most famously in Magritte's *Ceci n'est pas une pipe*). Caulfield acknowledges the inexpressive, style-less manner of the Belgian master as a model: 'Magritte not Monet!'. When he points out that 'in the prints, the imagery is not original in terms of art history', that their subject matter is, in an historical sense, *conventional*, Caulfield directs attention to the element of philosophical proposition in its employment. The relative simplicity of the visual effects in the prints, as compared with those in the paintings, with their *trompe l'oeil* trickeries, their false collage elements (doubly deceiving, being made of real paint), their imitation of actual surface textures of mock wood and bogus plaster work, suggests that the prints are less concerned with aspects of what may be called the incidental sociology of the paintings, the depiction of the everyday banal in all its kitschy splendour, than with a sharpness of focus upon the problematics of representation.

Caulfield's simple recurrent subjects, drawn largely from that same repertoire of café, restaurant and domestic objects, are, of course, aspects of his continuous dialogue with the 'essential' high Cubism. That he had thought deeply about its platonic Purist derivatives, as possibly providing a clear-cut schematic visual language apt to his purposes, is evident from several early paintings, in their use of grid patterns and geometric linear devices, and, quite clearly, in *Bottle and Drape* (1962) and *Still Life with Bottle, Glass and Drape* (1964). But it is clear that from early on Caulfield has been most persistently indebted to the uncluttered 'concrete and concise' clarities of Juan Gris's great paintings of 1915 and after, with their incisive decorative colourism and elegant hard simplicities, their coolness of wit and clearness of purpose, and with those conceptual processes behind his painting that Gris described as 'the mathematics of picture making' and the 'physics of representation'. Temperamentally, Caulfield is more at home with such an essentially intellectual art than with the emotional incertitudes and ambiguities of Braque and Picasso even at their most analytic, or with the ludic exuberances of their 'synthetic' cubism. And in the prints Caulfield is almost always at his most cool and reserved, and always at his most elegantly and economically propositional. Among early critics who recognised these qualities in his prints, Barbara Reiss (writing in 1973) was herself elegantly economic: '. . . [they] play on perceptible ironies between surface realities and 3-D illusions, between 'abstraction' and 'representation', between the work-as-fact and its poetic wit about contemporary and historical art and concepts and his own (and others') reproduction of them.'

It was a comic persona of Apollinaire who, in an ironic dialogue, first referred to Gris as 'the demon of logic', and as so often, with a phrase, struck a critical nail on the head. It is to that aspect of the great Cubist's achievement that Caulfield's work responds with such distilled virtuosity in the prints. They constitute a sustained and concentrated engagement with the very problems that preoccupied Gris in his greatest work, the still-lifes of 1916-19. These opposed representation to pictorial architecture, or 'decoration' ('. . . but all painting has always been decoration' he wrote to Kahnweiler in 1921, at a time when his own painting was most abstractly synthetic) and confronted the problematic contradiction between the image as an ordering of the perceived world, an analytical tool for seeing things as they are (which is something known as well as seen) and the painting itself an invented object *in the world*, with its own intrinsic dynamic structure and 'logical' order. 'The logic of a work of art is in its structure,' wrote Gris's friend, the poet Pierre Reverdy, in 1919. 'The moment the ensemble holds together and is balanced, it is logical.'

This play on the first two of Reiss's 'perceptible ironies' can be traced to Caulfield's earliest work, and reflects a temperamental predilection for the impersonal presentation of visual facts, for the autonomy of the object and anonymity of facture, and for pictorial 'logic'. No less than his paintings his prints have a characteristic poise and balance, a pictorial inevitability that comes from a perfect sureness of compositional judgement and control: they maintain with wordless aplomb an impeccable high definition performance. It is a kind of conjuring: Caulfield is the great entertainer of his generation, an undisputed master of visual illusion. The catalogue of his prints presents an astonishing repertoire of cunning artifice. But there is a great deal more to it than that. In art one thing leads to another; *to conjure* is to call up, it is a kind of invocation. The objects and spaces so magically summoned into visibility are imbued with reference and implication, become significant of things not visible; those things for which Caulfield finds such inimitably precise denotations ('It is enough to invent signs,' said Matisse) are laden with connotations, celebratory, nostalgic, ironic, disquieting, comic. The lamps and windows, the deserted restaurant interiors with their sharp-angled geometrics of light and shadow, the billowing curtains, empty coat-stands, vases of flowers, which in the prints of the early 1970s are indicated with such signal – often black and white – economy, are evocations of a world in which quiet dramas of happiness and sadness are played out, dates are kept or unkept, conviviality enjoyed or solitude endured.

Images of familiar things in recognisable places attract inevitable associations, provoke reflection on the emotions they arouse, the values they represent. Those in *Some poems by Jules Laforgue* with images by Patrick Caulfield, the limited edition book, with accompanying portfolios of prints, published in 1973 by Petersburg Press, were prepared by the artist over a period of three years from 1969. Taken together, they comprise Caulfield's most sustained meditation on the inconsequentiality of the everyday, the ineluctable modality of the visible, the inescapable turning of time. They add up to an inventory of absences. Isolating into sharp focus the most banal objects, 'contemporary' style coat-hooks, a plain wall-clock, a menu, kitchen unit doors, a glass of water, etc., he presents them (they are things from their own time, they bring the poems into the present) as items of the furniture and accoutrements of the life of the self-mocking poet/lover, locked by *ennui* and indecision into a ridiculous solitude in hotel rooms, cafés and public gardens, ever-conscious, as evenings fall and chances of ecstasy are missed, of mortality:

Ah! until nature has pity on us,
I'll take my life monotonous.

She left yesterday. Perhaps I mind?
Ah yes! So that's what hurts!

As winter comes on

There's nowhere to sit down, all the benches are wet;
Believe me, it's all over once again,
All the benches are wet, the woods are so rusty,
And so many horns have sounded ton ton . . .

'Laforgue' wrote Hugh Kenner, 'was first of all a *role*.' Recognising this persona, Caulfield creates the sets, the lighting and the props for the melancholy drama enacted in the poems. Like the best stage designers his sets signify even in the absence of the actors: a wrought-iron balcony balustrade imitates the rollers breaking on the distant unseen coast; the bare branches uplit by sodium lights against a violet nightfall take on the colour of rust; the railings hasten diagonally to top left to measure the passing of the hurrying unknown lady of the avenue. *Some poems* is an Eliotesque masterpiece, reminding us of the great poet's own debt to Laforgue, having precisely the dandyish aplomb, the Baudelairean bravura in the face of the spiritual and material paucities of modern life, of the writer of *Prufrock and Other Observations*:

The lamp said,
'Four o'clock,
Here is the number on the door.
You have the key,
The little lamp spreads a ring on the stair . . .'

Perhaps in reaction to the extreme economy of the Laforgue images, and also to the clear-cut austere black and white elegance of *Black and White Café* (1973) and of the series of six prints that closely followed it, Caulfield began, in 1974, to complicate the imagery of his prints. The process begins with *Jug* and *Jar*, of that year, whose vaguely Mediterranean setting suggests also a shift of mood. The early printed work, as we have seen, was animated by a playful-ironic art-historical referencing, often quite specific, and the prints of the early 1970s had continued these games, with droll allusions to Bridget Riley (the interiors with striped wallpapers of 1972, one of which contains what is, surprisingly, the first of the pipes in the prints), a homage to Braque (*Two Whiting*, also 1972), and subtle references to geometric abstraction in the black and white series of 1973. In the two 1974 prints, for the first time, colour bleeds from the surround into the image, a cubist-derived device that Caulfield has continued to use ever since as a means to demonstrate the fictitious nature of the printed image, and to show that a single undifferentiated colour may simultaneously serve both decorative and descriptive purposes, can at once magically define image and ground, create the illusion both of a form and of a circumambient fictive space, and assert the objective actuality of the printed plane.

The mood-change is confirmed in the so-called 'Provence' series of six *Garden with Pines* prints, which follows in 1975. In these, we may feel that Caulfield is drawing directly on a particular experience of a real place, and discovering more than enough to beguile the eye and the mind in the diversity and complication of his re-constructions, in the virtuosity of his inventions. Each of these prints is a variation on a theme, in which the foreground objects, in each case treated quite distinctively, are set against a constant figure, the tangled pines beyond the window, for which the same stencil was used. In each case the border colour spills into the image, but in every print in a quite different way. Thus behind the lamp (whose shade has a sheer-silk effect created uniquely on every copy by a smearing of inks: a jokey comment on the contemporary vogue for prints with hand-coloured interventions) there is light thrown into the trees with pale green variegations; a blue sky is glimpsed through the trees in *Signature Pots*, and a dawn light in *Rosé Bottle*, palely illuminating the napkin and empty bottle of last night's supper (the label is the first of only two such photo-collage effects in the prints; it opposes to the sky and twisted pines a subterranean architectural counter-rhythm); several hot reds describe the sunset intensity of *Evening Menu*; in *Terracotta Vase* the sky is the same hue as everything else in the image. Ringing such changes is something printmaking processes make possible, but in this case Caulfield's play with the image, though obviously quite different, brings to mind Picasso's reduction method linocuts, in which an image is revealed and complicated by successive printings of a progressively cut single block. (Remarking this at the time, Alan Cristea, Caulfield's print dealer at Waddingtons, made a gift of a linocut set to the artist. As far as is known it was never used.)

The complication of the imagery in the prints continues to increase from 1976 through 1978, culminating in *Picnic Set*, (1978), with Caulfield making ever more complex demands upon Chris Prater at Kelpra. In a series of extravagant images Caulfield found in the medium itself, and in his own delight at the wonderful diversity of things that are encountered in what Randall Jarrell called 'the dailiness of life', more than enough material for his research into the nature of the visible world and the problematics of its representation, and for his enthralling demonstrations of the relation of imitation to sign, and sign to reality. Creating a graphic imagery utterly his own, both comic and witty, at once ironic and celebratory, naturalistic and decorative, documentary and symbolic, he finds less occasion for ironic reference to other art.

The still-life, however, continues to provide the essential theme, with its signifying richness, its historical functions. *Still Life Ingredients* (1976), brings together pot, jug, and other kitchen implements with onions, tomatoes and vegetables: ingredients both formal and thematic, for art and for life. In a typical visual pun the red pots in *Glazed Earthenware* (also 1976) are printed in a glazed ink. In the former the light throws the daytime shadows of leaves over the ensemble; in the latter the utensils throw their own shadows of the evening: in both, the sign of time. In *Bananas with Leaves* (1977), the apple-green apple-tree leaves that throw blue shadows over the bananas are of the border colour bled into the image, transformed into 3-D relief and creating depth of field by an edging of darker green: flat colour become form by sleight of hand; the eye deceived into contradictory readings, colour as fact, colour as fiction. With *Picnic Set* (1978) the series comes to a glorious climax in the most complicated image of all. The *gravitas* of the genre has already been comically subverted in the three *Sausage* images of the same year: salami *vanitas*. *Picnic Set* presents us with a radiant holiday image: the light streams down from top right through the laden vineyard on to the table prepared for an *alfresco* picnic lunch. The photo-collage labels are windows on to the scene at large (in what is a marvellously ingenious implied version of the ever-receding image), the white spots on the red plates are counter-pointed by the red spots on the glasses, the mottled shadows defined by the sunlight beam are fragments of the greater vineyard shade. That shaft of sunlight is the phenomenon of a moment. Life, it is said, is not a picnic; but even picnics must come to an end.

After the exuberances of these prints of the mid-late 1970s, Caulfield has returned to an imagery that has become progressively more simple, schematic and direct. This begins with the images of jars and pots of 1979-80, whose printed textures, imitating hand-made papers, mocked the vogue in American printmaking at the time for the real thing. These are beauties of graphic economy, drawn with consummate skill, in which the vessels are set against here a window, here a stone step, here a doorway on to a Chinese vista of mountains, all suggested with the quickest of gesture or simplicity of line. (The beautiful *Fruit and Bowl* is the odd-man-out in this suite, its bowl and drapery and fruit in radiant colours suggesting Cézanne done into Matisse.) The process continues through to the suite of *Jugs* (and the *Pitcher*) of 1981-82, in which the now-familiar technique of merging the colour of the spatial background with the colour of the object form is brought to new heights of stylish sophistication. The manner of the later prints is established in these brilliant decorative images, which manage to be at once capricious and monumental.

In two major series, the *Wall Plates* of 1987, and *White Ware Prints* of 1990, the light that streams from top left in *Picnic Set*, and which is in that image a crucial element in an elaborate scenario, is reduced to the most beautifully precise sign in images of startling abstract refinement. Caulfield's abiding preoccupation with light is a component of his deepest philosophical and thematic concerns. For light is the very element of the visual, it is the determinant of colour, it discloses space. To consider visual representation and its paradoxes is to contemplate before anything else the phenomenon of light. In these later prints, the ellipses of spotlight, the sharp-angled chevrons of white through windows, the thrown light that catches the white pots in the stark paradox of *a white silhouette*, serve not only to exemplify the power of pictorial illusion and artifice to trick the eye and the mind into perception and conception, but as potent metaphors. There is more to them than meets the eye. The light that illumines things is a messenger of time; time lives in space. Within these correlatives we measure out our lives. These images are saturated with time, the obsession of the melancholic. If we are tempted to think there are grander themes than those essayed in these elegant propositions, then we should remember again that these were the preoccupations of all the greatest artists of still-life. The realities of which they are such potent reminders are perennial; no artist of his generation has contemplated the comedy of life with greater intelligence, wit or courage than Patrick Caulfield.

Mel Gooding, November 1998

Notes and references

Caulfield's remark is quoted by Pat Gilmour in 'Kelpra Studio: The Rose and Chris Prater Gift' (London, The Tate Gallery, 1980). His exclamation 'Magritte not Monet!' occurred in conversation with the present writer. Gris is quoted from his lecture *On the Possibilities of Painting* (1924), and from a letter to Kahnweiler in 1921; Apollinaire from *This Evening the Cubists will Open Their Exhibition* in *L'Intransigeant* on 10 October 1912; Reverdy from 'Self Defence' (Paris, 1919): I am indebted to Christopher Green's Introduction to 'Juan Gris' (Whitechapel Art Gallery, London, 1992), especially his essay, *Gris's Objects*. Barbara Reiss's essay appeared in Studio International, December, 1973. Hugh Kenner is quoted from 'The Pound Era' (Berkeley and Los Angeles, 1971).

The number preceding each title indicates the catalogue raisonné reference

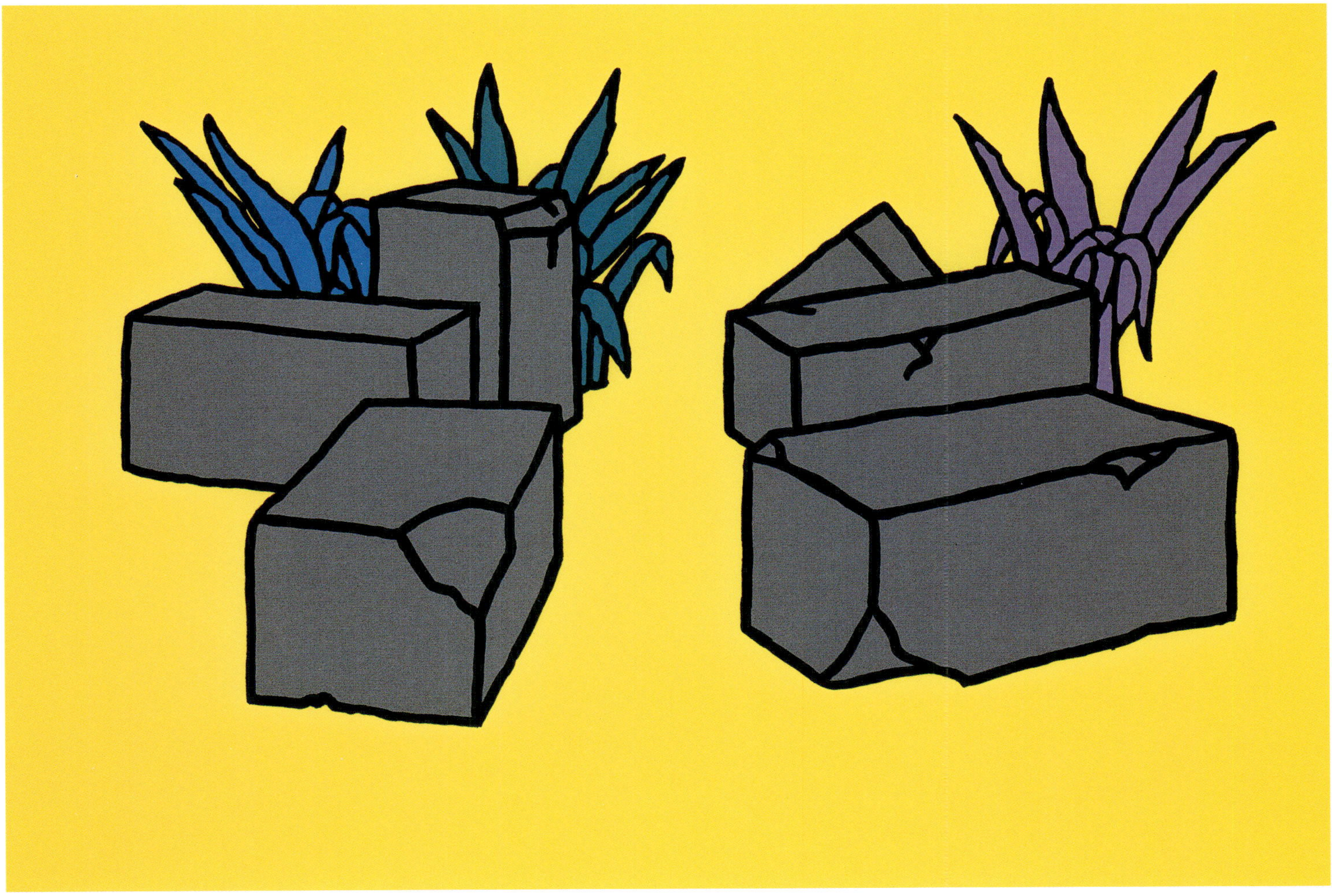

1. **Ruins** 1964

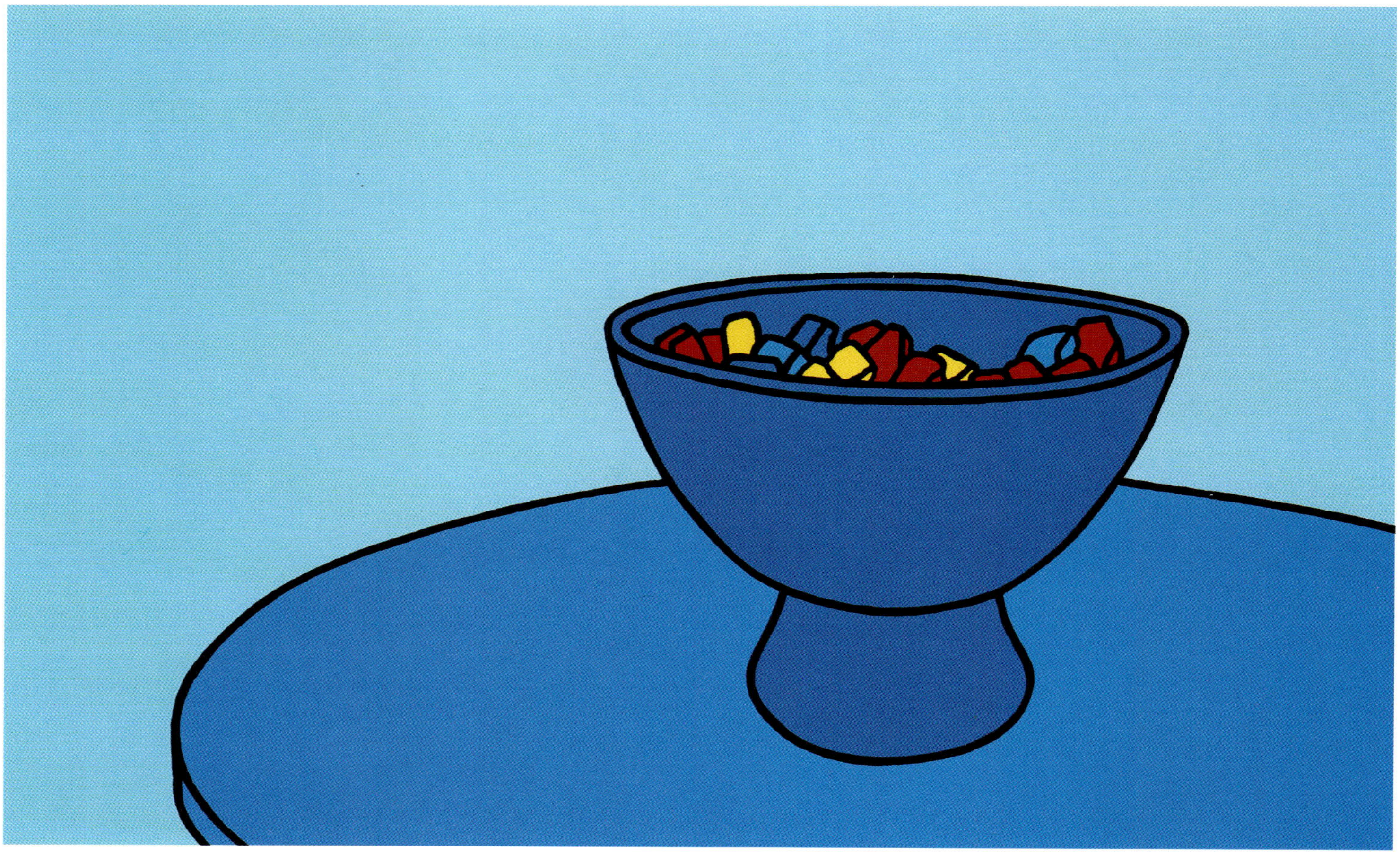

5. **Sweet Bowl** 1967

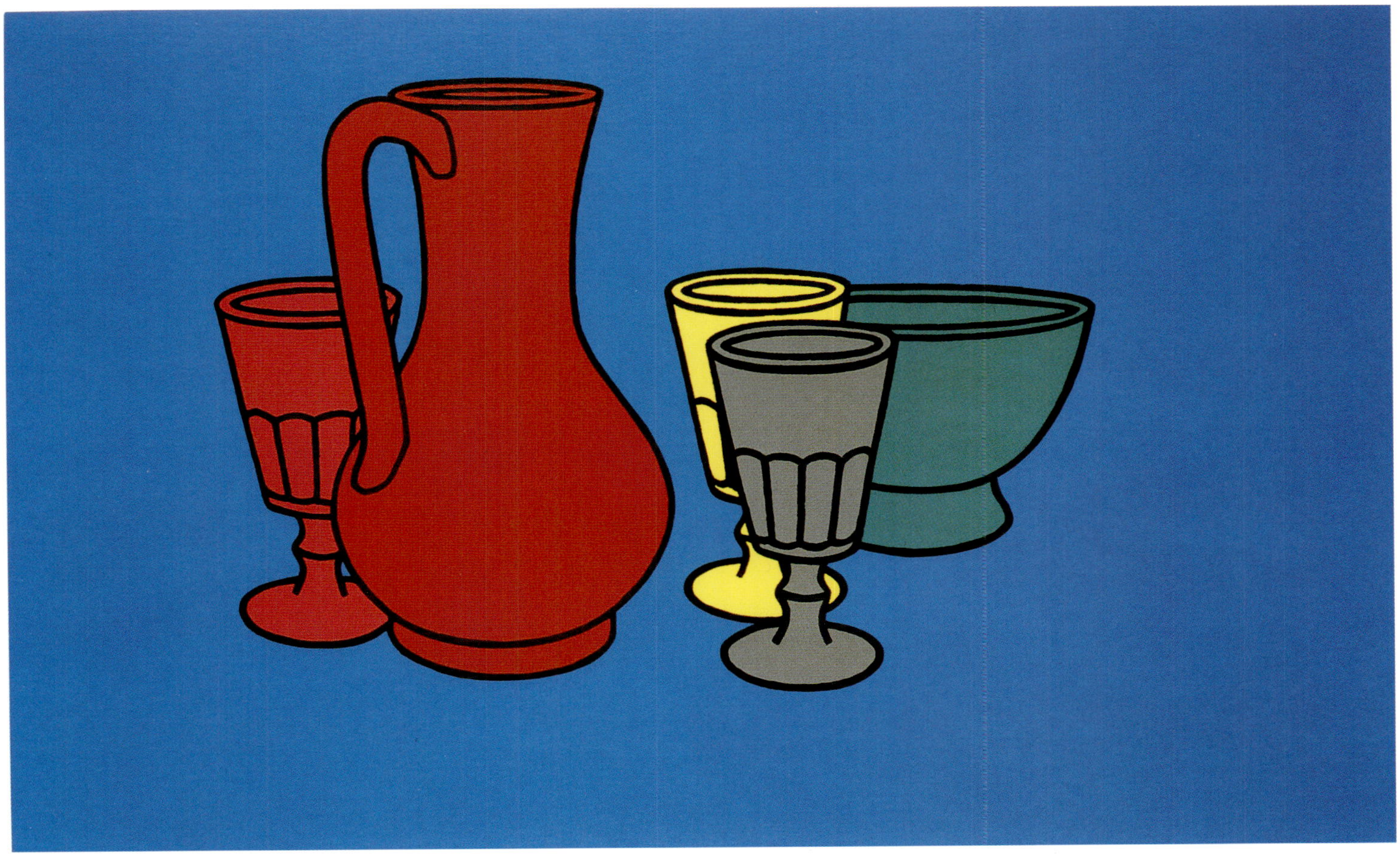

7. **Coloured Still Life** 1967

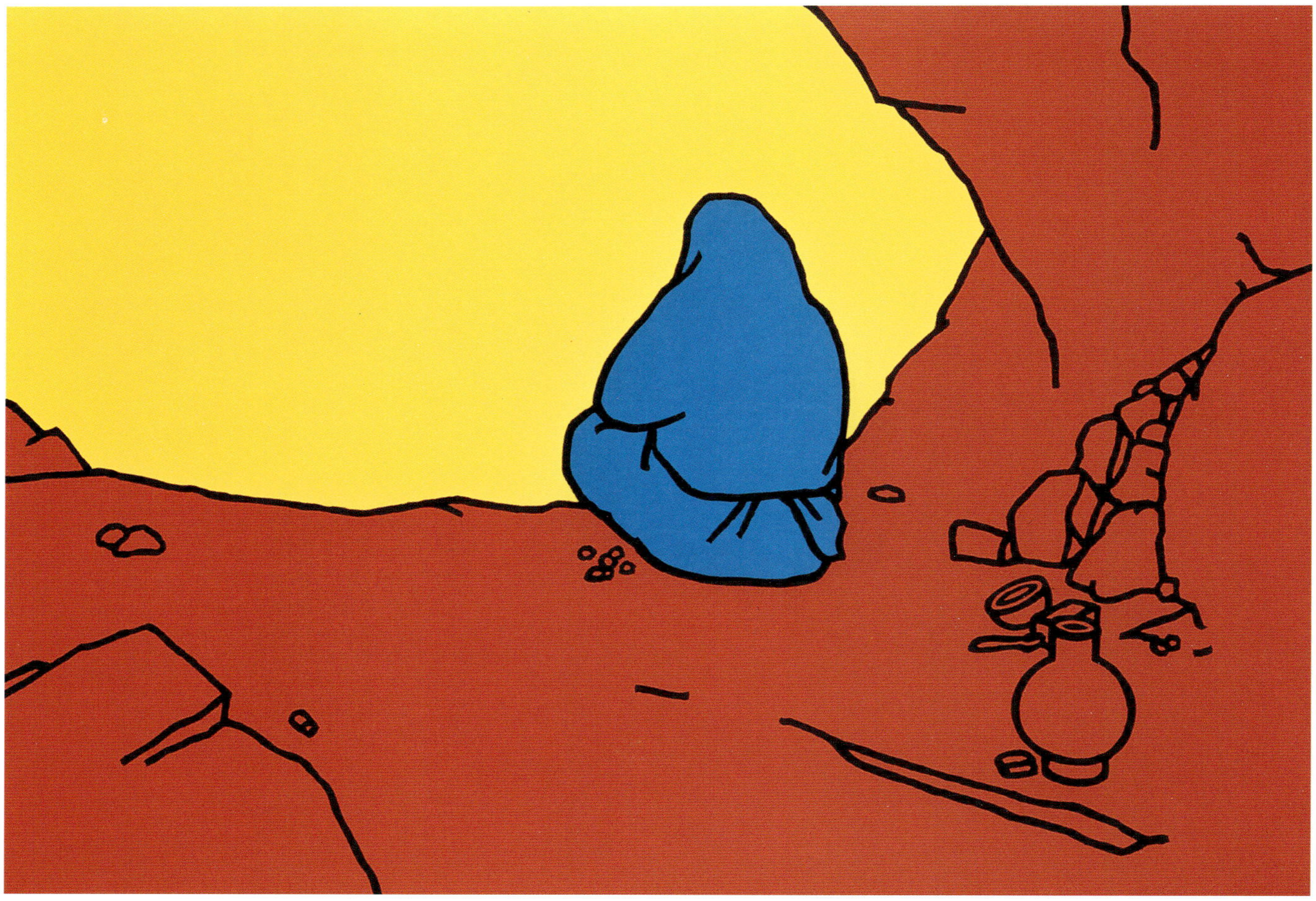

2. **The Hermit** 1967

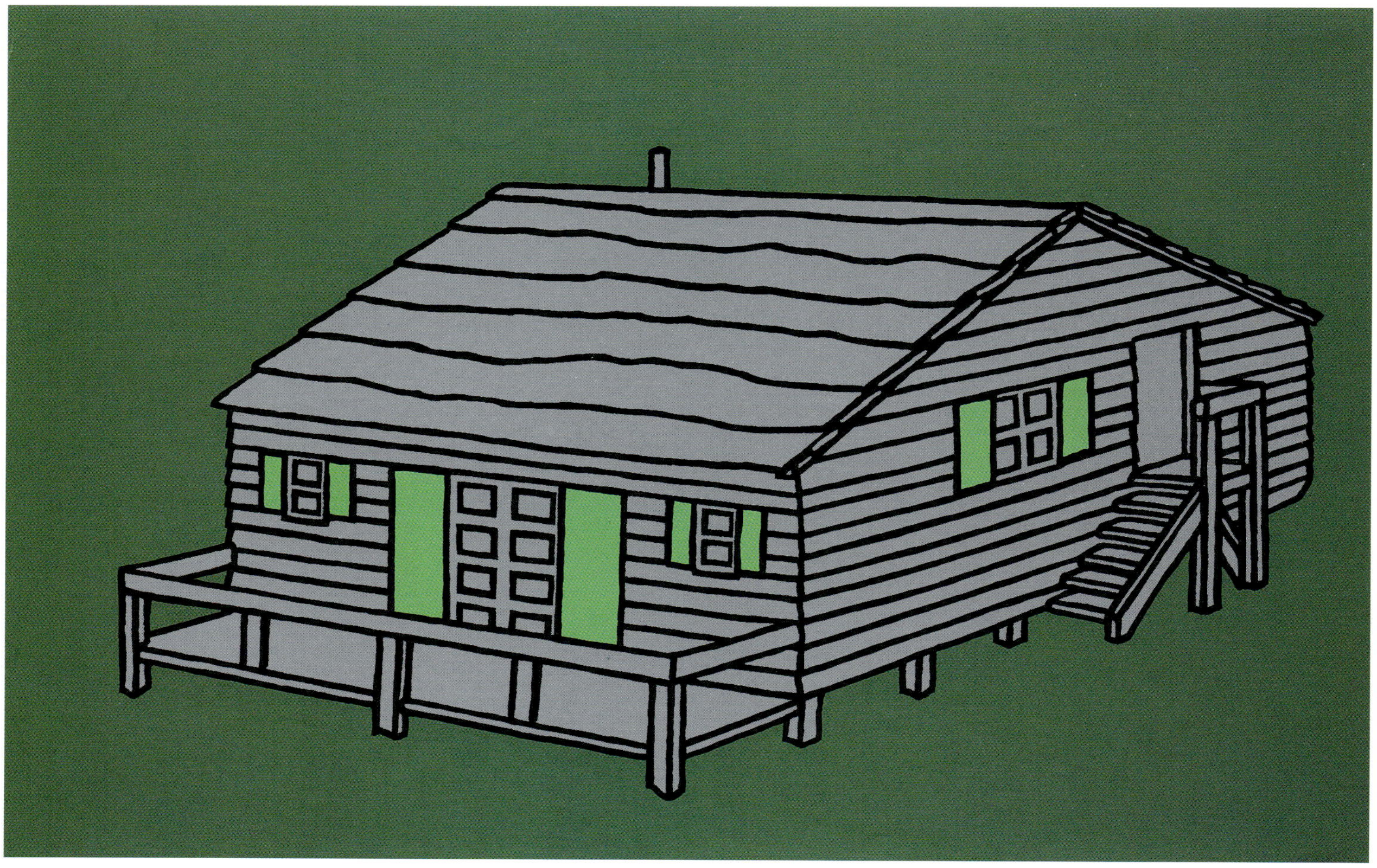

6. **Weekend Cabin** 1967

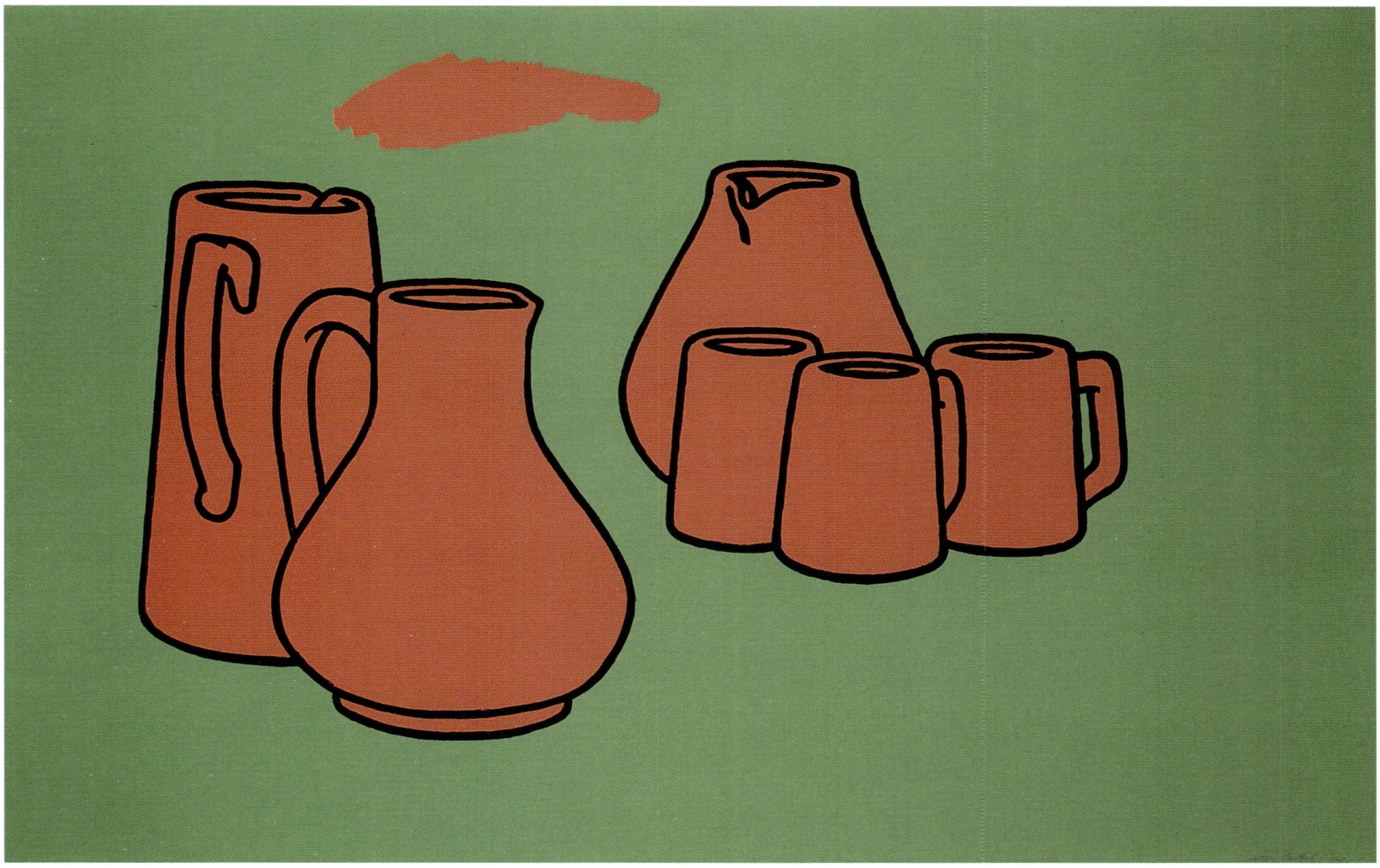

4. **Earthenware** 1967

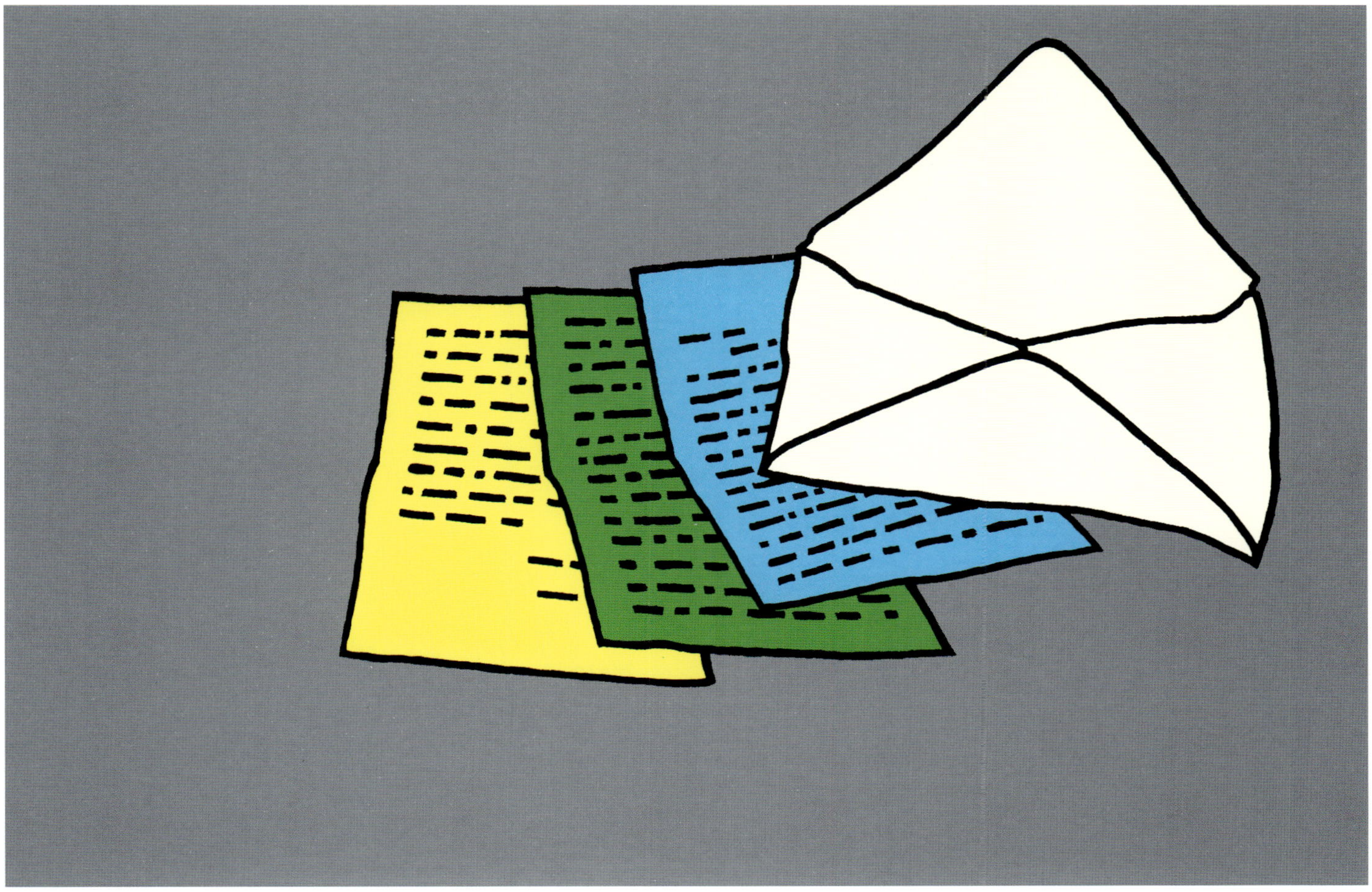

3. **The Letter** 1967

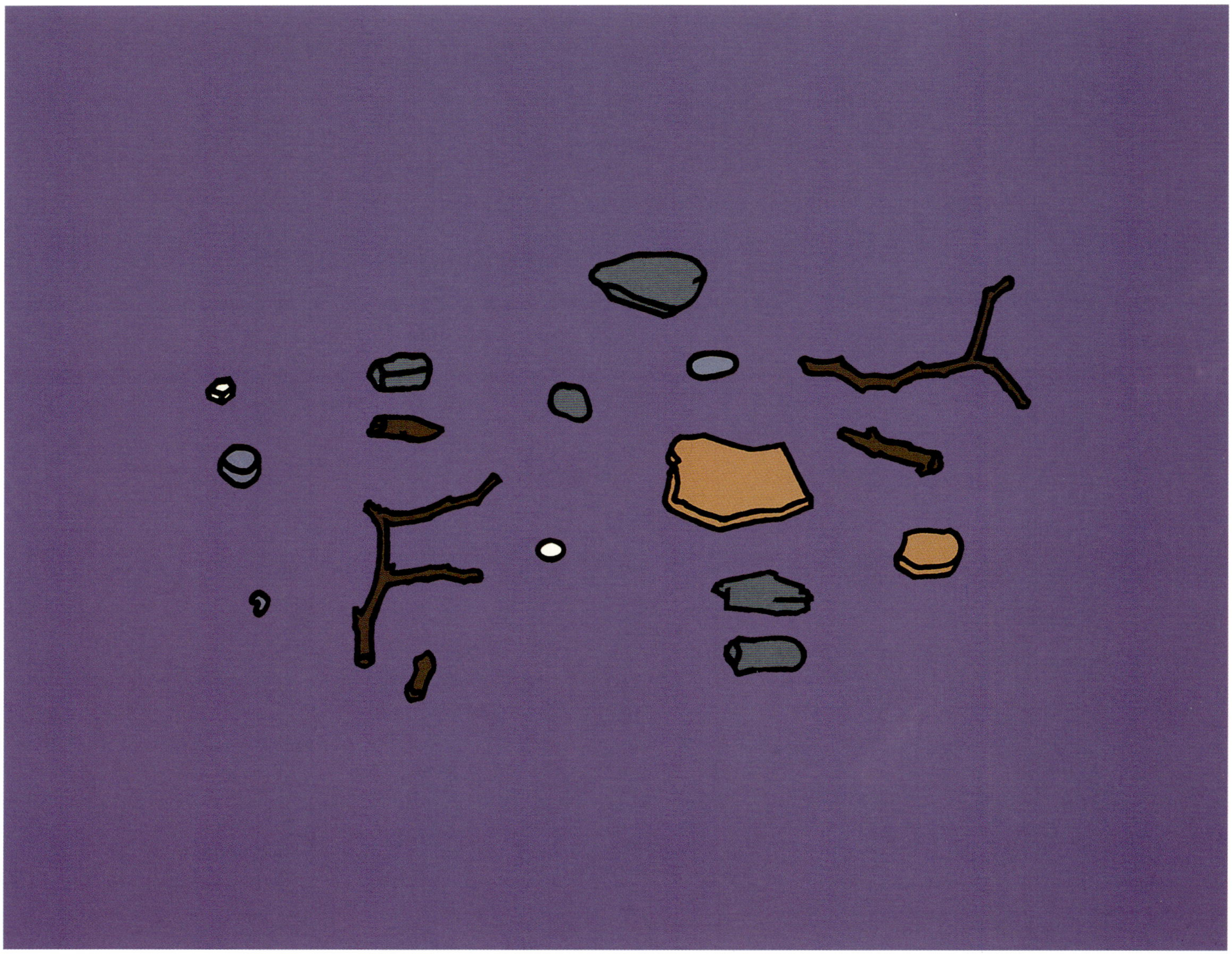

10. **Found Objects** 1968

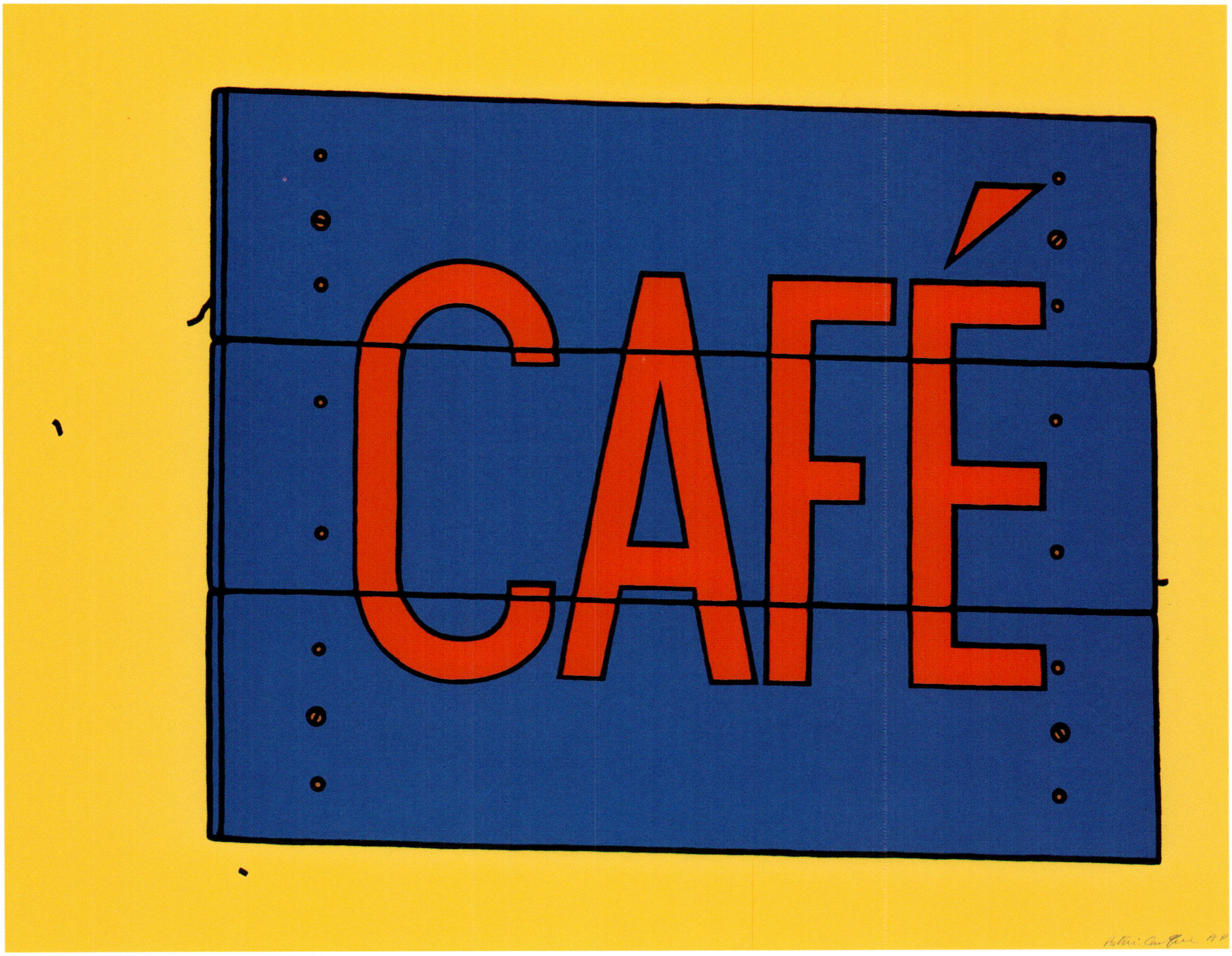

12. **Café Sign** 1968

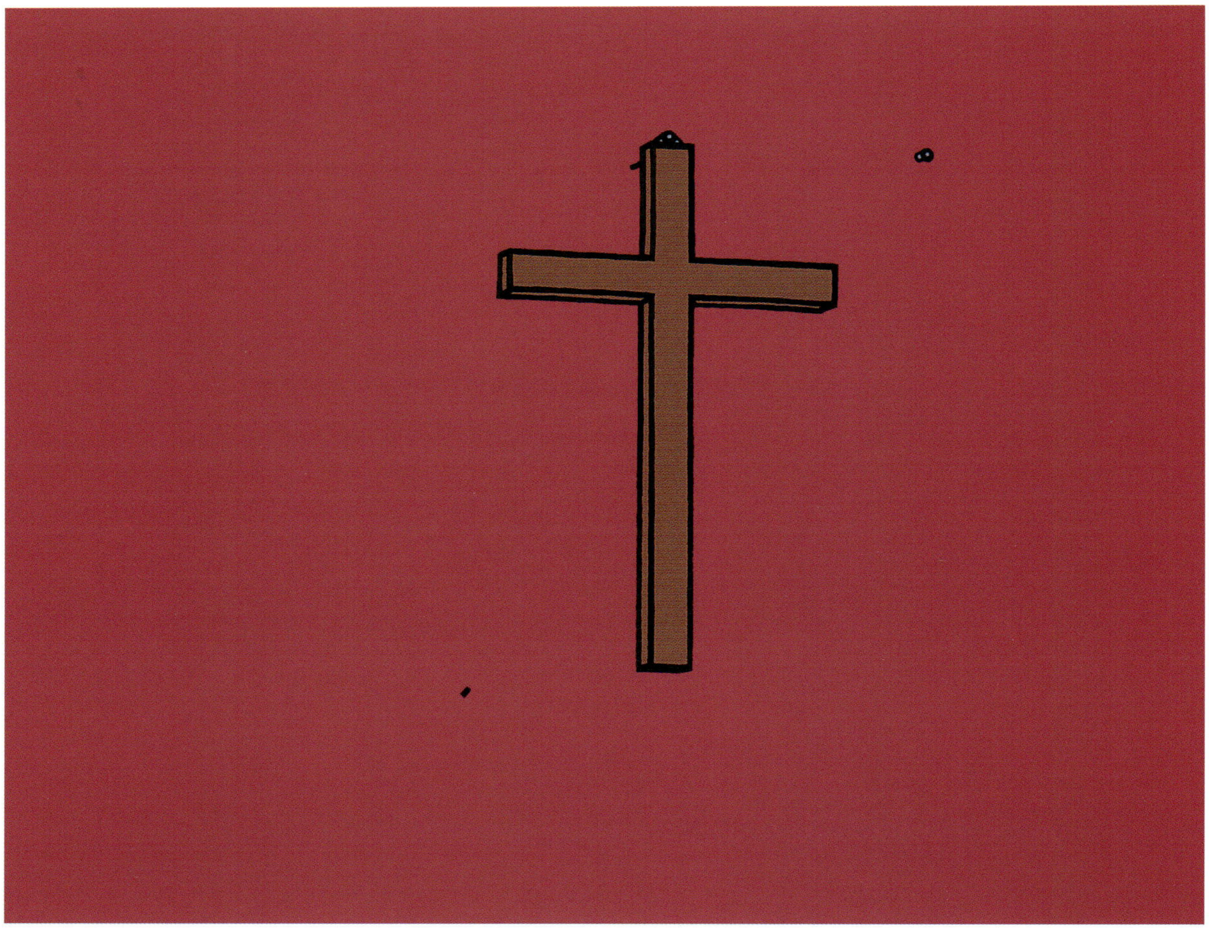

8. **Crucifix** 1968

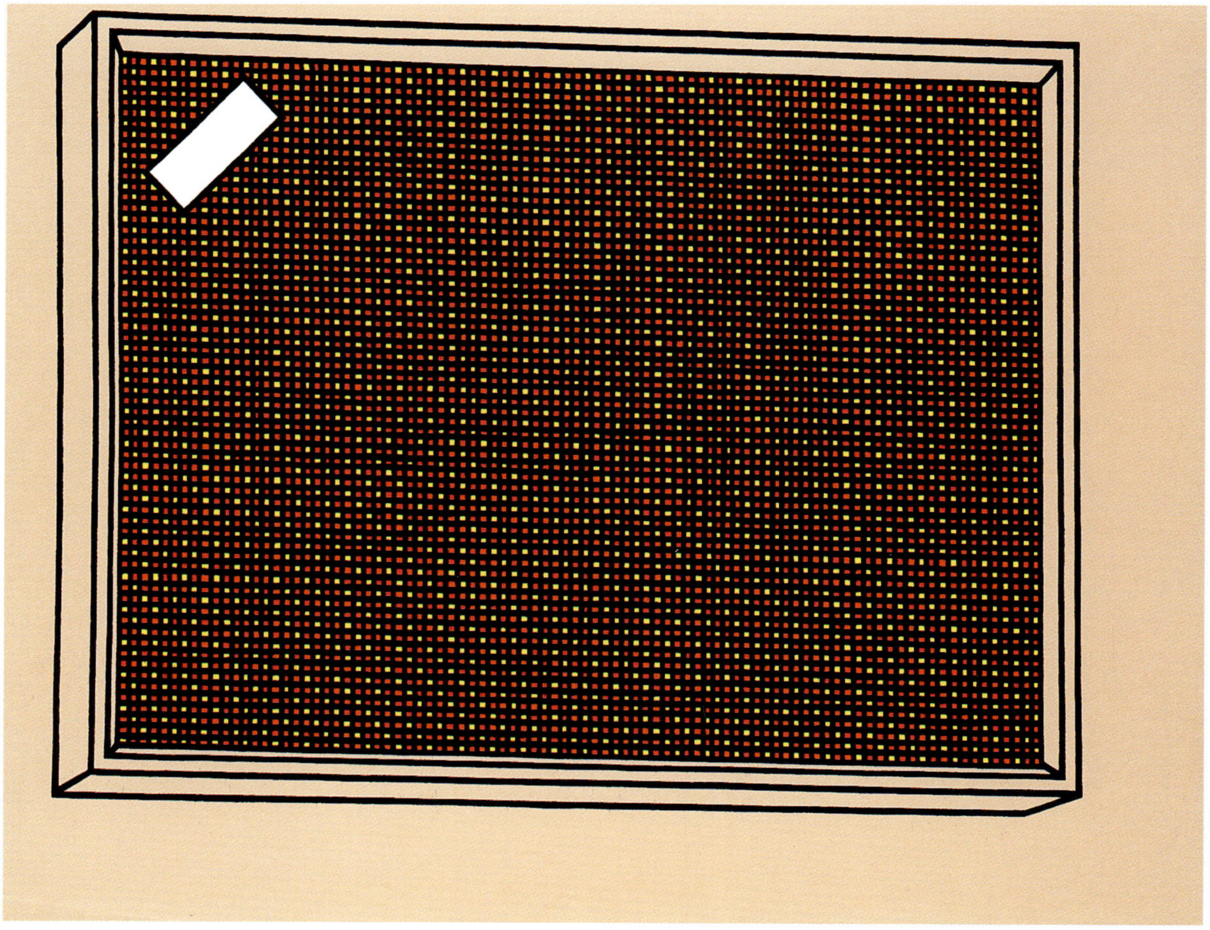

11. **Loudspeaker** 1968

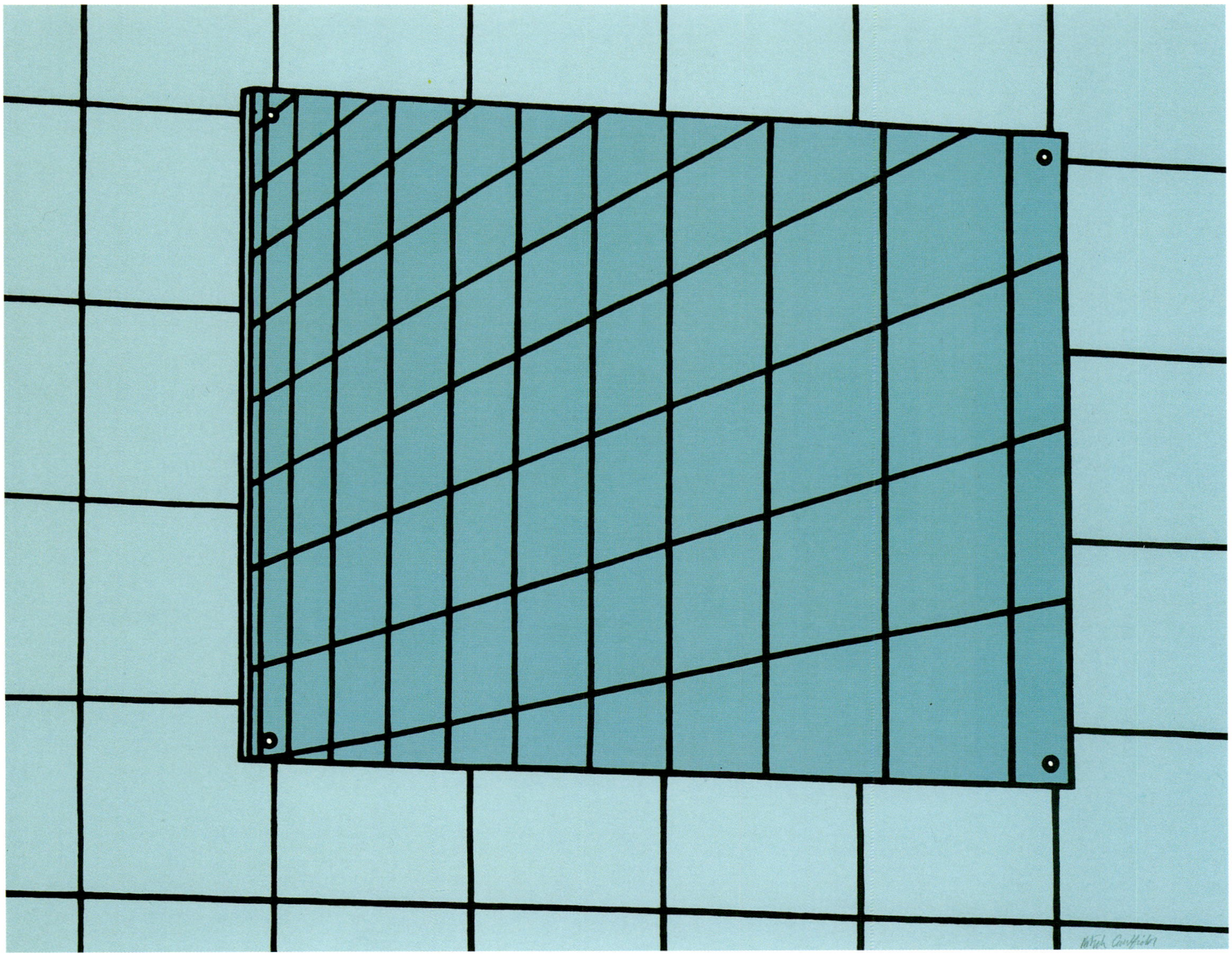

9. **Bathroom Mirror** 1968

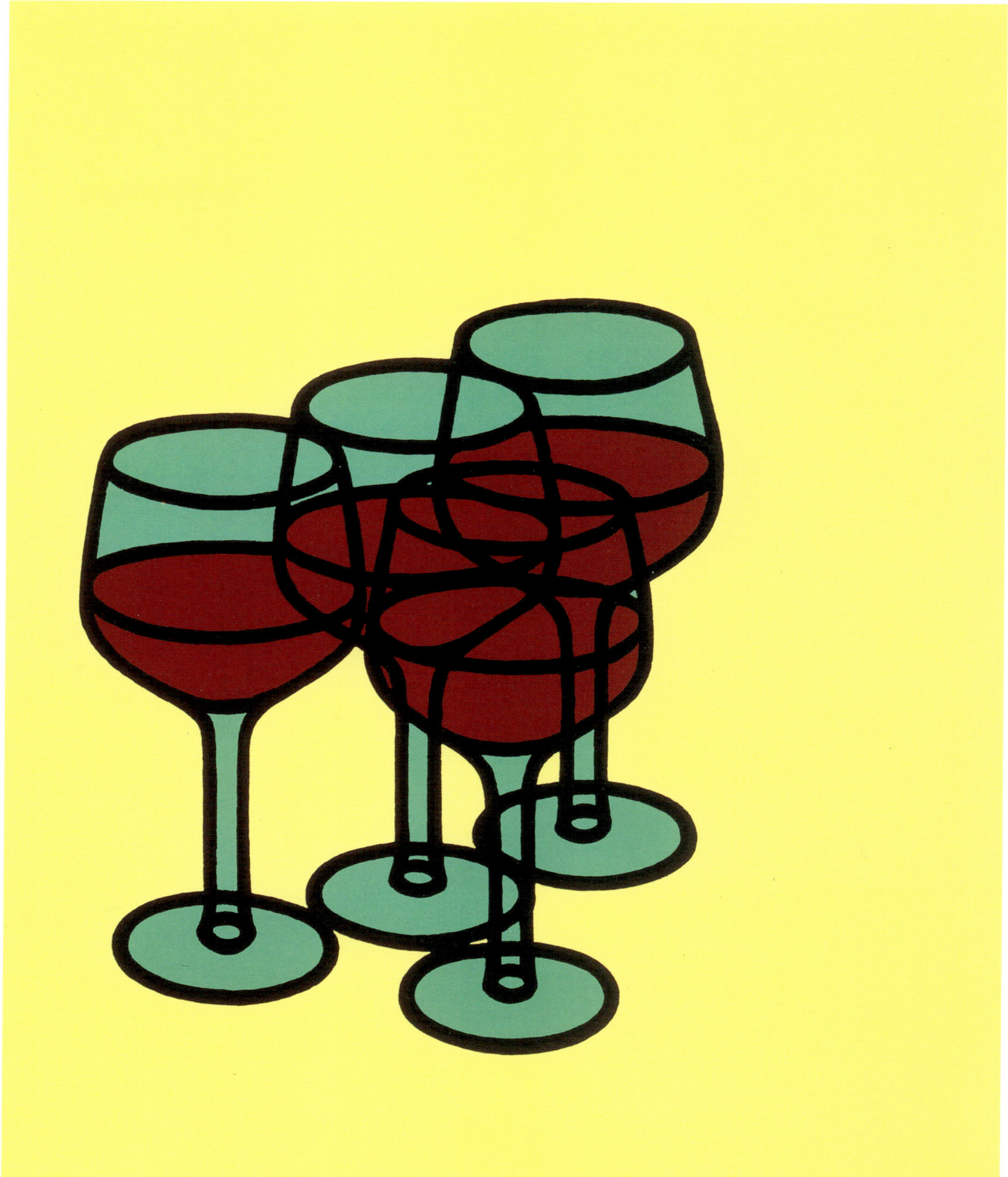

16. **Wine Glasses** 1969

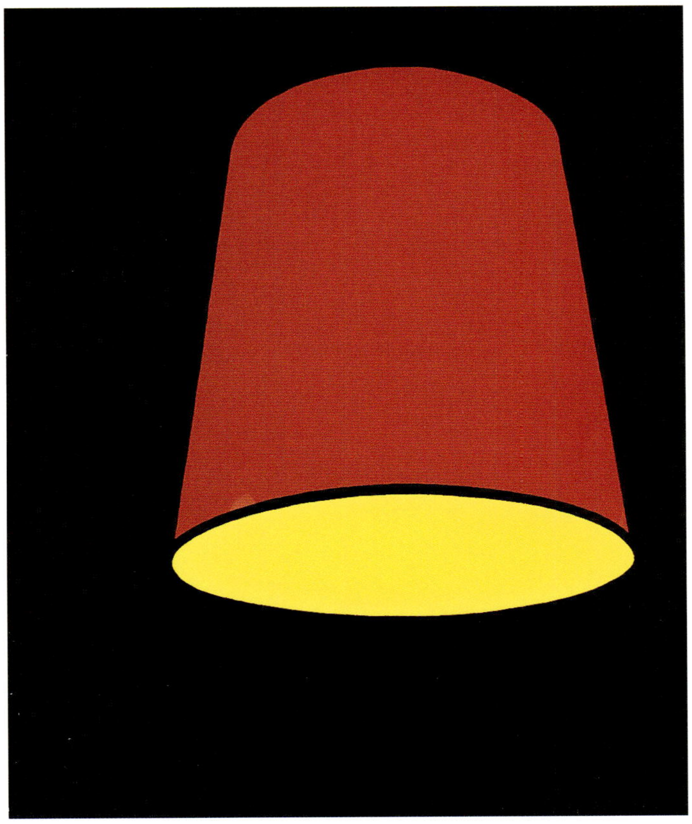

13. **Lampshade** 1969

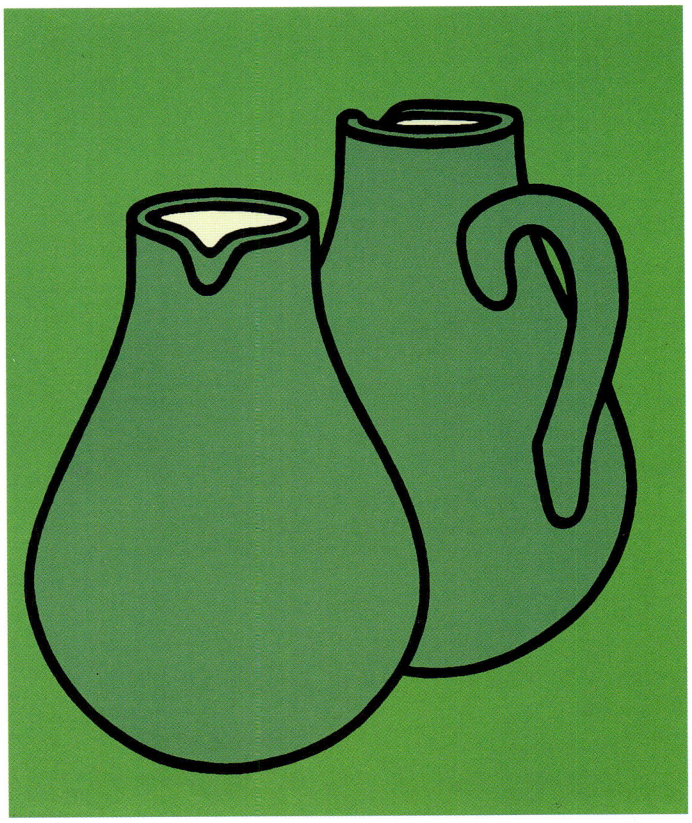

14. **Two Jugs** 1969

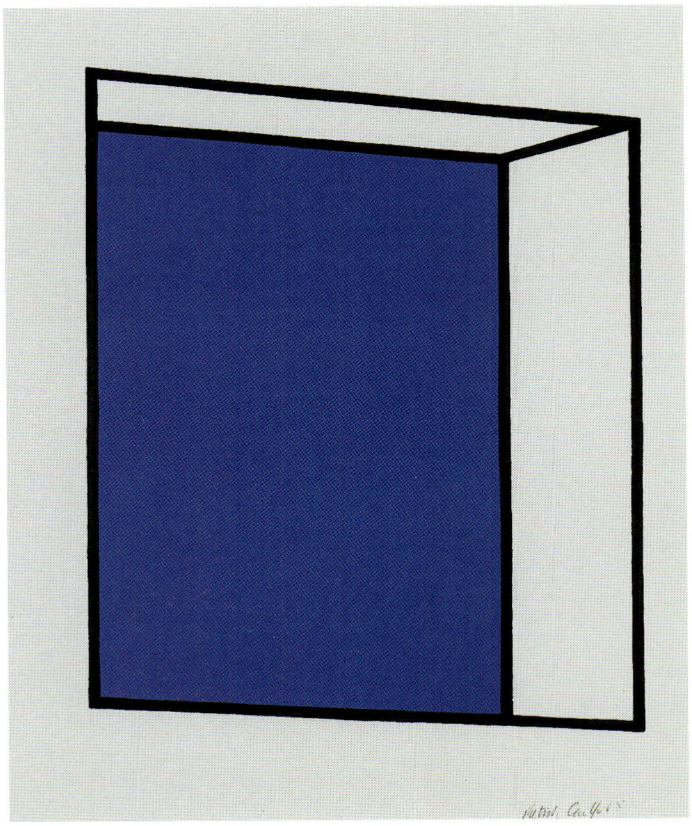

15. **Small Window** 1969

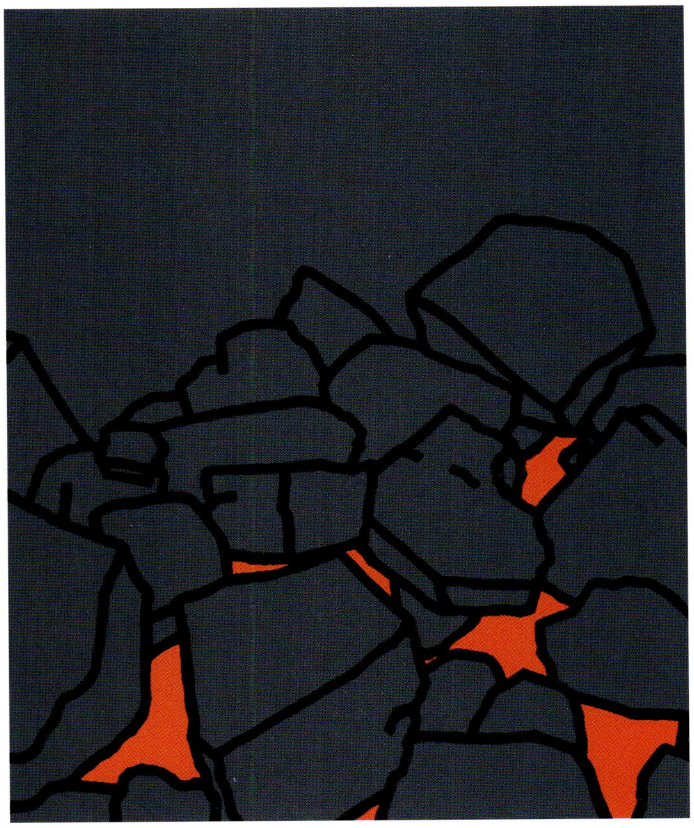

17. **Coal Fire** 1969

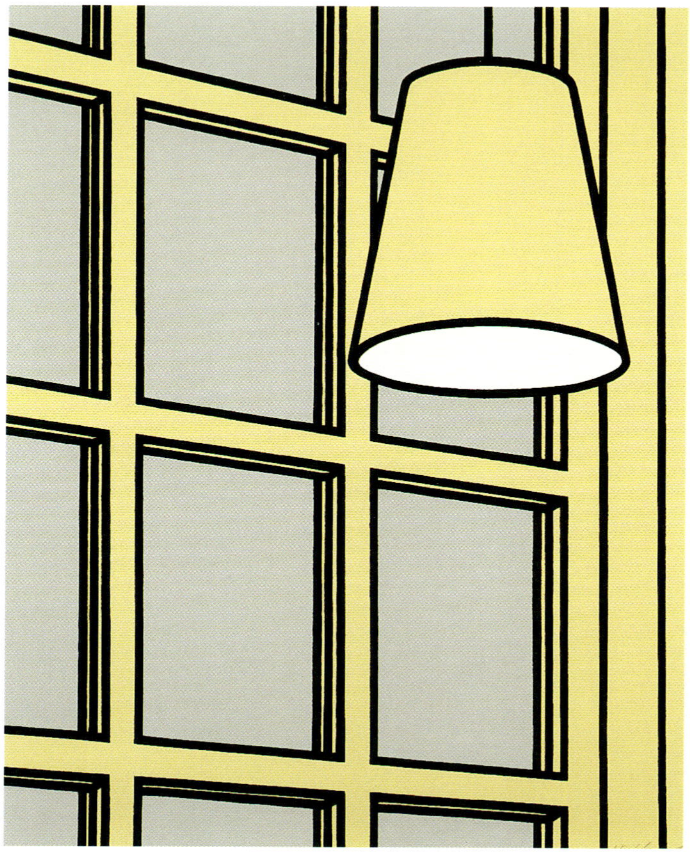

18. **Interior : Morning** 1971

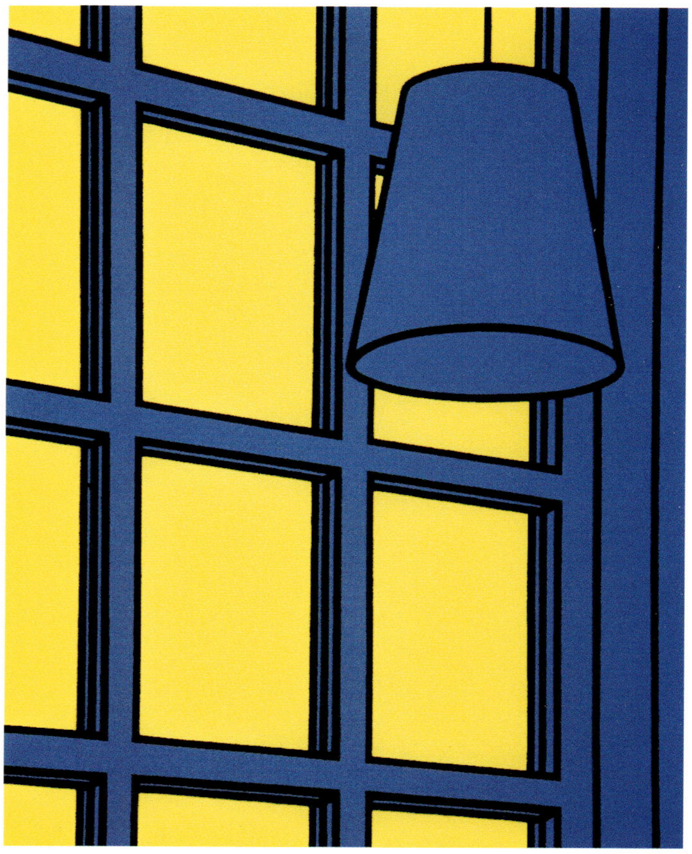

19. **Interior : Noon** 1971

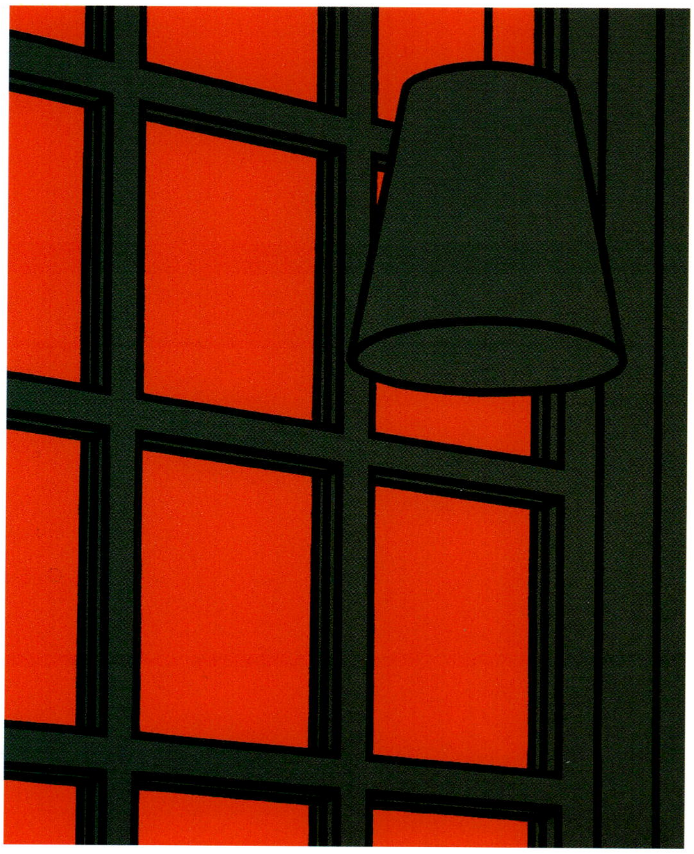

20. **Interior : Evening** 1971

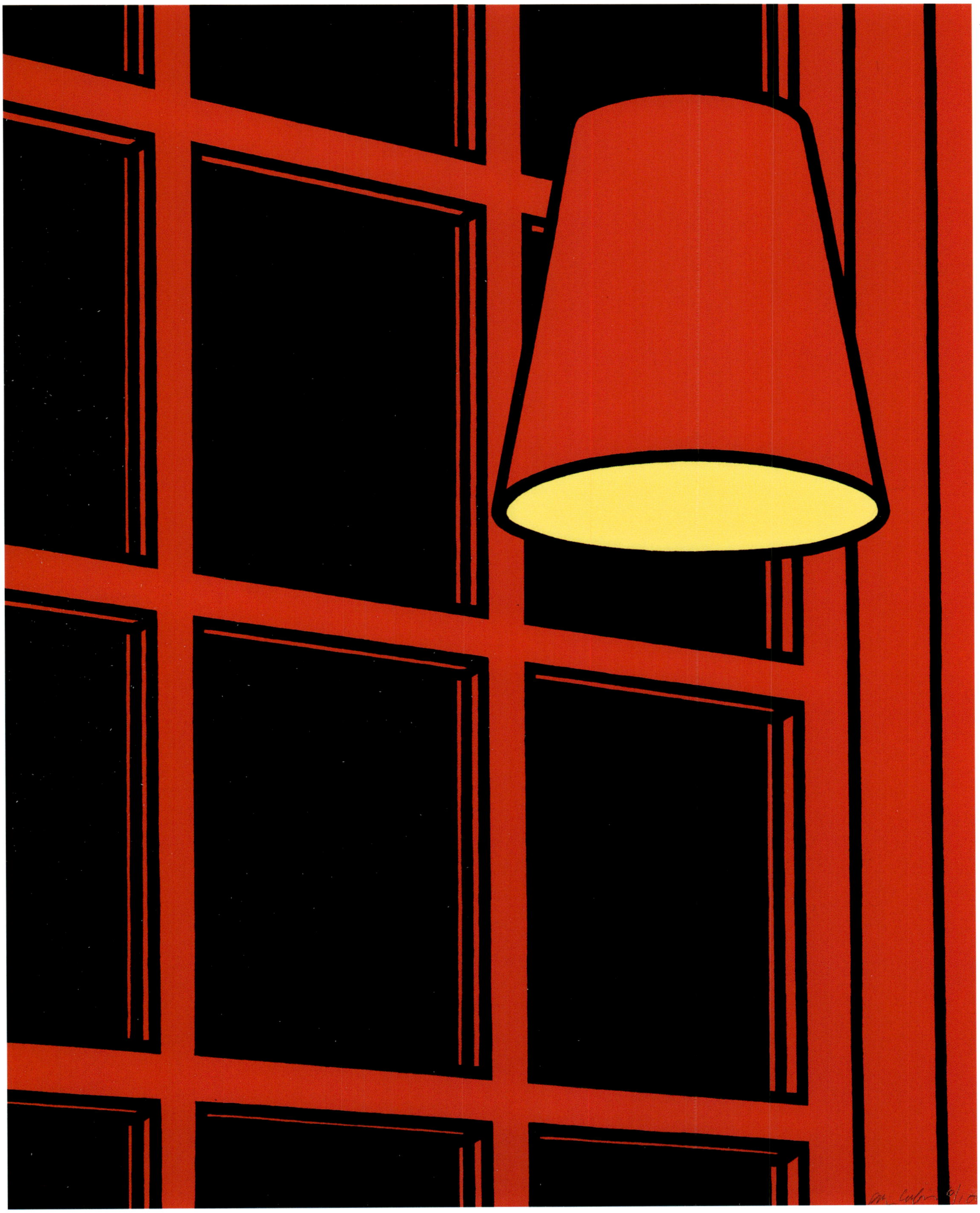

21. **Interior : Night** 1971

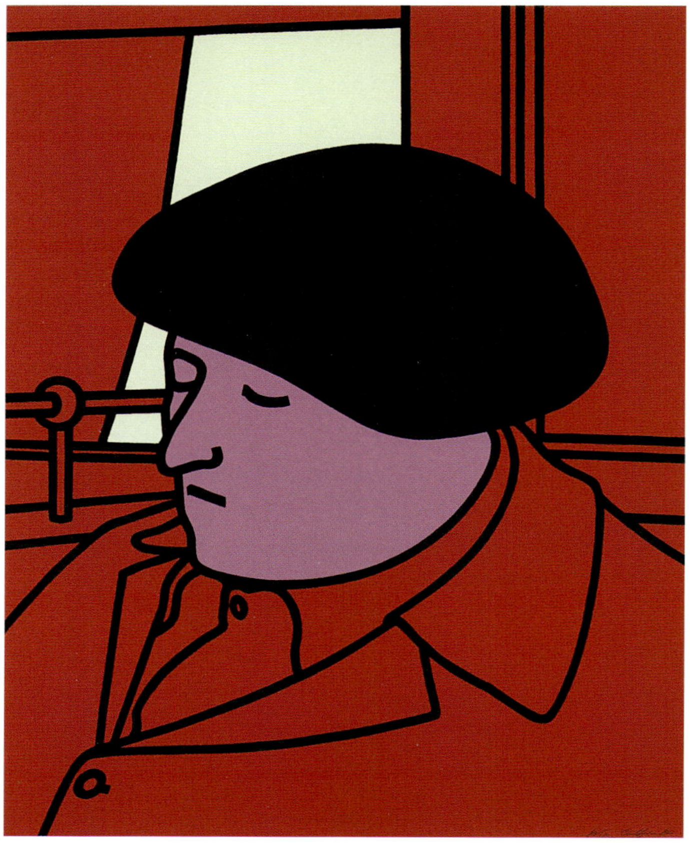

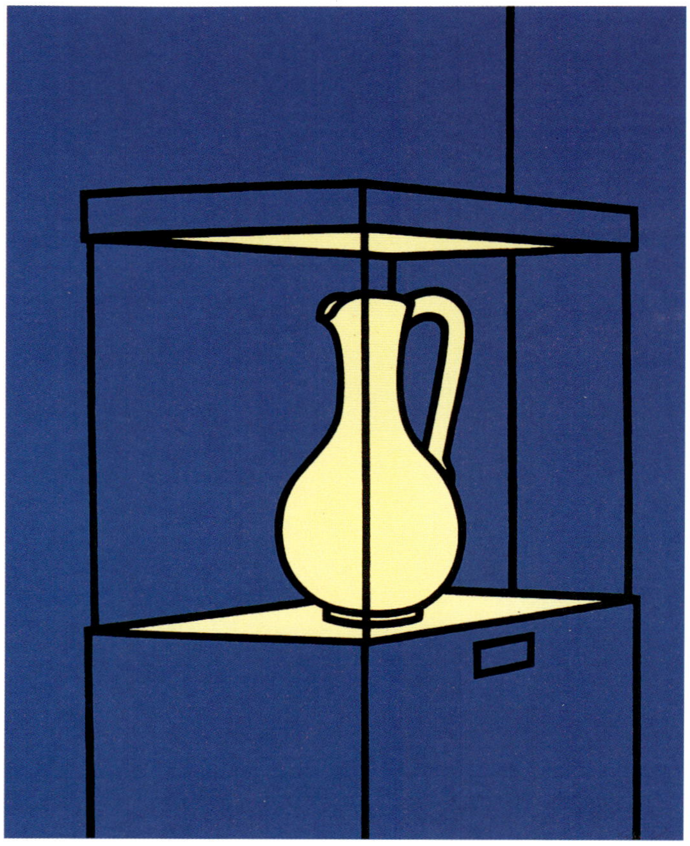

22. **Portrait of a Frenchman** 1971

23. **Vase on Display** 1971

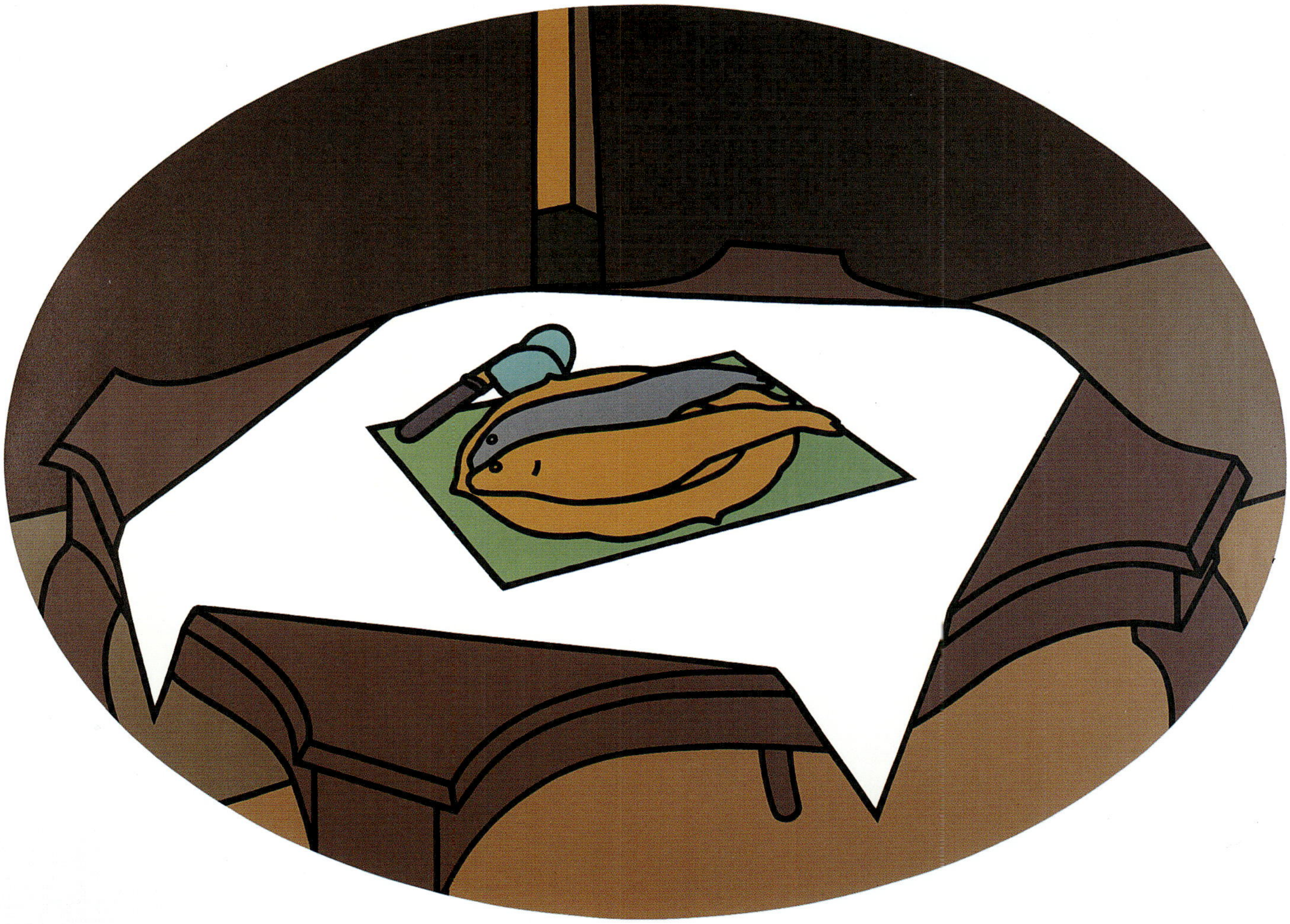

24. **Two Whiting** 1972

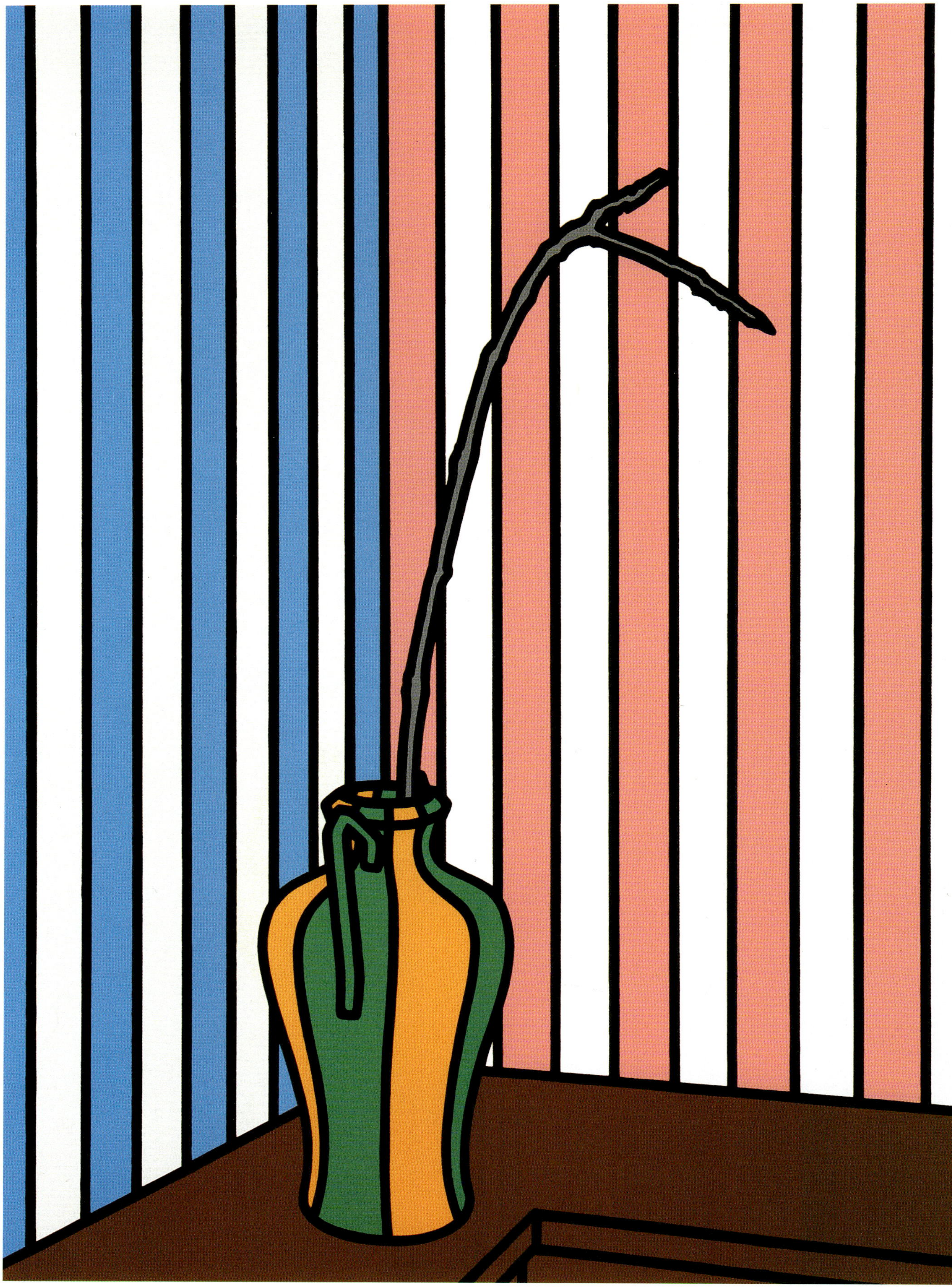

26. **Fig Branch** 1972

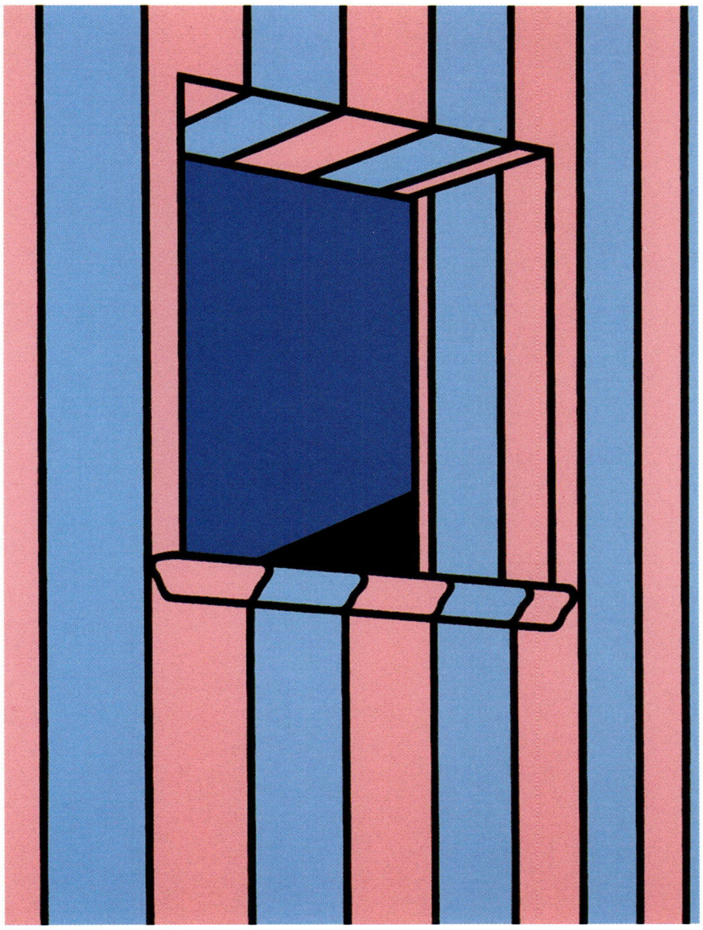

25. **Window at Night** 1972

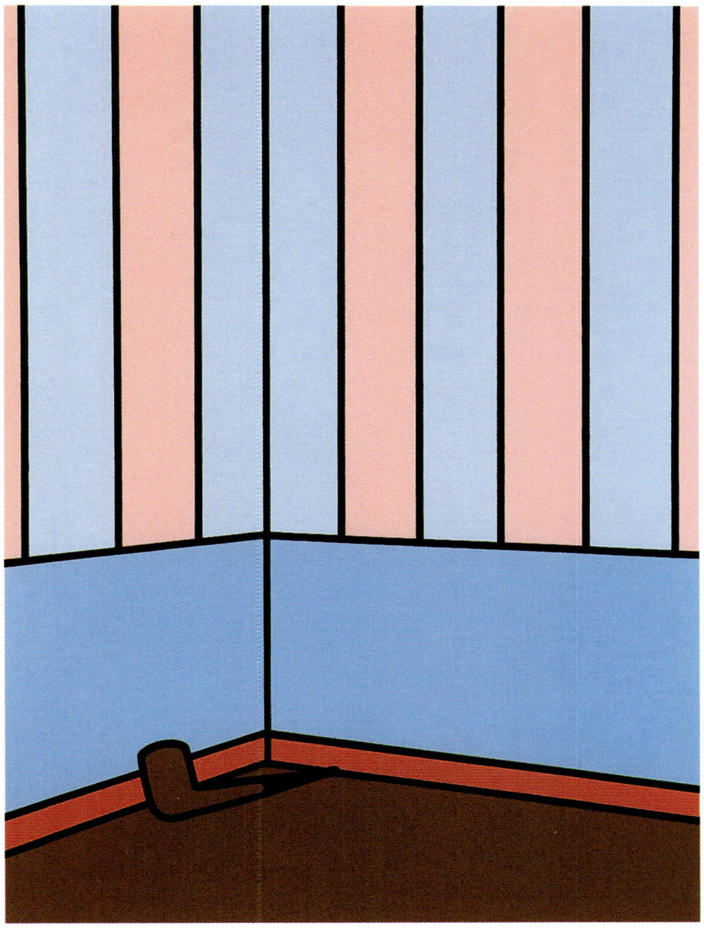

27. **Pipe** 1972

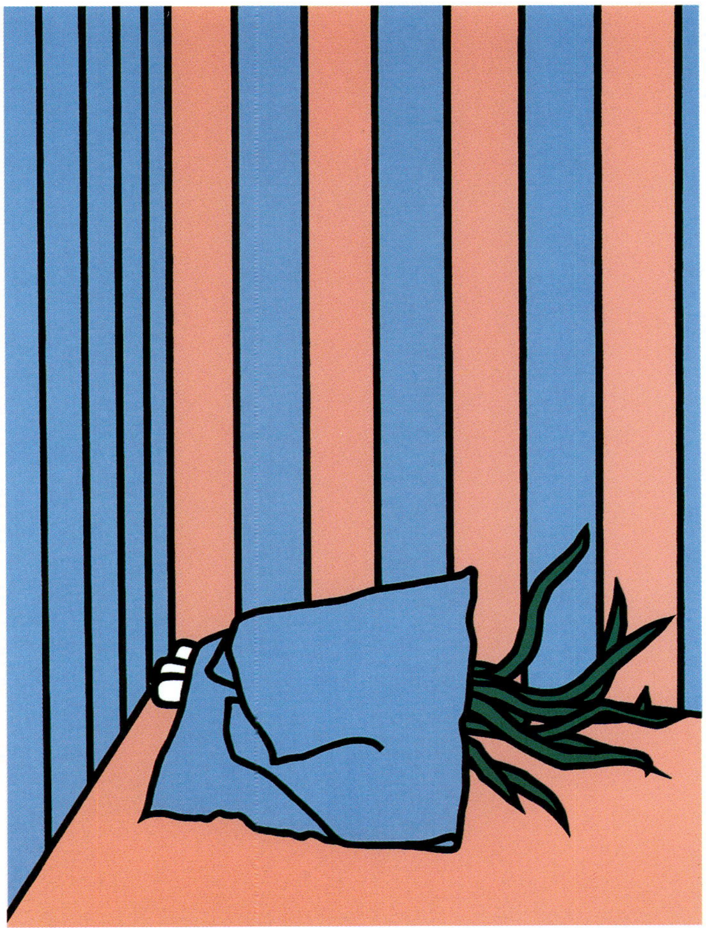

28. **Napkin and Onions** 1972

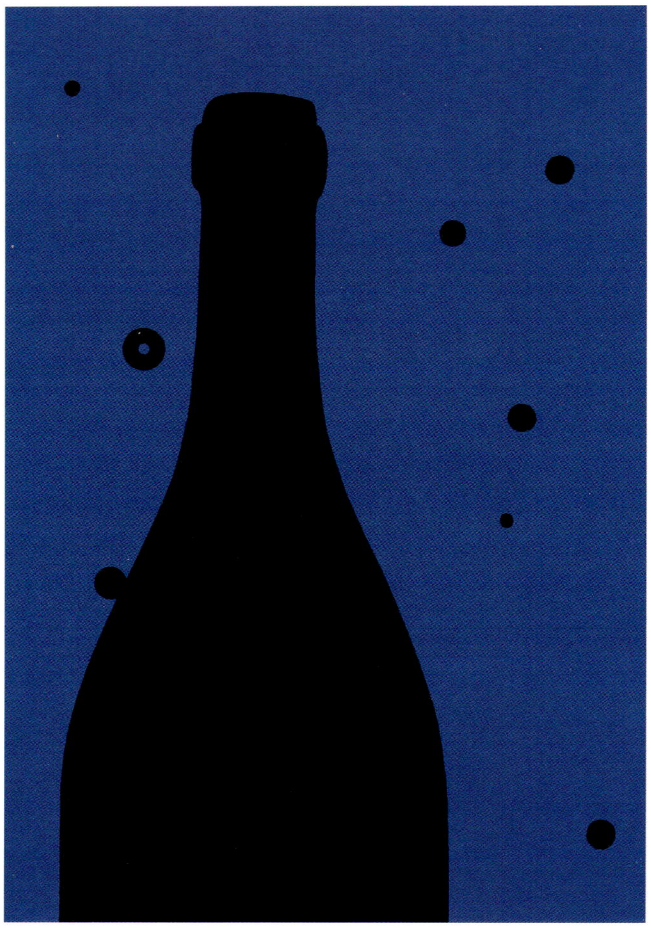

30. **Night Sky** 1973

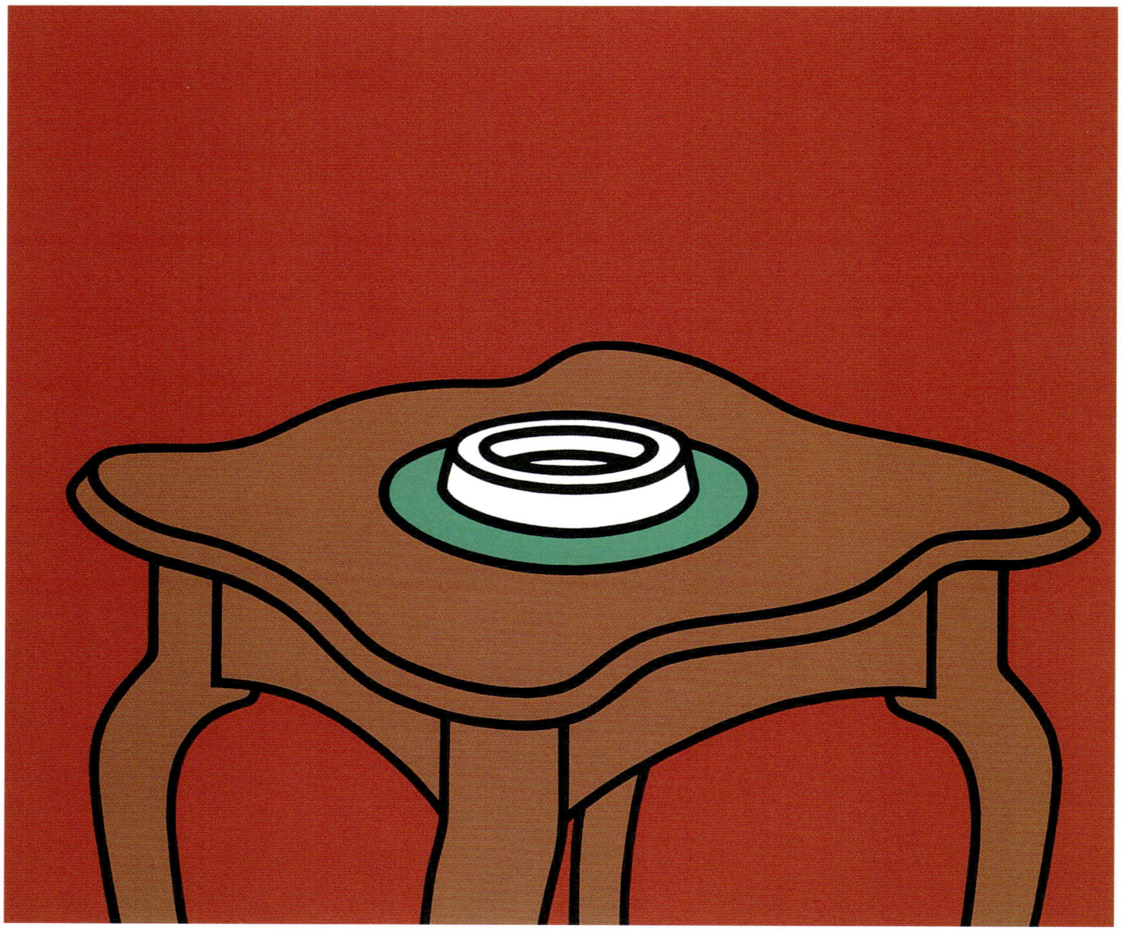

29. **Occasional Table** 1972

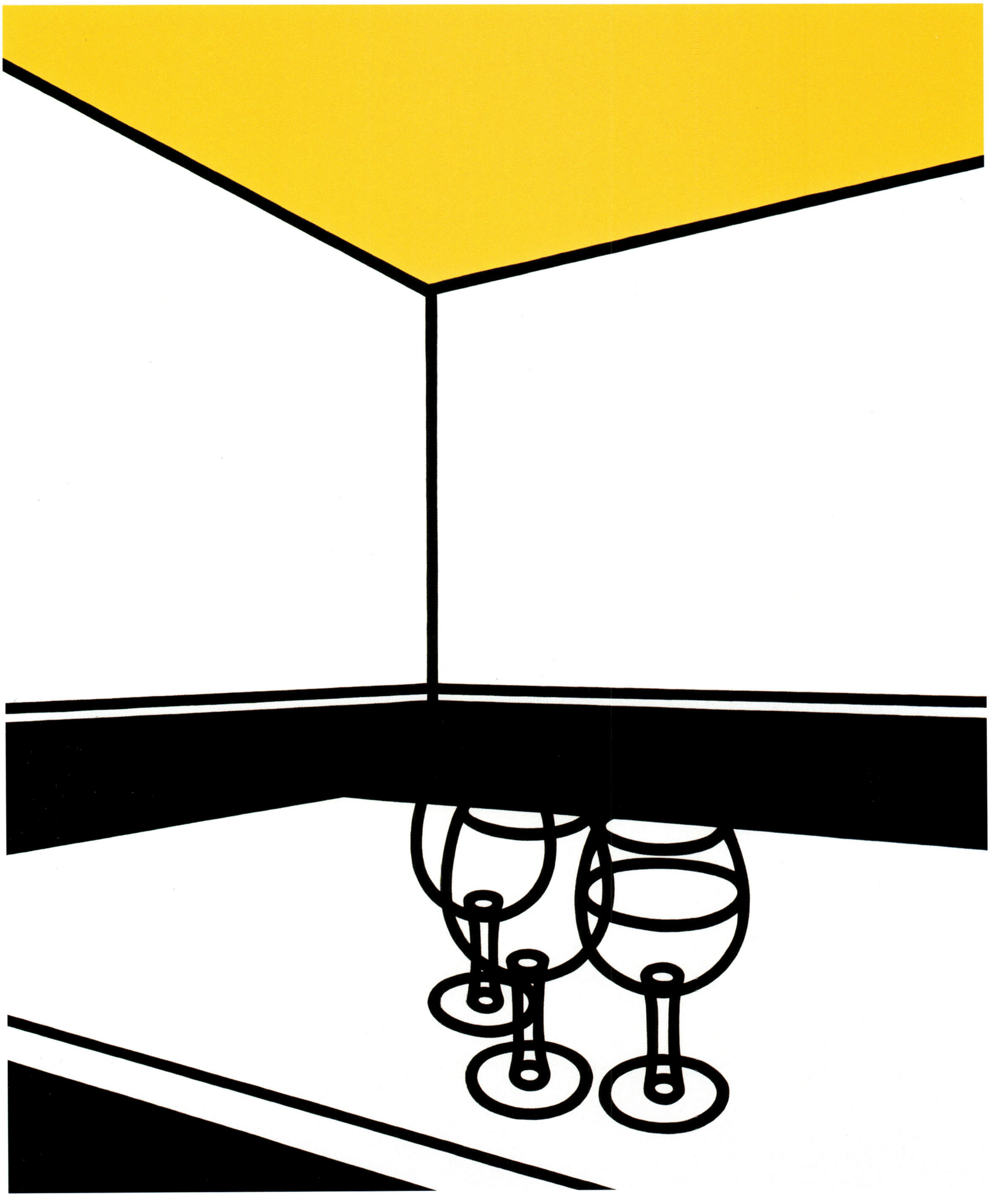

31. **Black and White Café** 1973

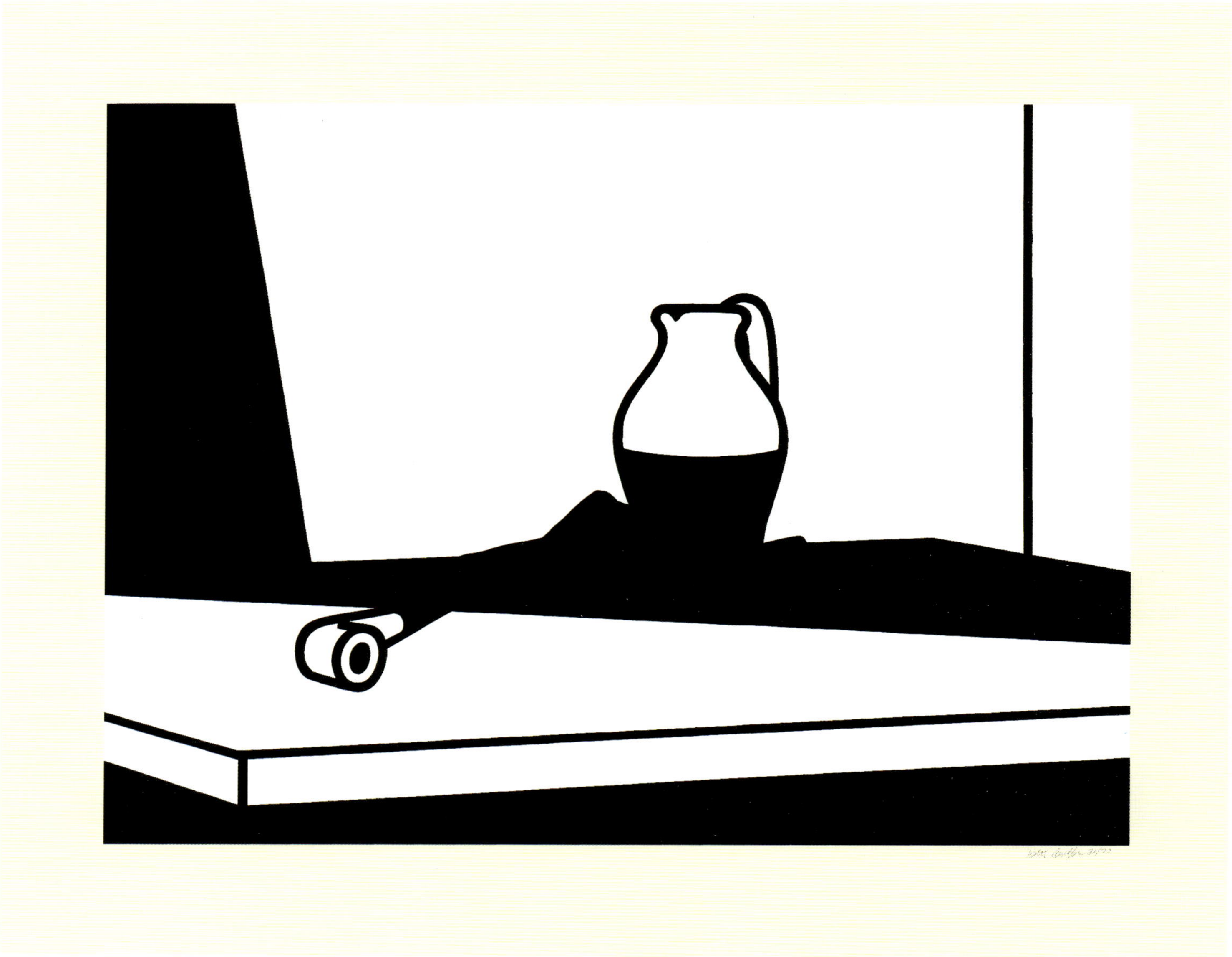

37. **Pipe and Jug** 1973

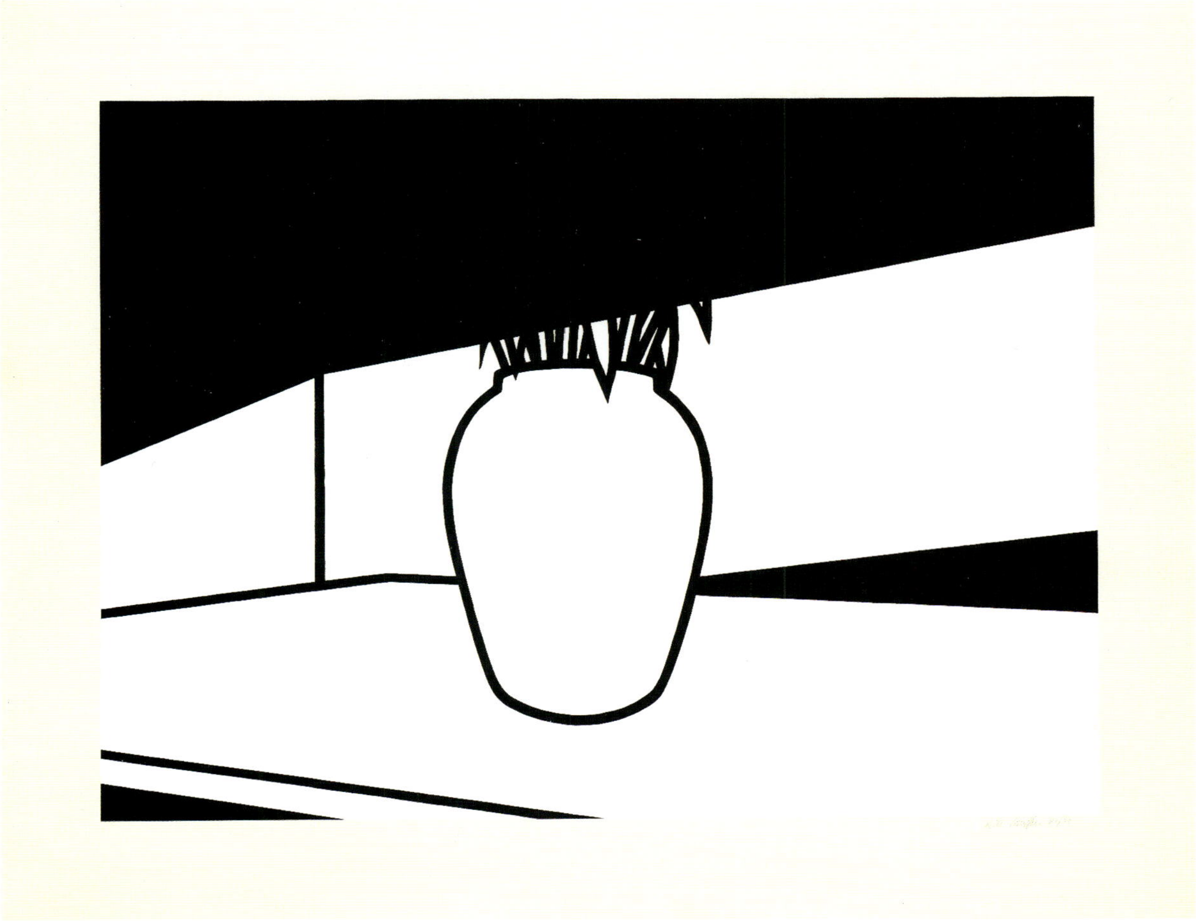

32. **Tulips** 1973

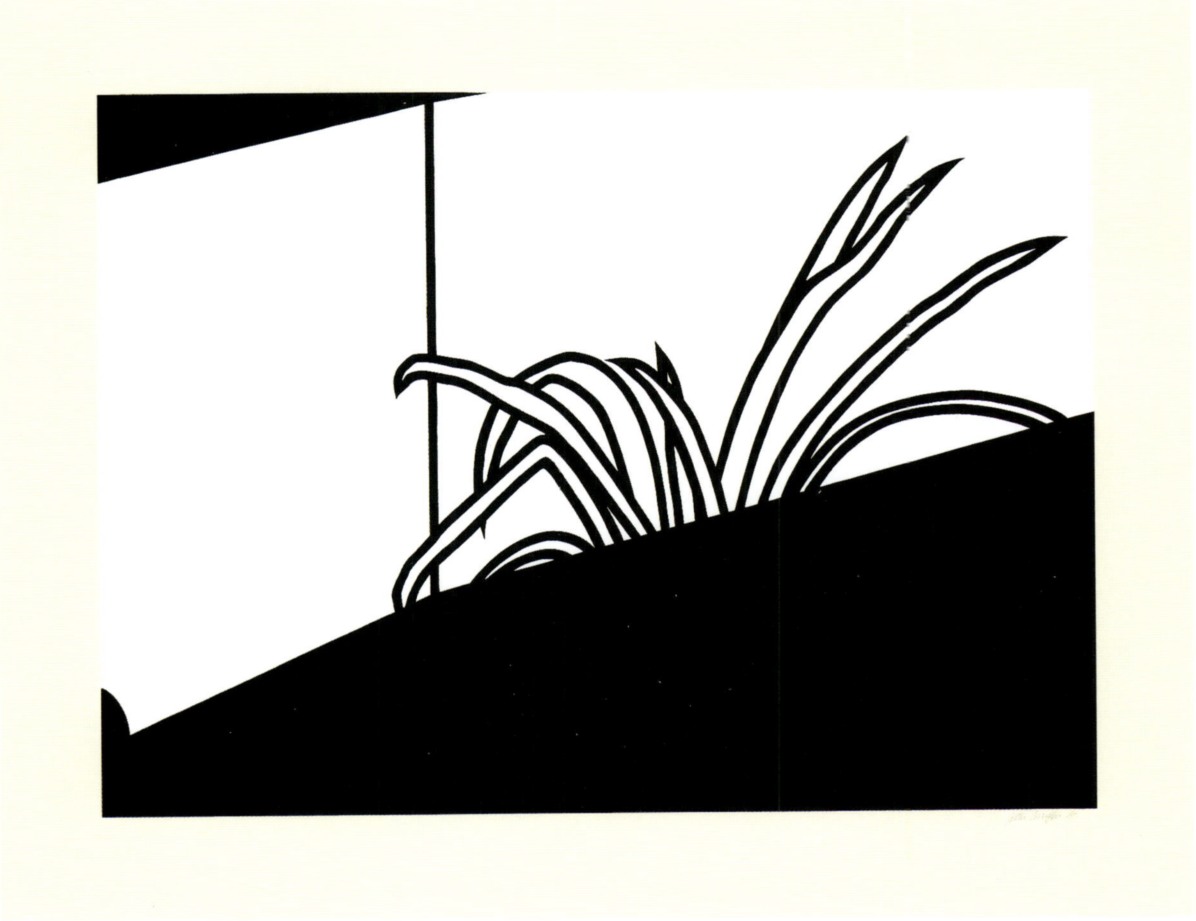

35. **Spider Plant** 1973

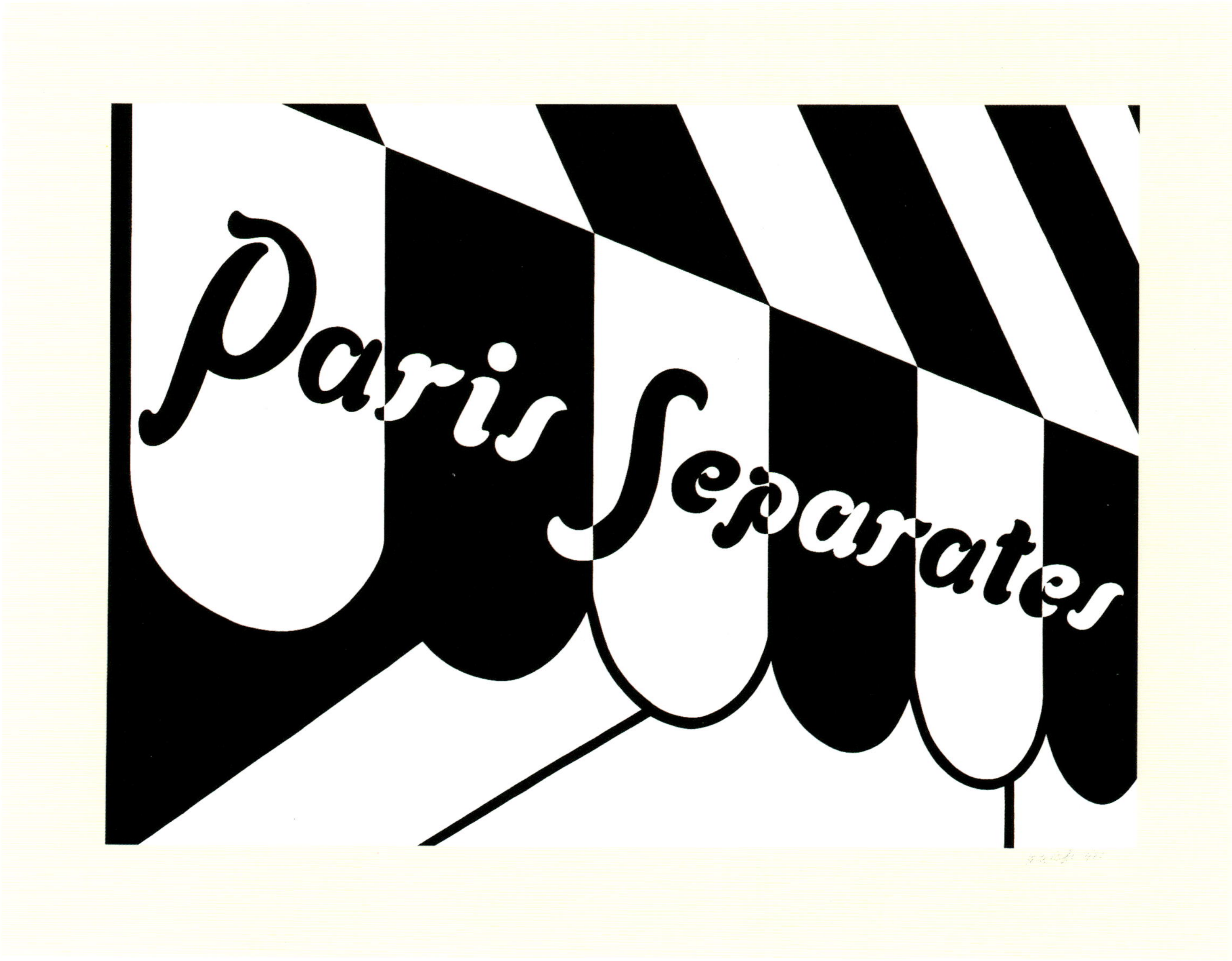

36. **Paris Separates** 1973

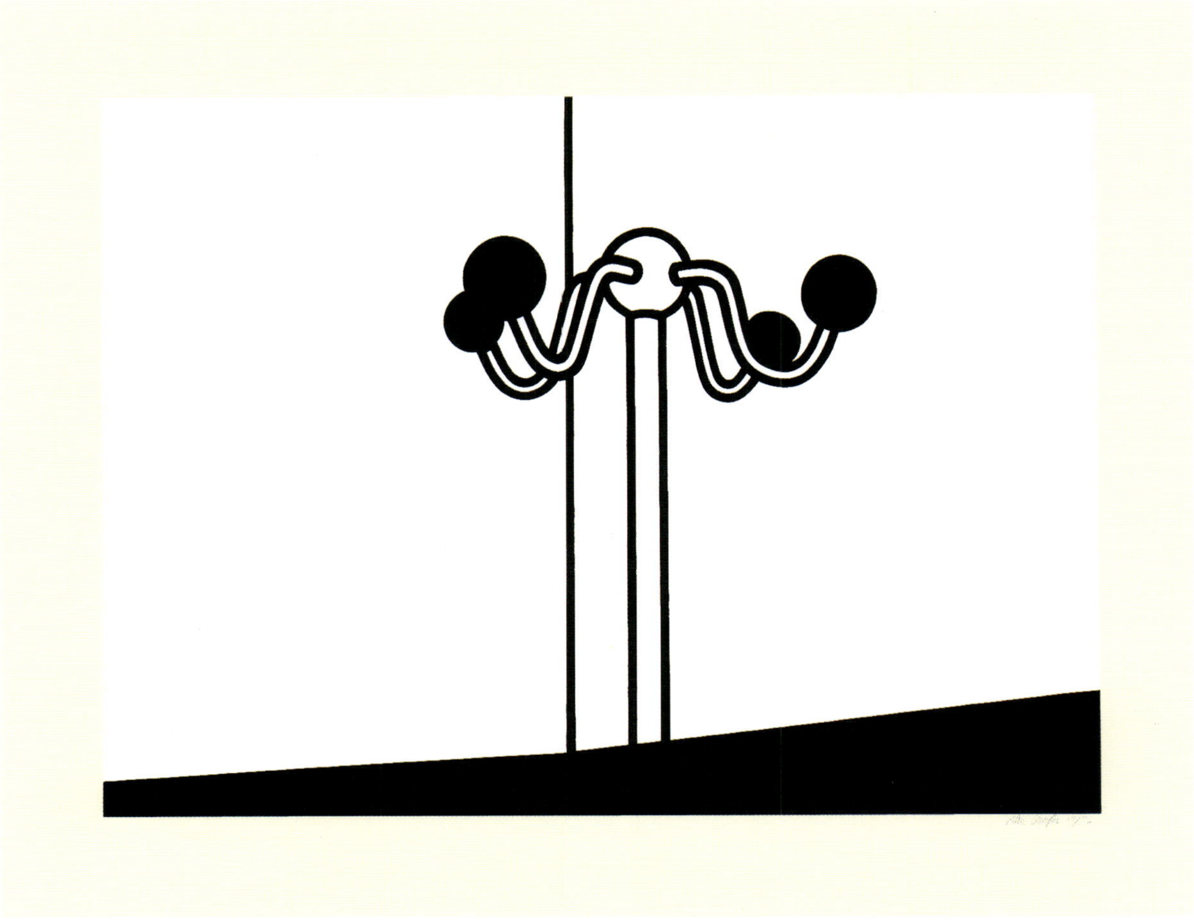

33. **Coat Stand** 1973

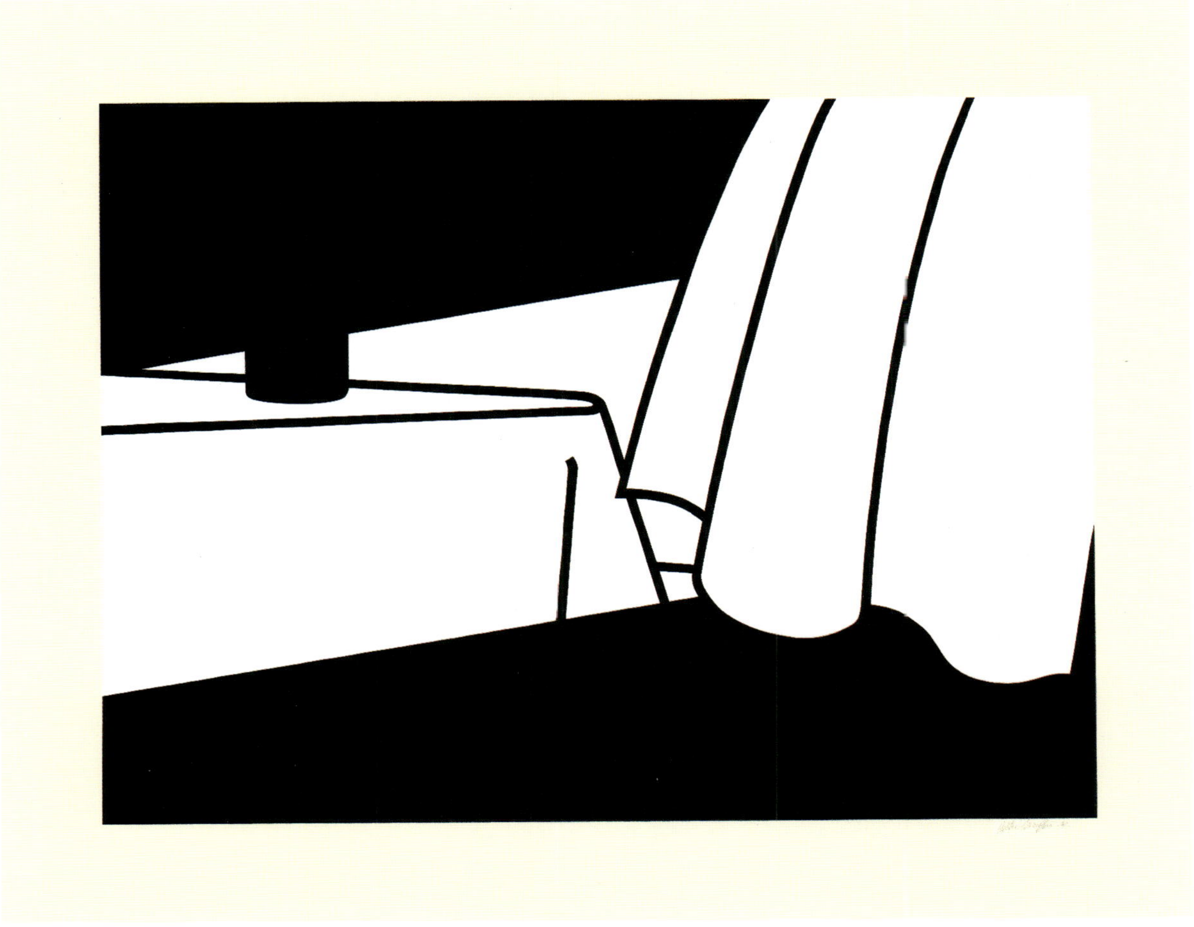

34. **Curtain and Bottle** 1973

38. **Some Poems of Jules Laforgue** 1973

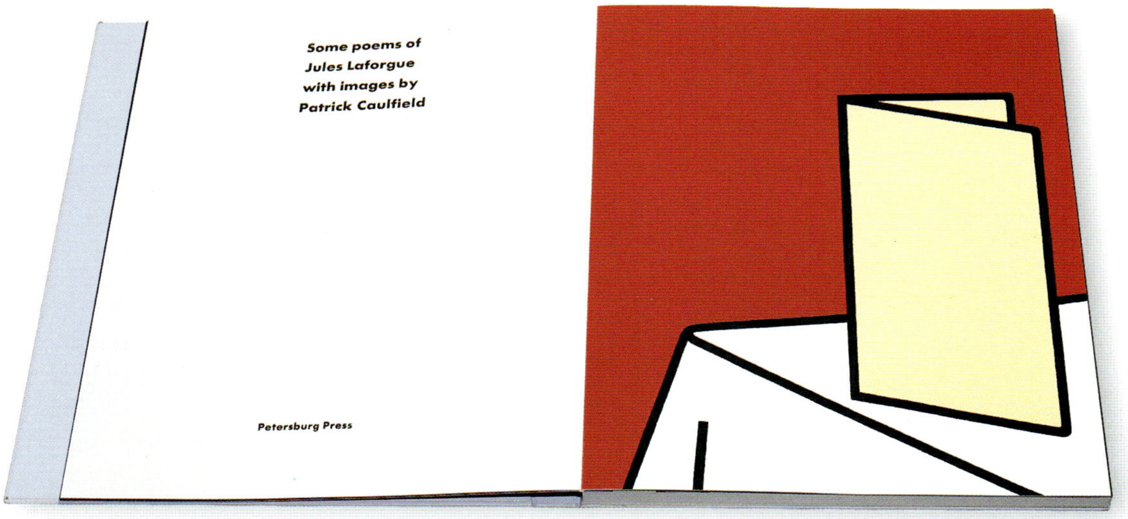

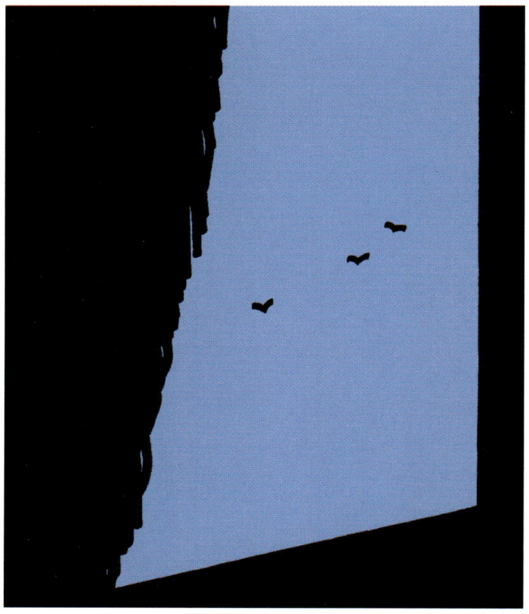

38a

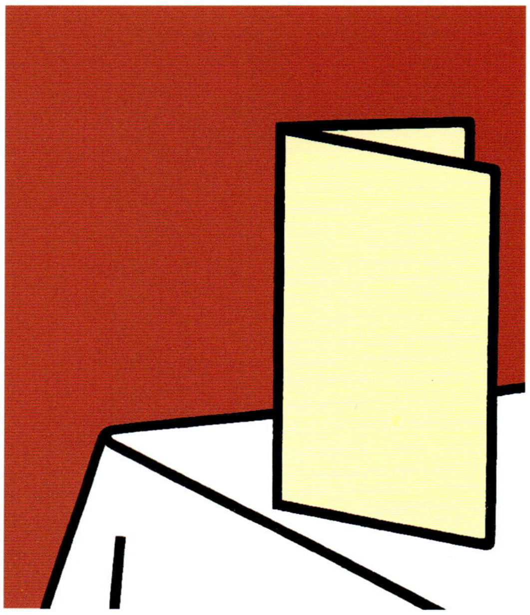

38b

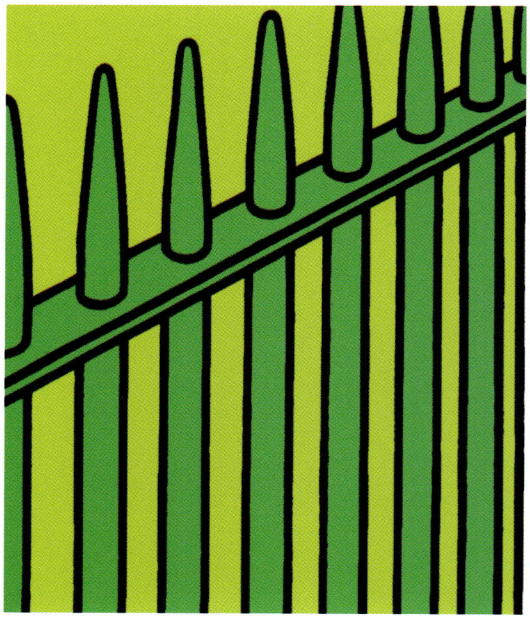

38c

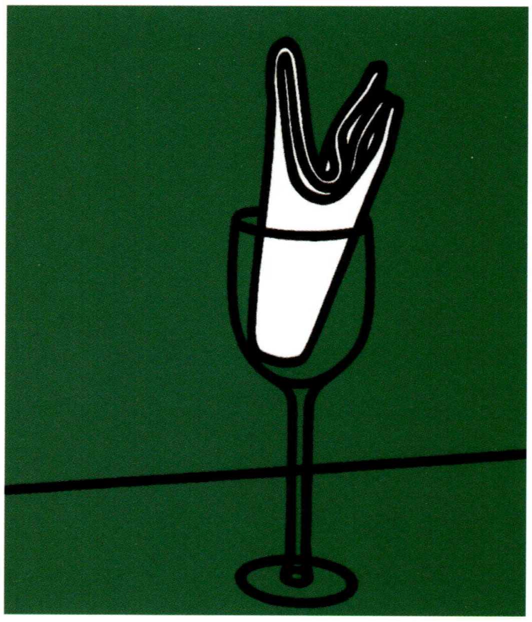

38d

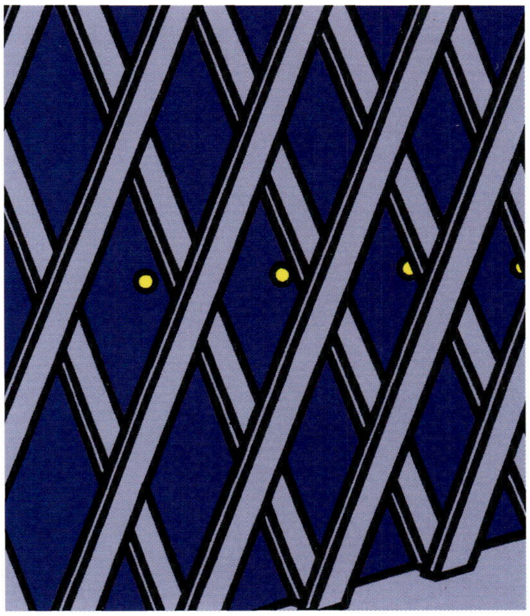
38e

38f

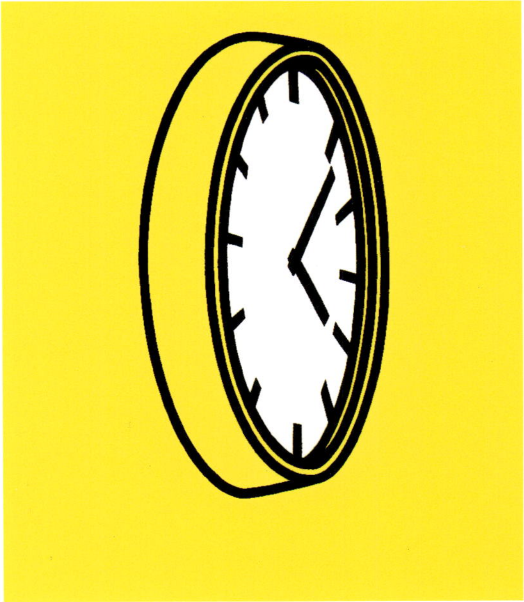
38g

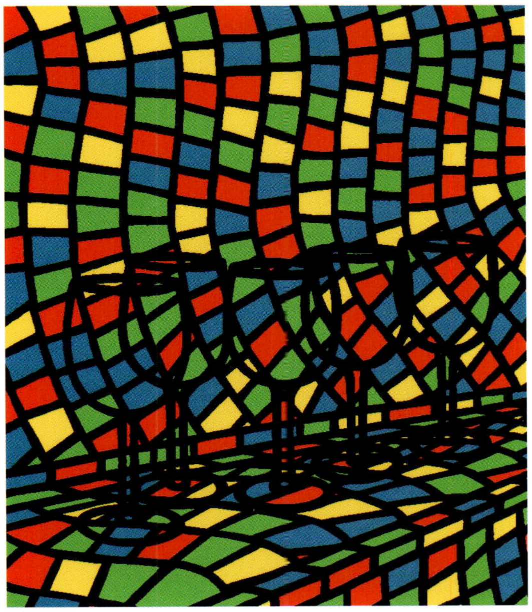
38h

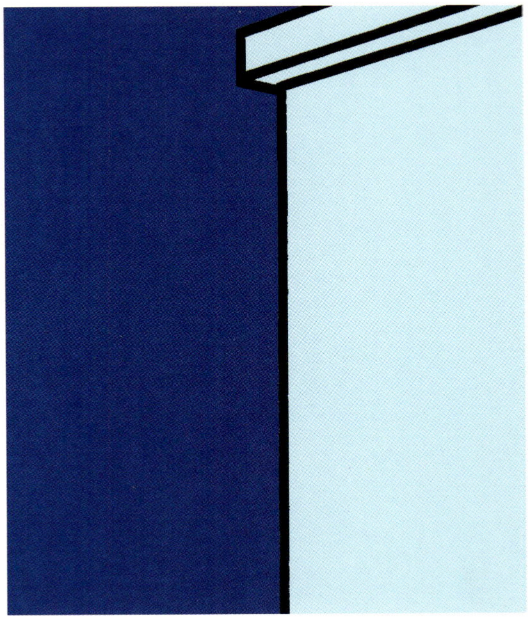
38i

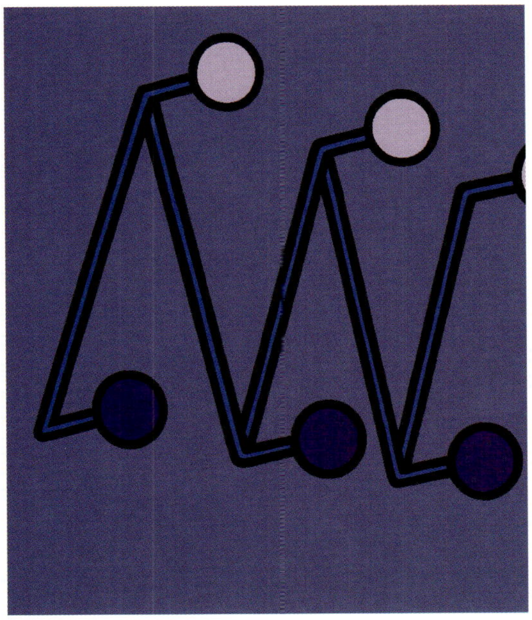
38j

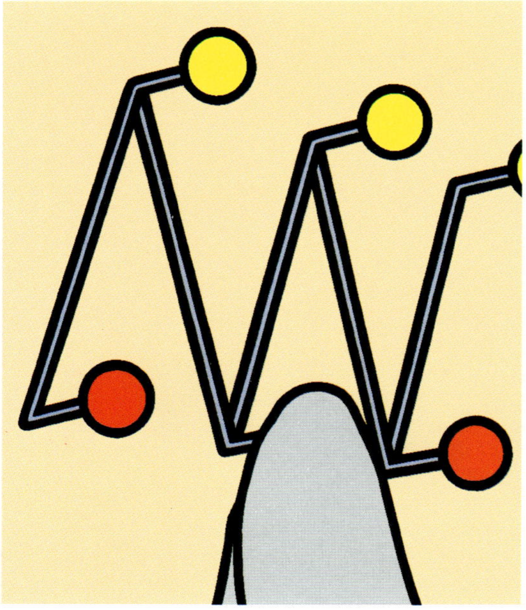
38k

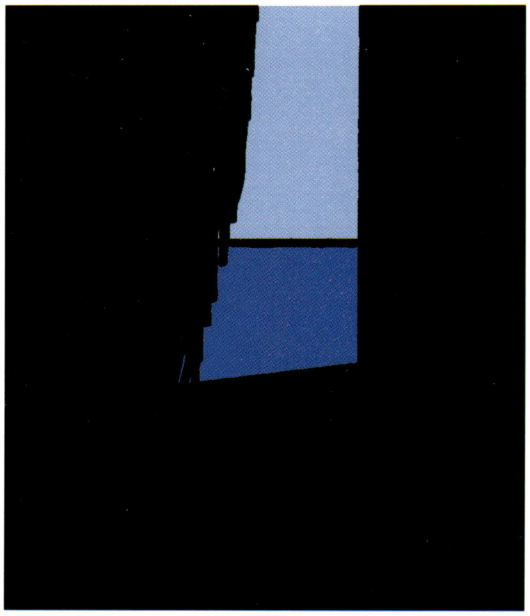
38l

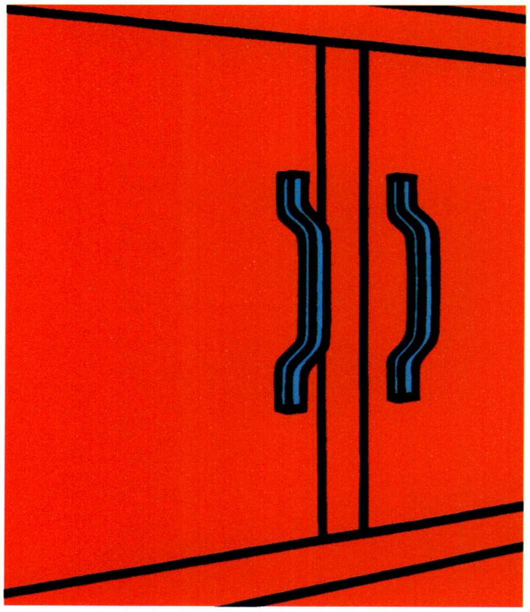
38m

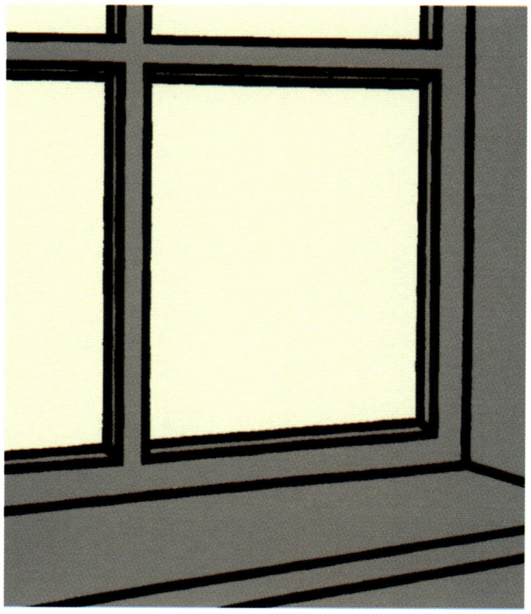
38n

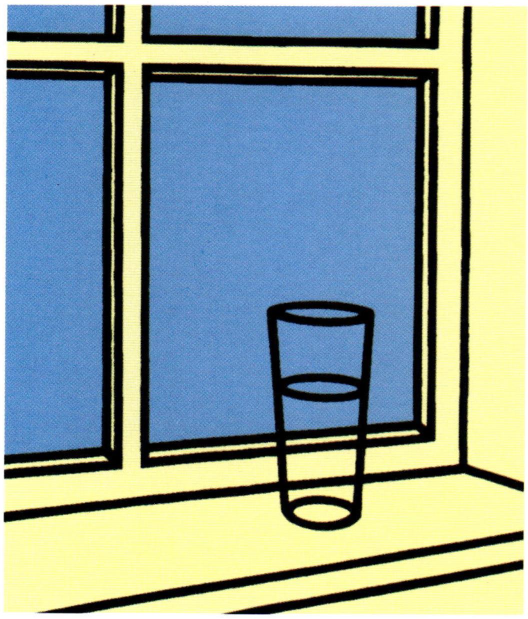
38o

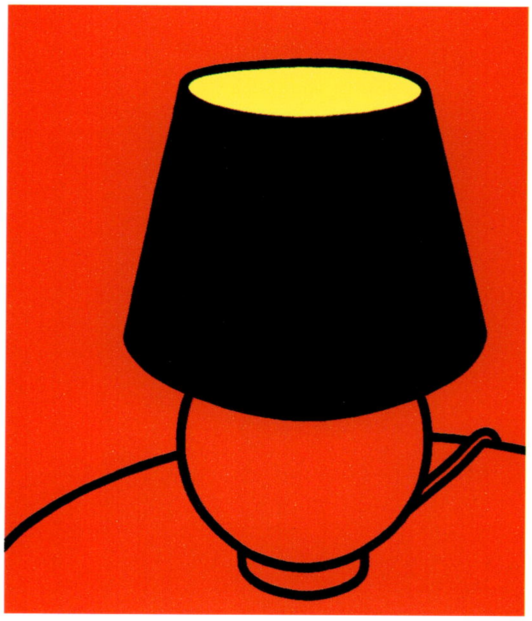
38p

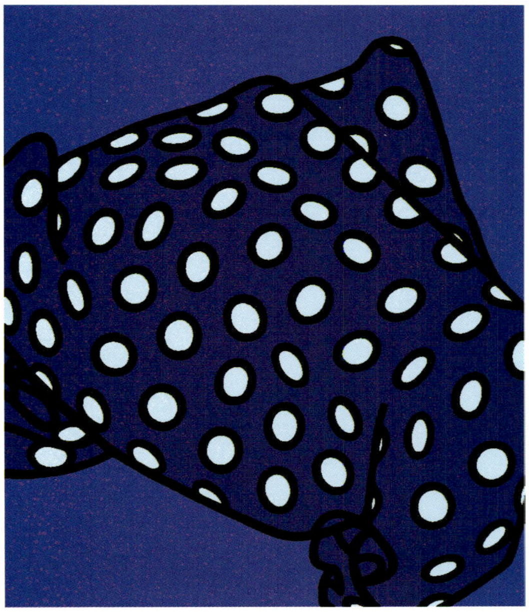
38q

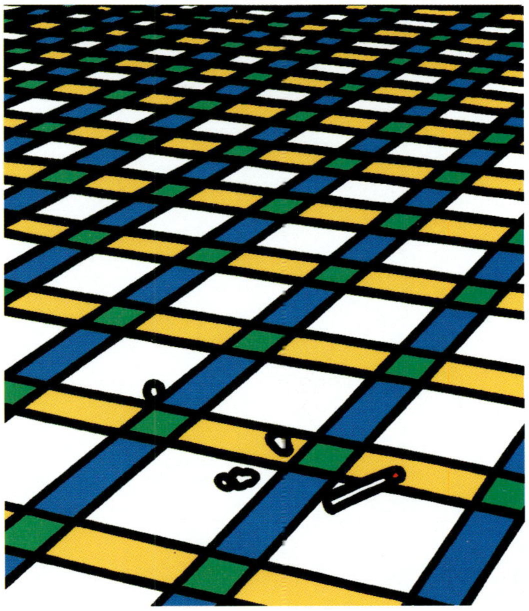
38r

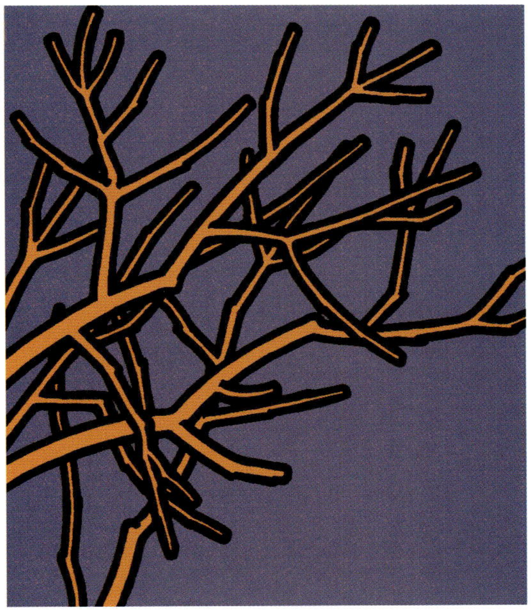
38s

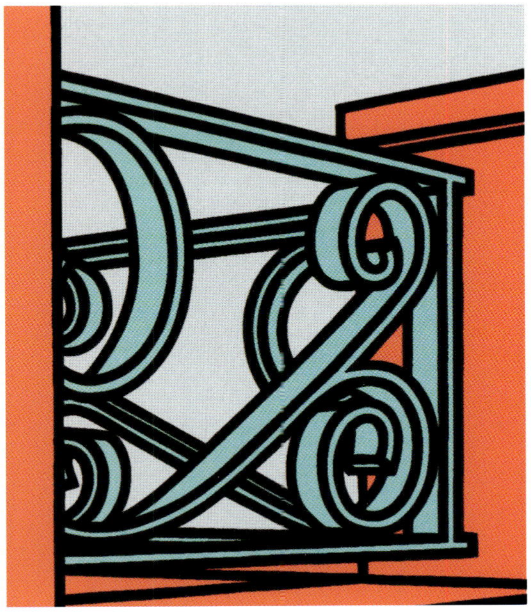
38t

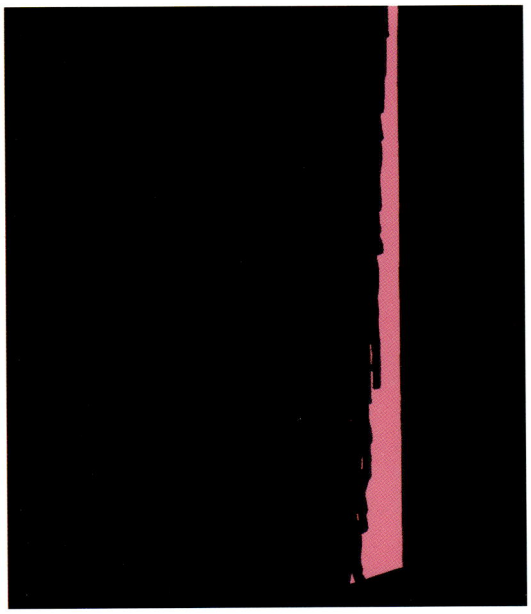
38u

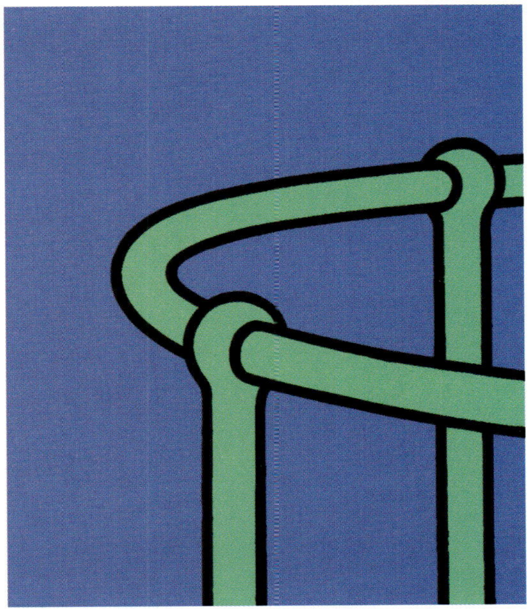
38v

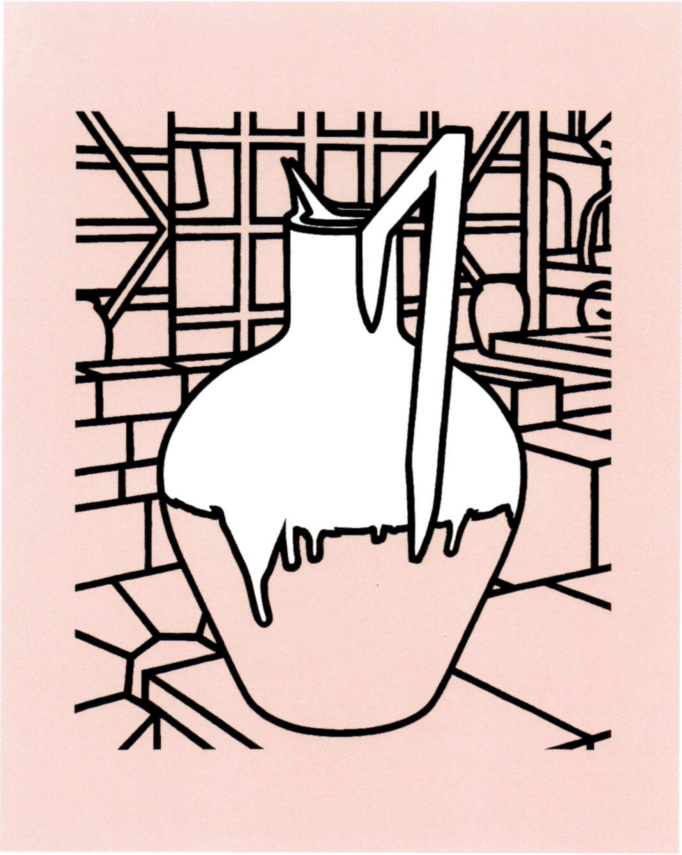

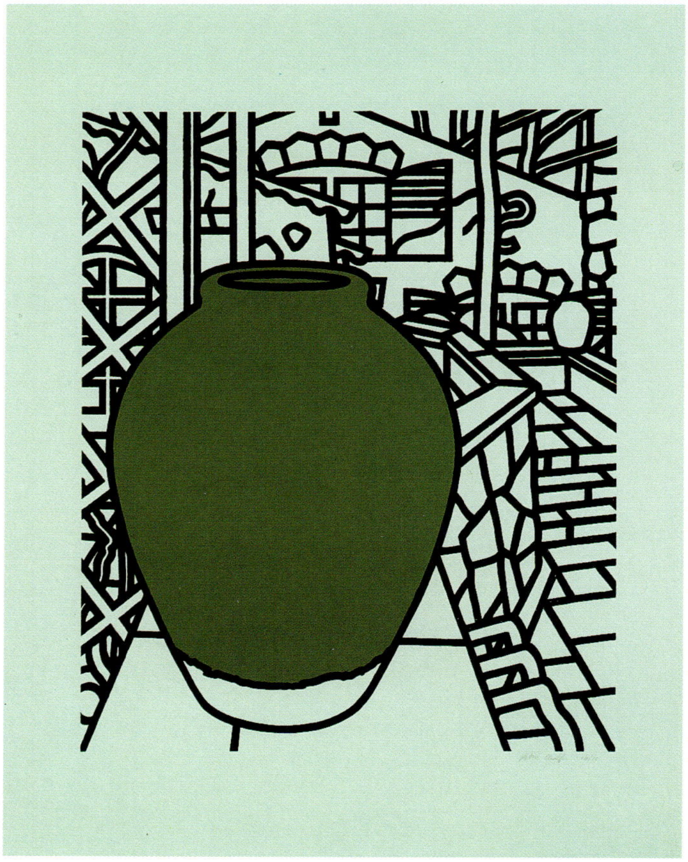

39. **Jug** 1974

40. **Jar** 1974

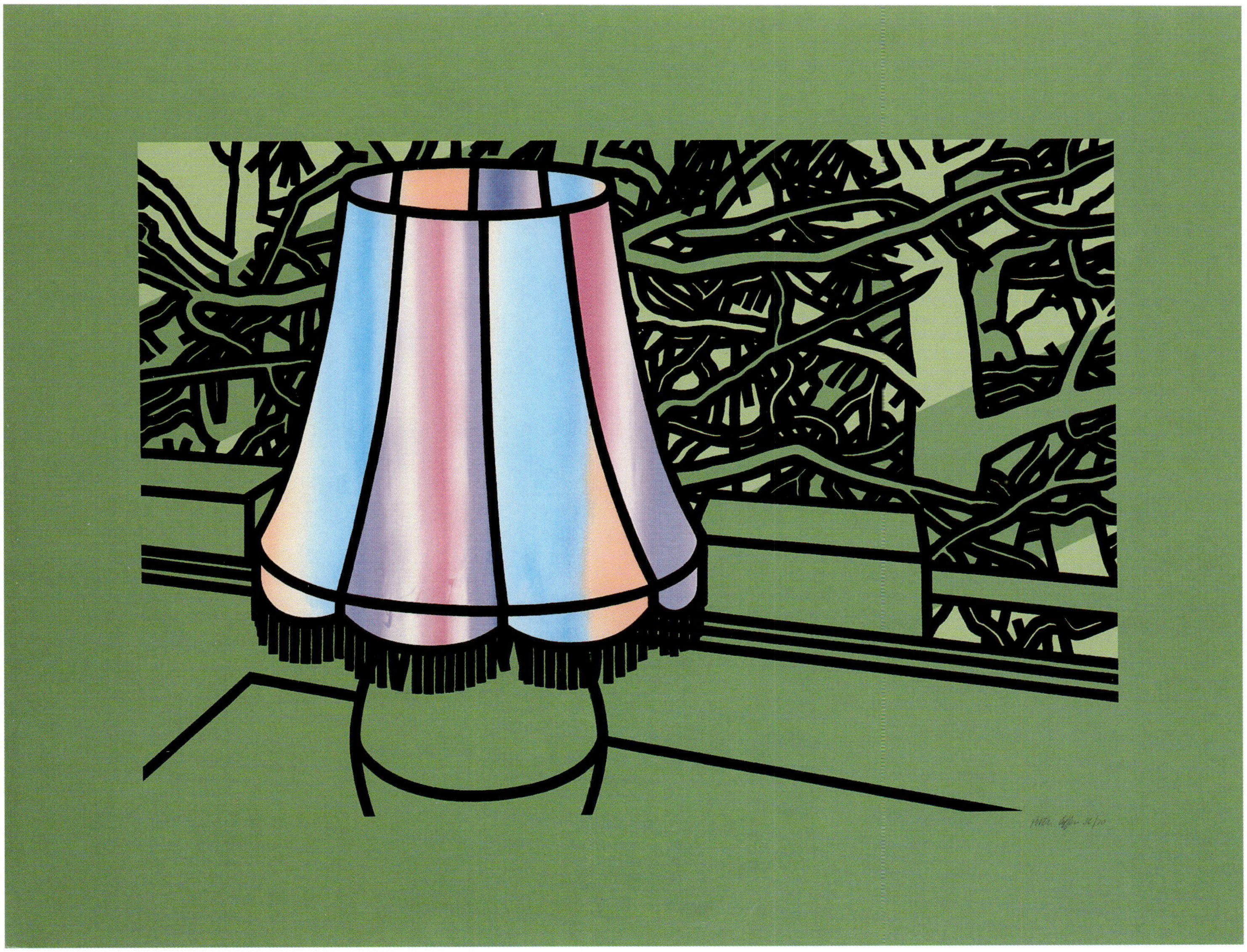

45. **Lamp and Pines** 1975

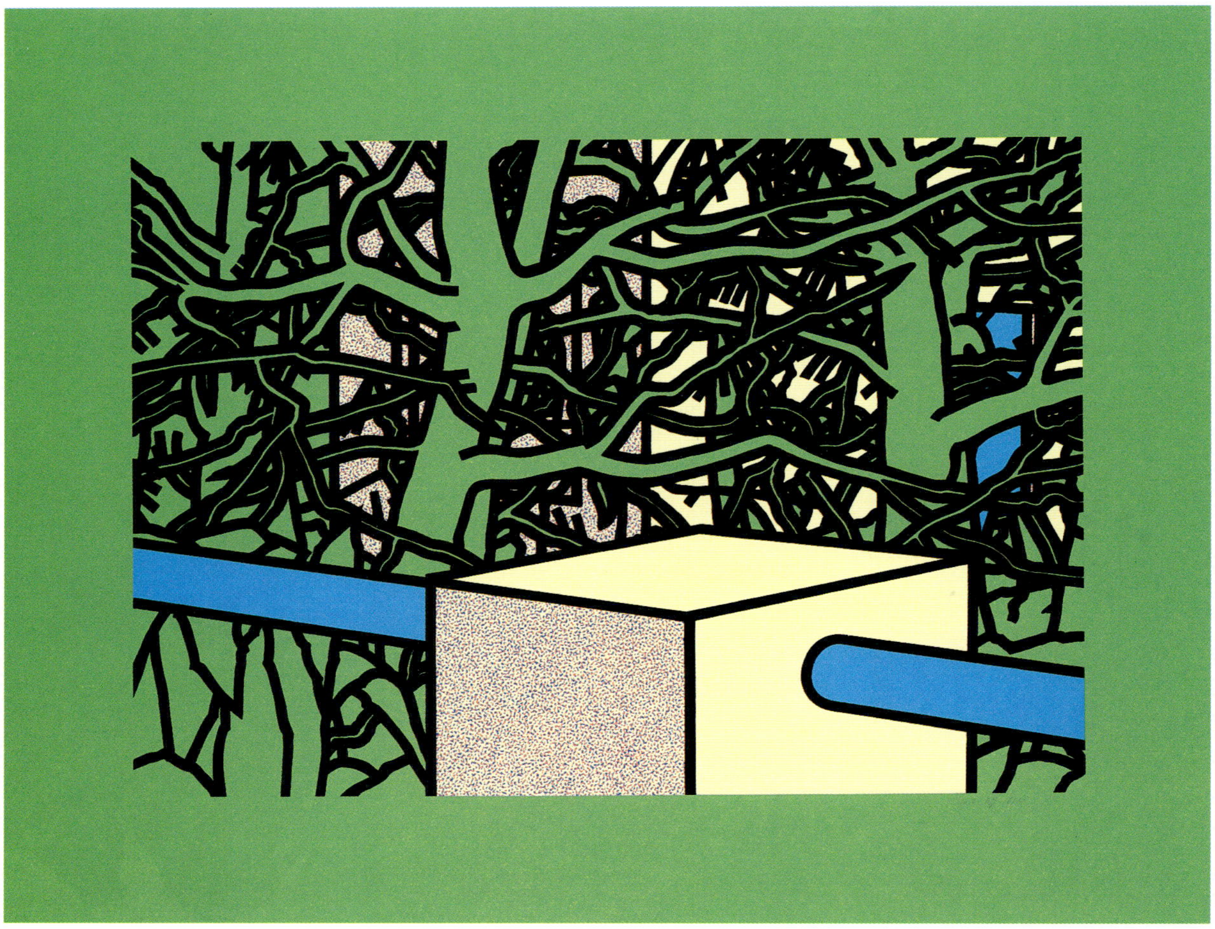

41. **Garden with Pines** 1975

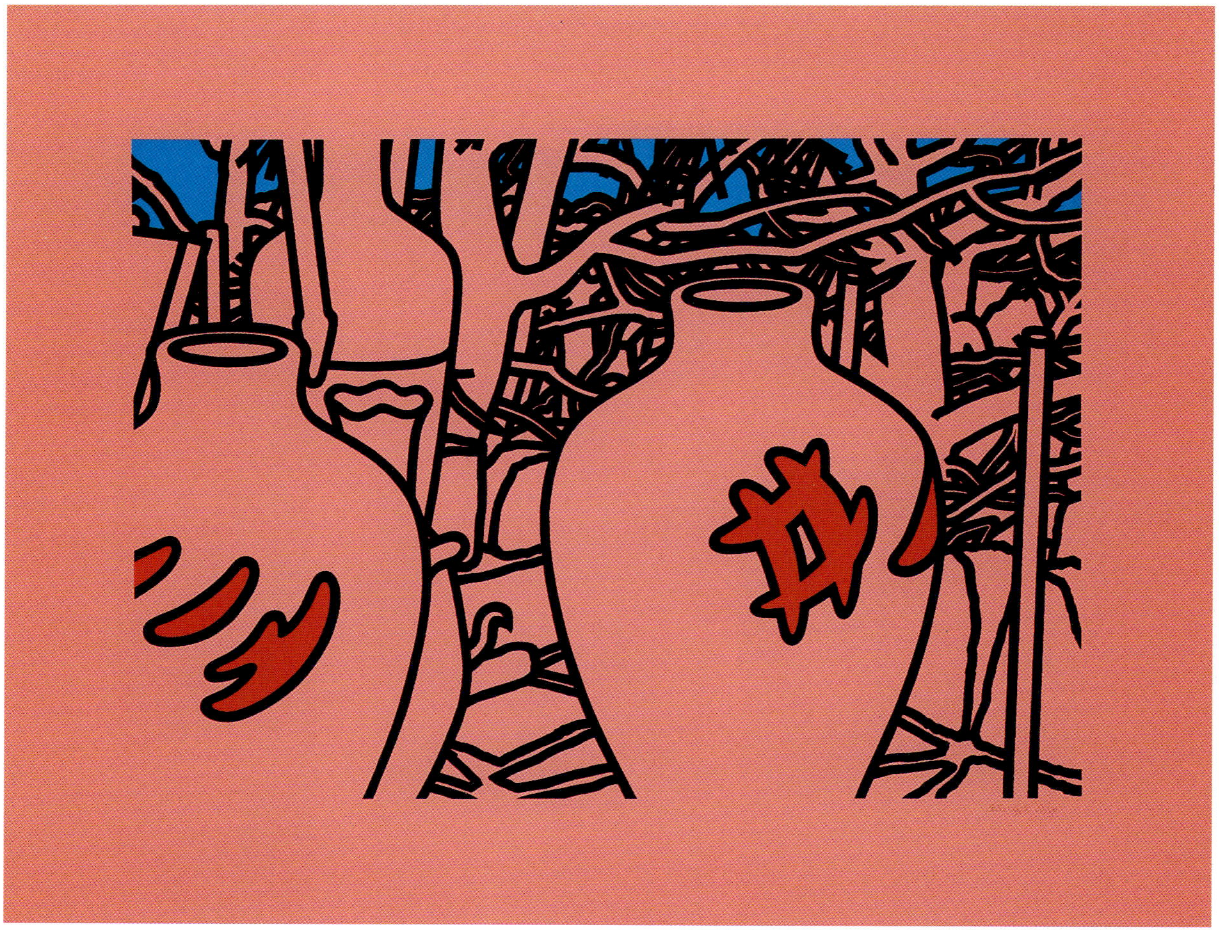

42. **Signature Pots** 1975

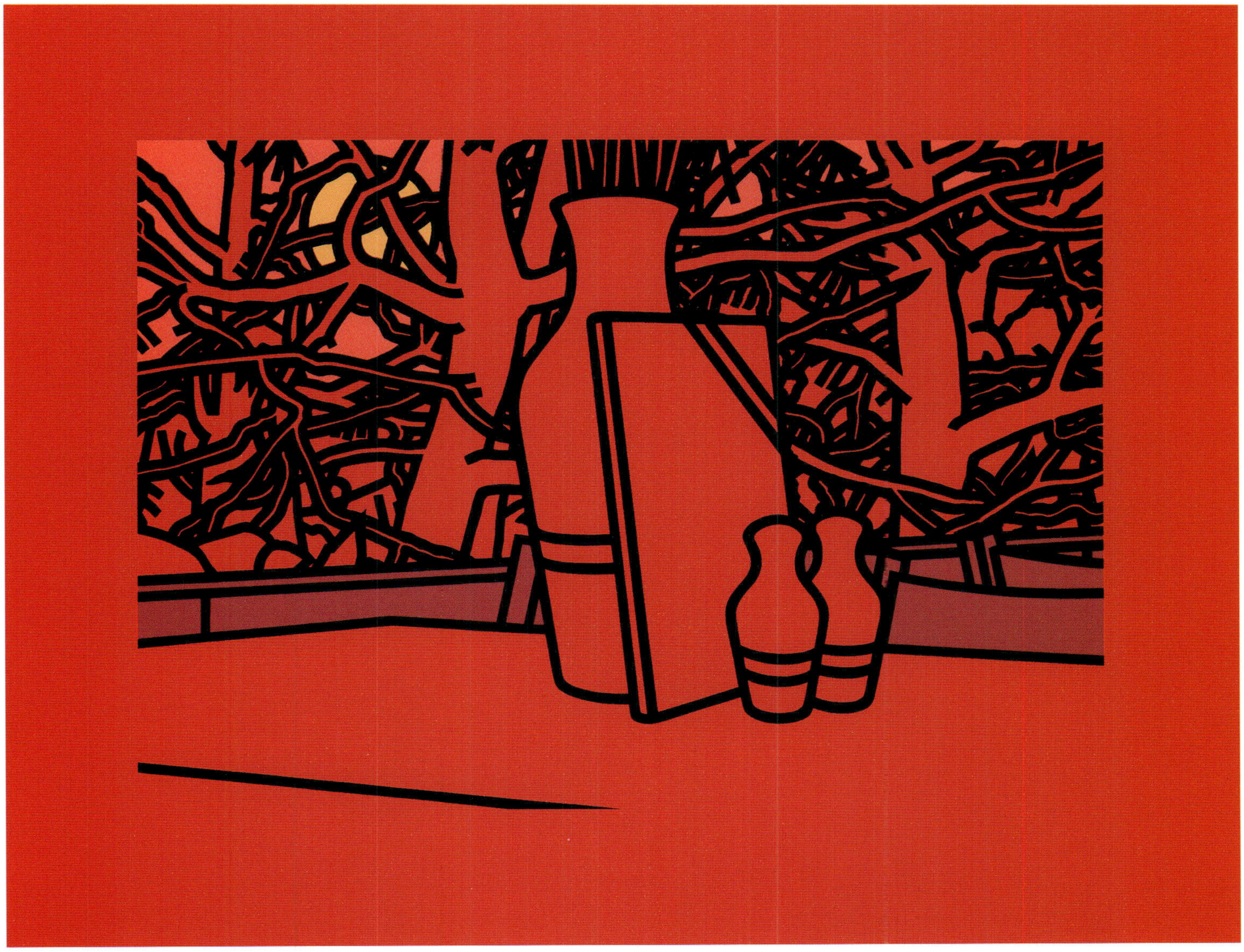

46. **Evening Menu** 1975

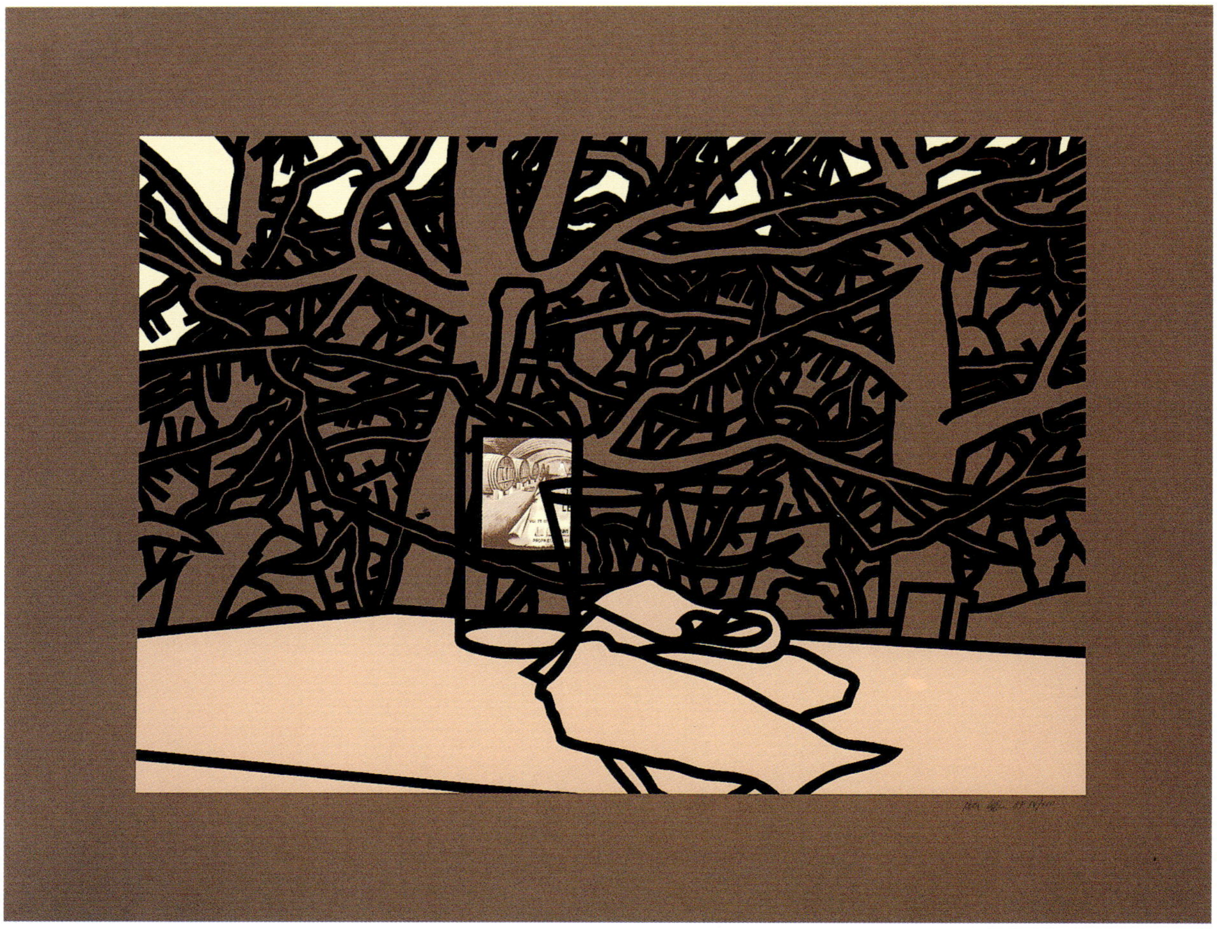

43. **Rosé Bottle** 1975

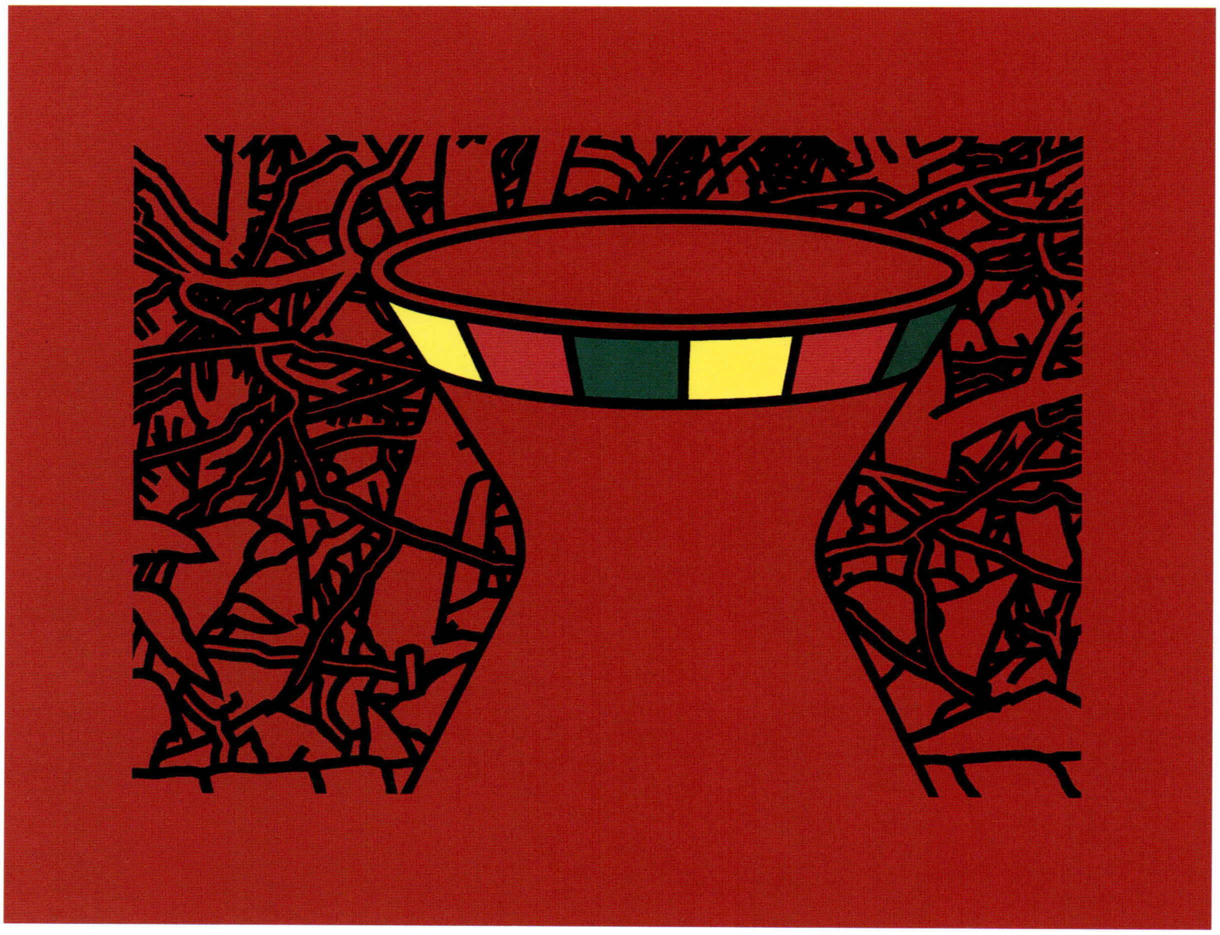

44. **Terracotta Vase** 1975

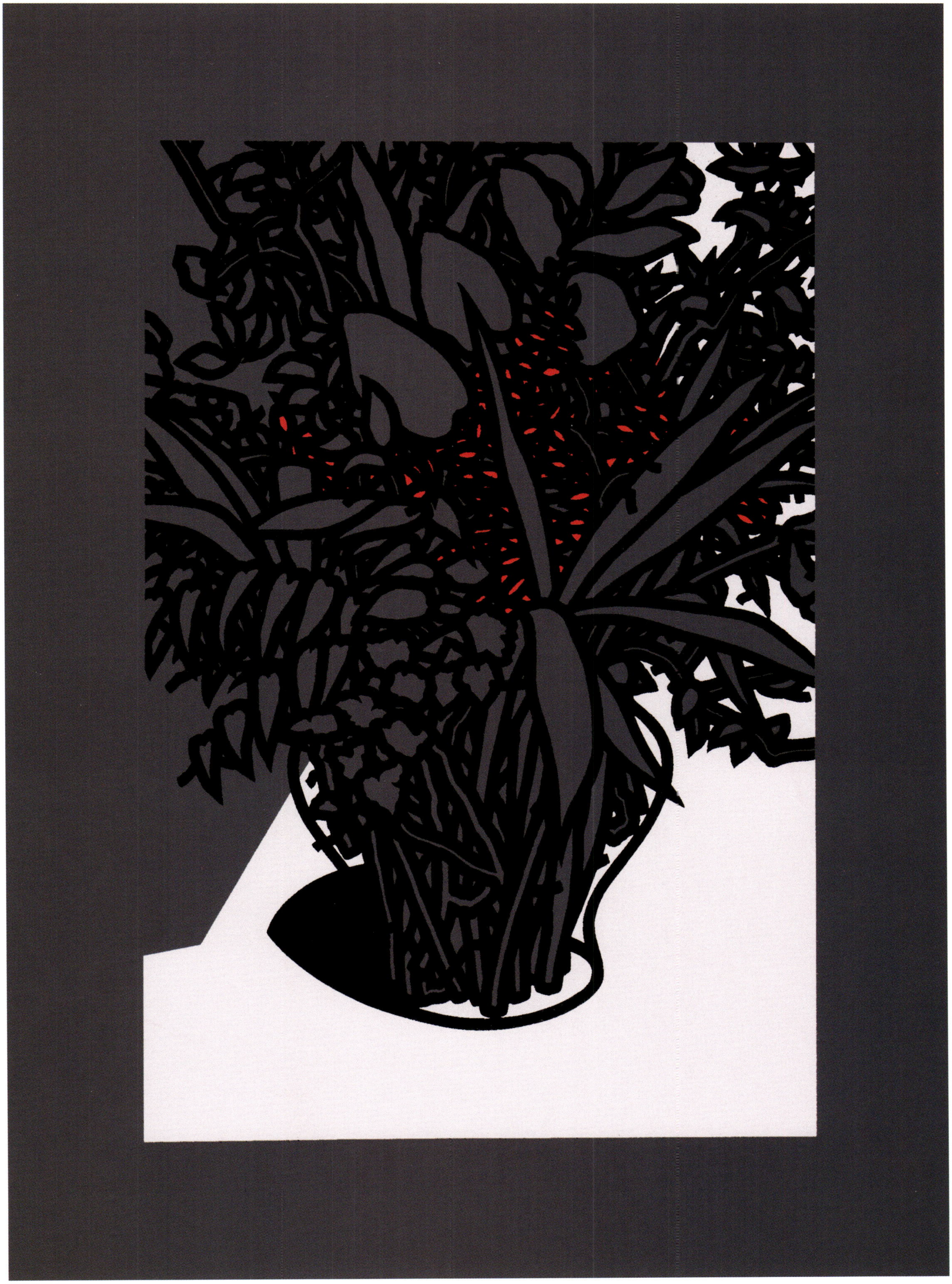

47. **For John Constable** 1976

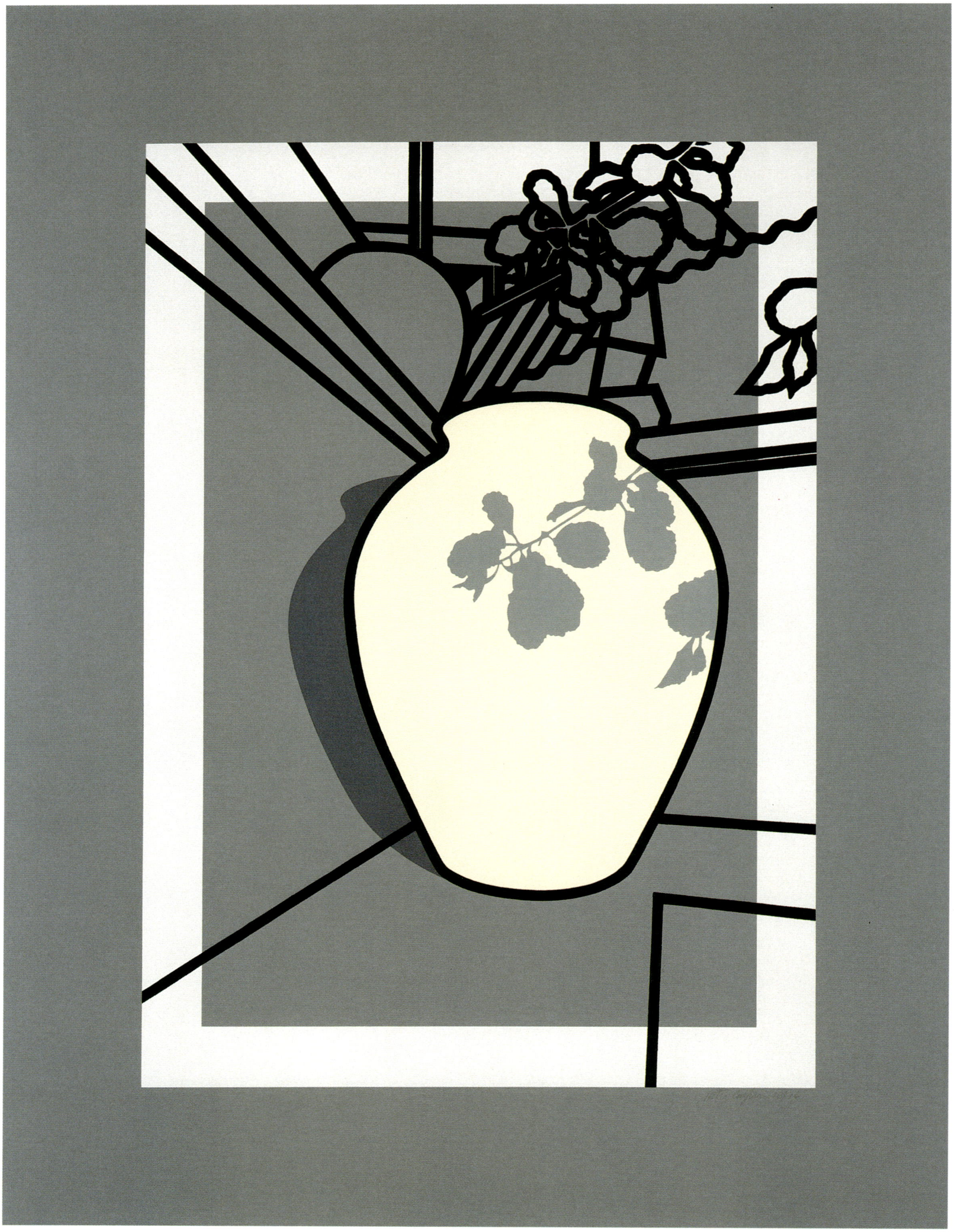

48. **White Pot** 1976

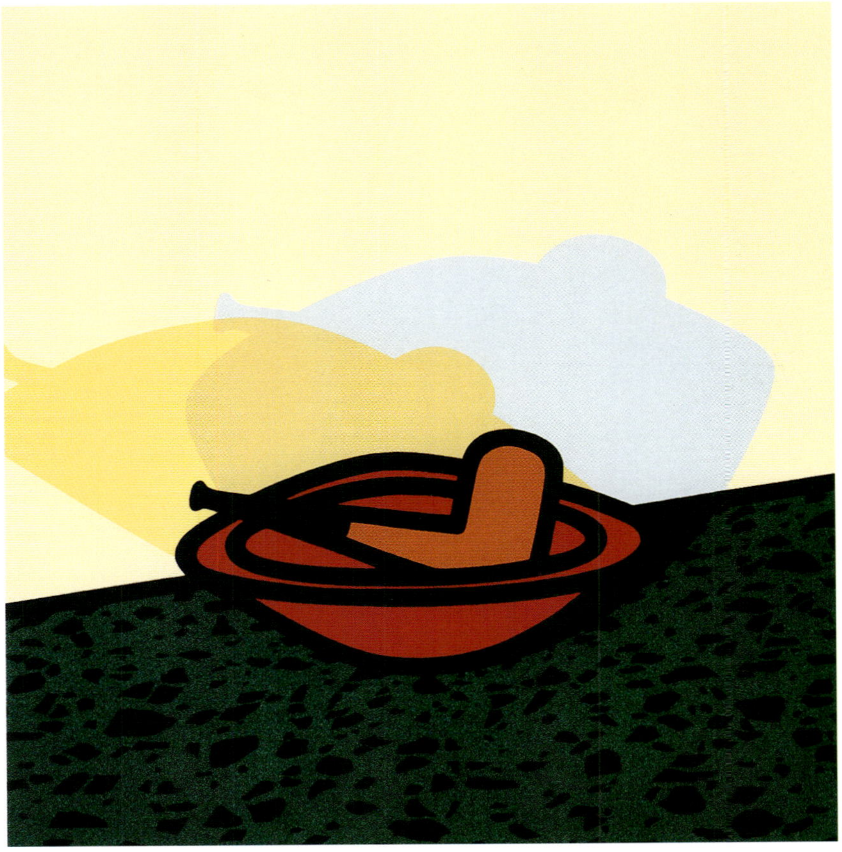

50. **Pipe in Bowl** 1976

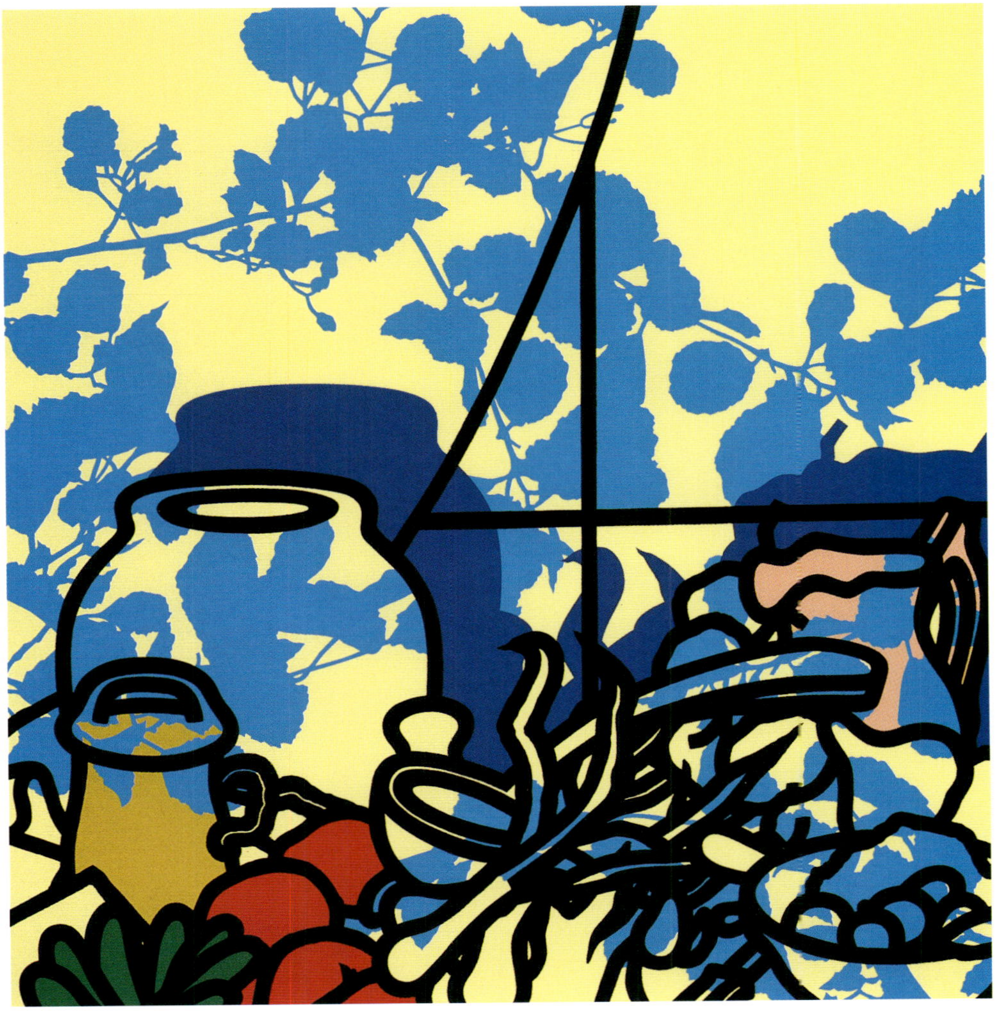

49. **Still Life Ingredients** 1976

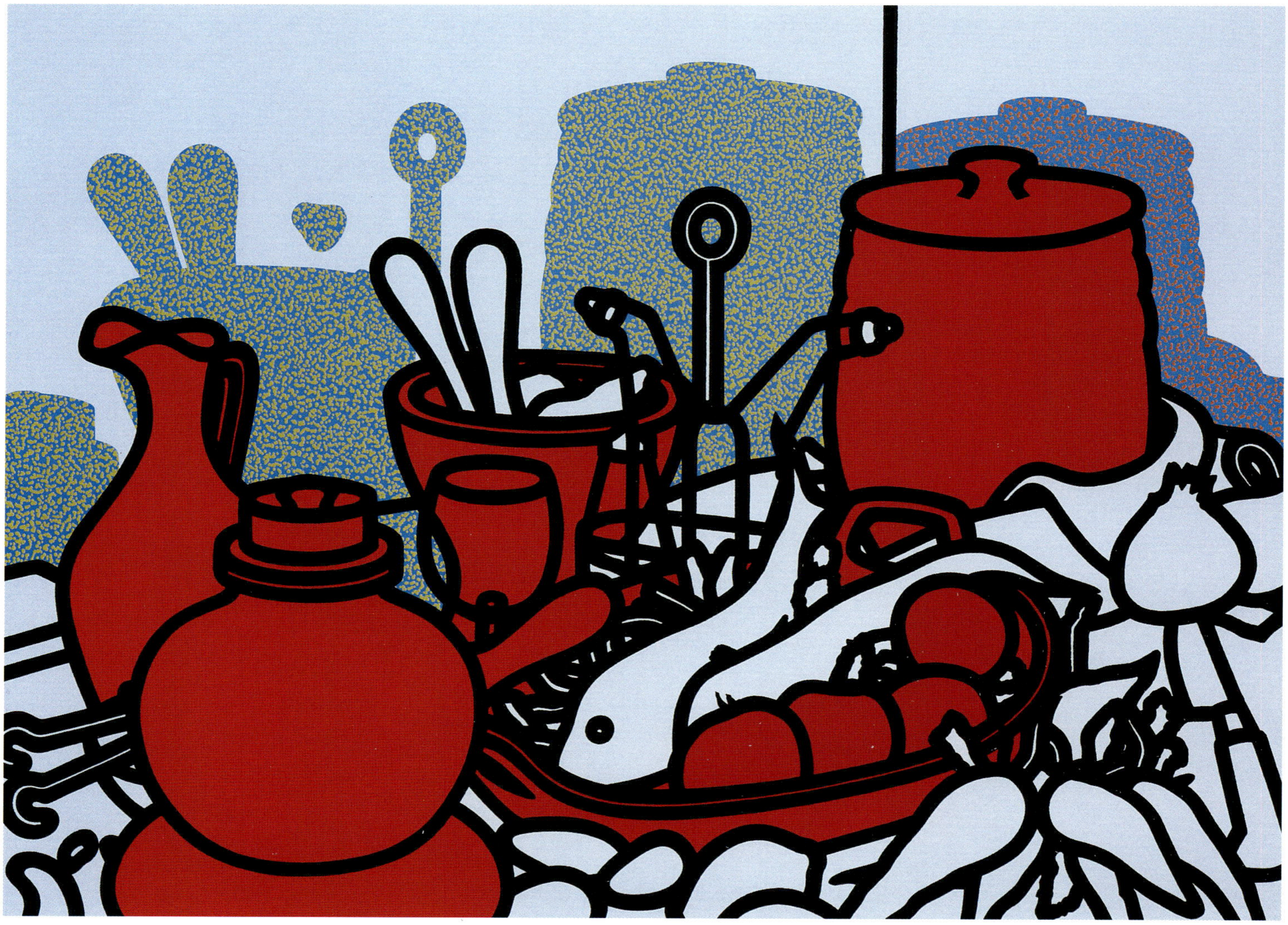

51. **Glazed Earthenware** 1976

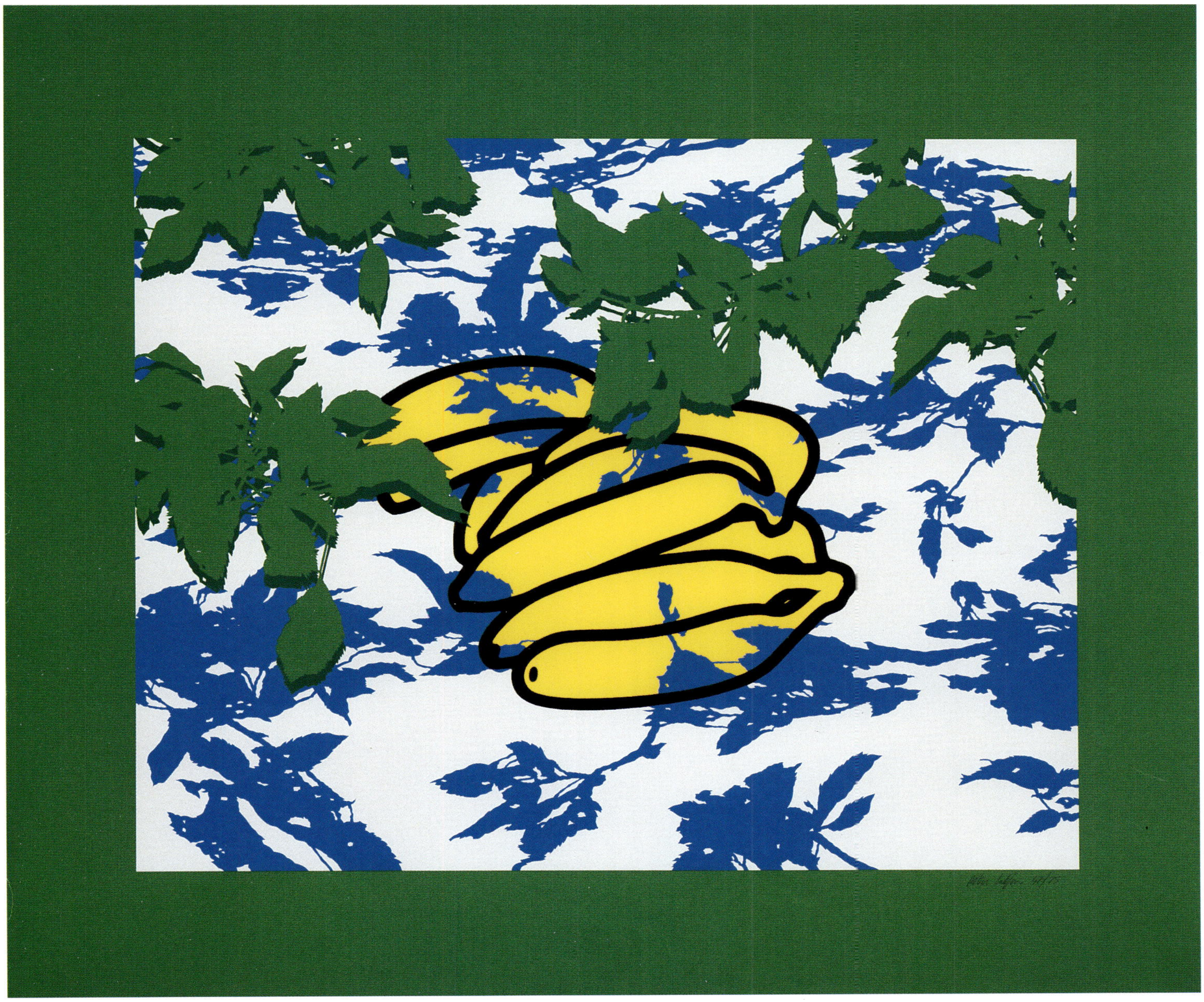

52. **Bananas with Leaves** 1977

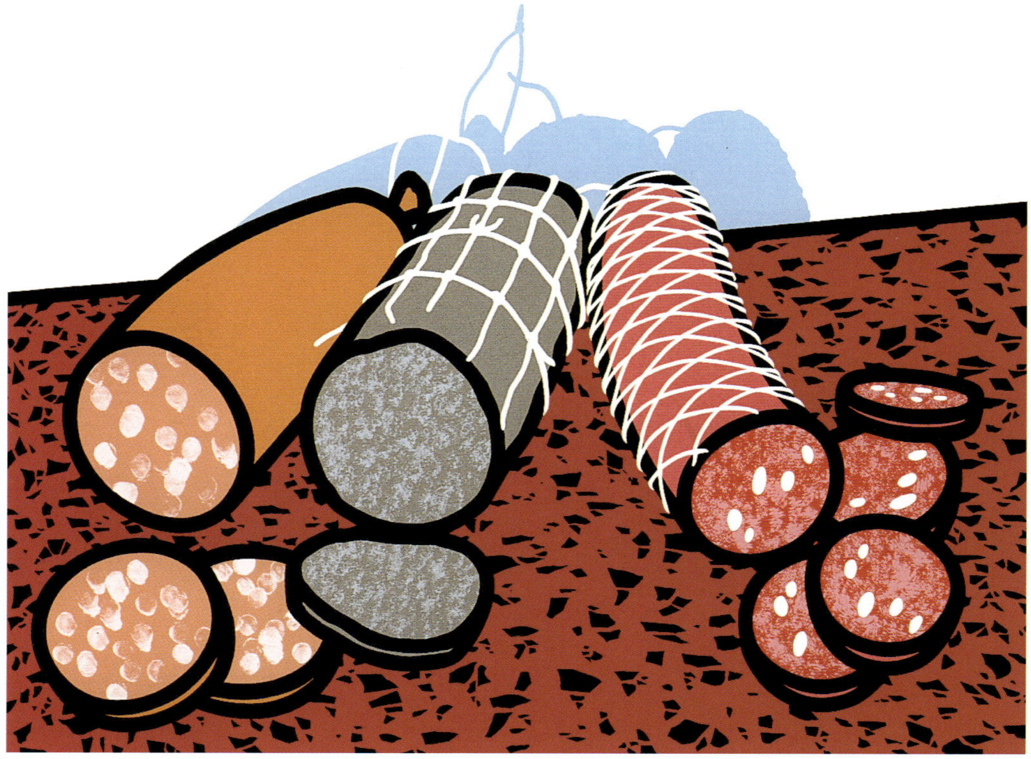

54. **Three Sausages** 1978

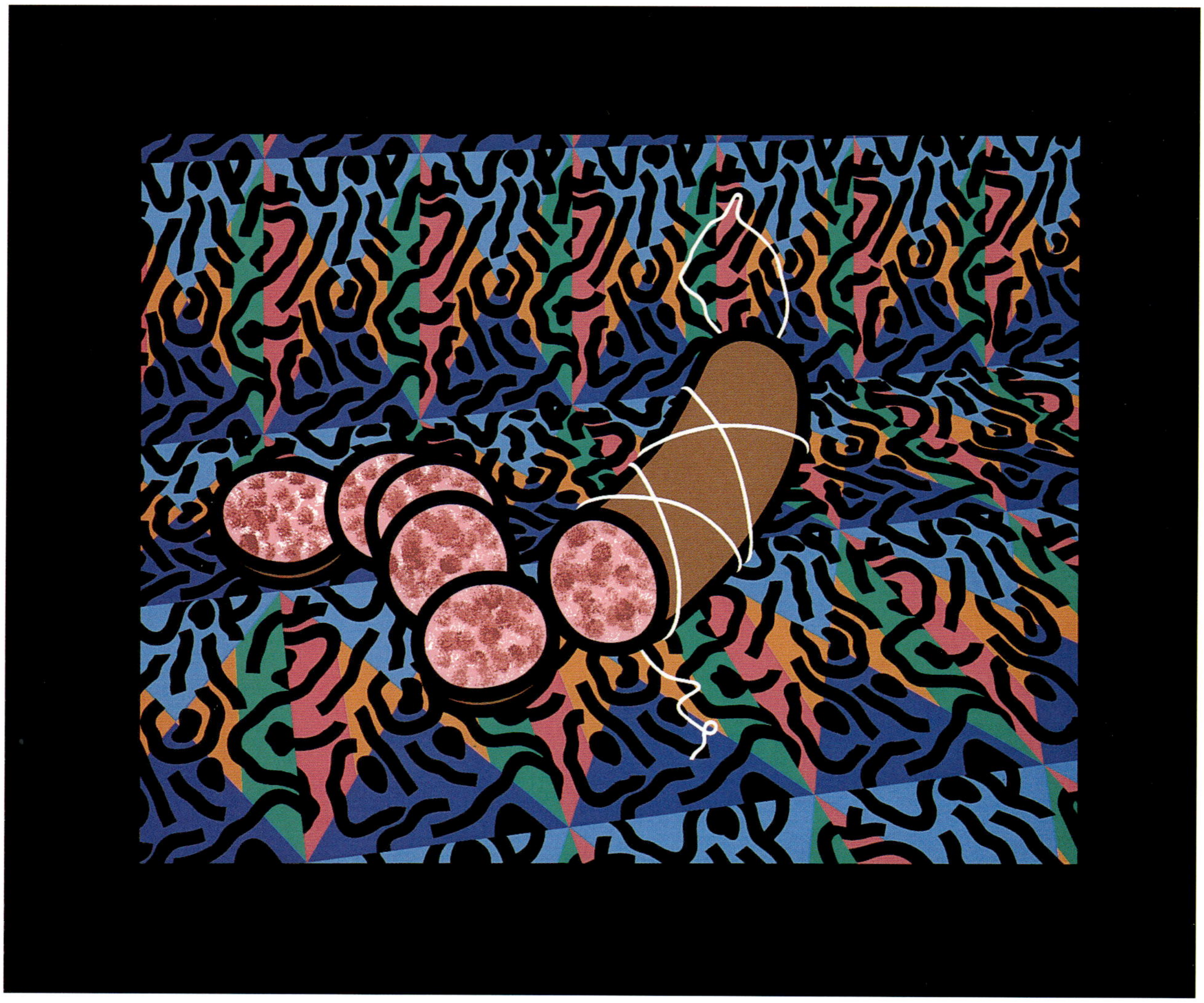

53. **Sausage** 1978

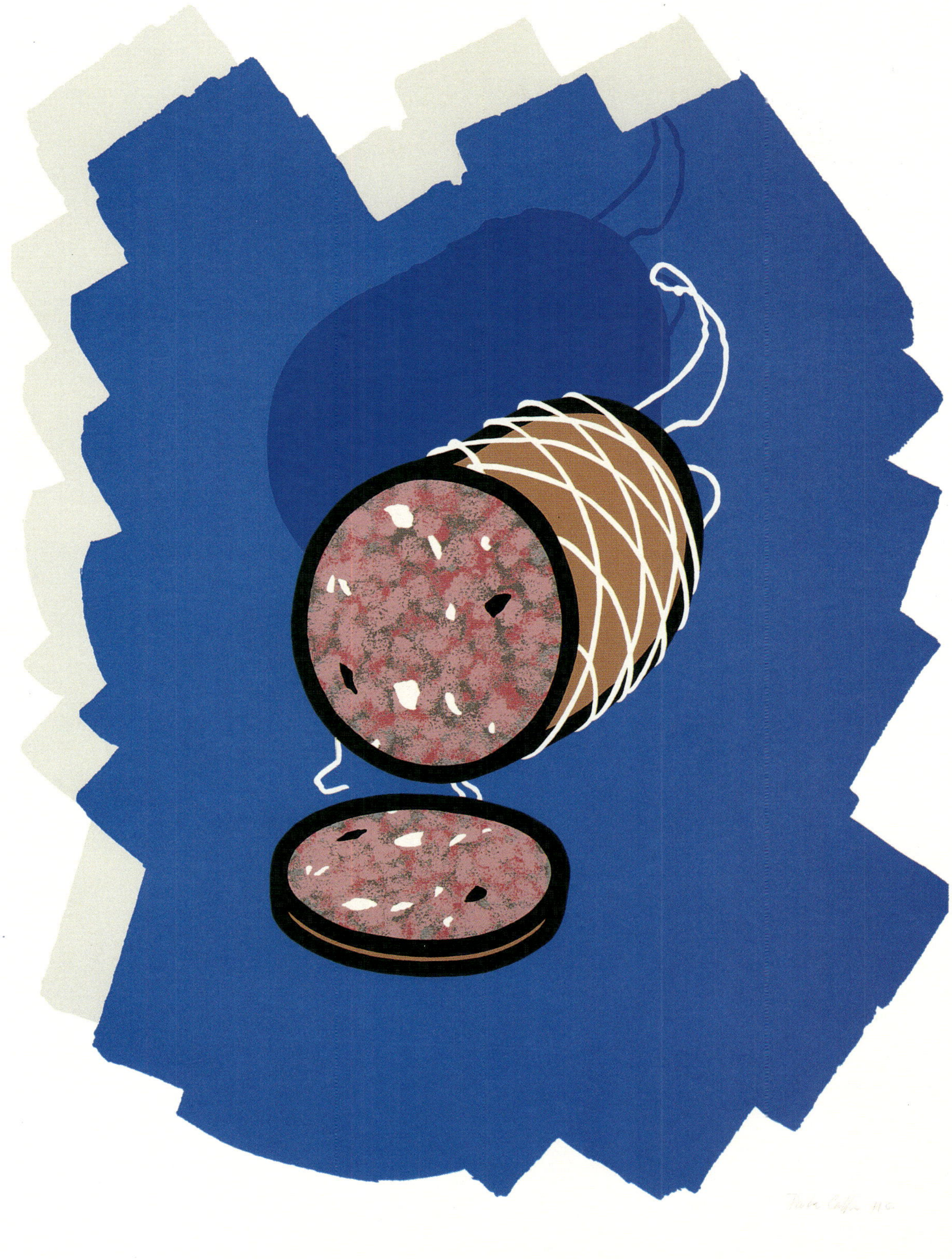

55. **Big Sausage** 1978

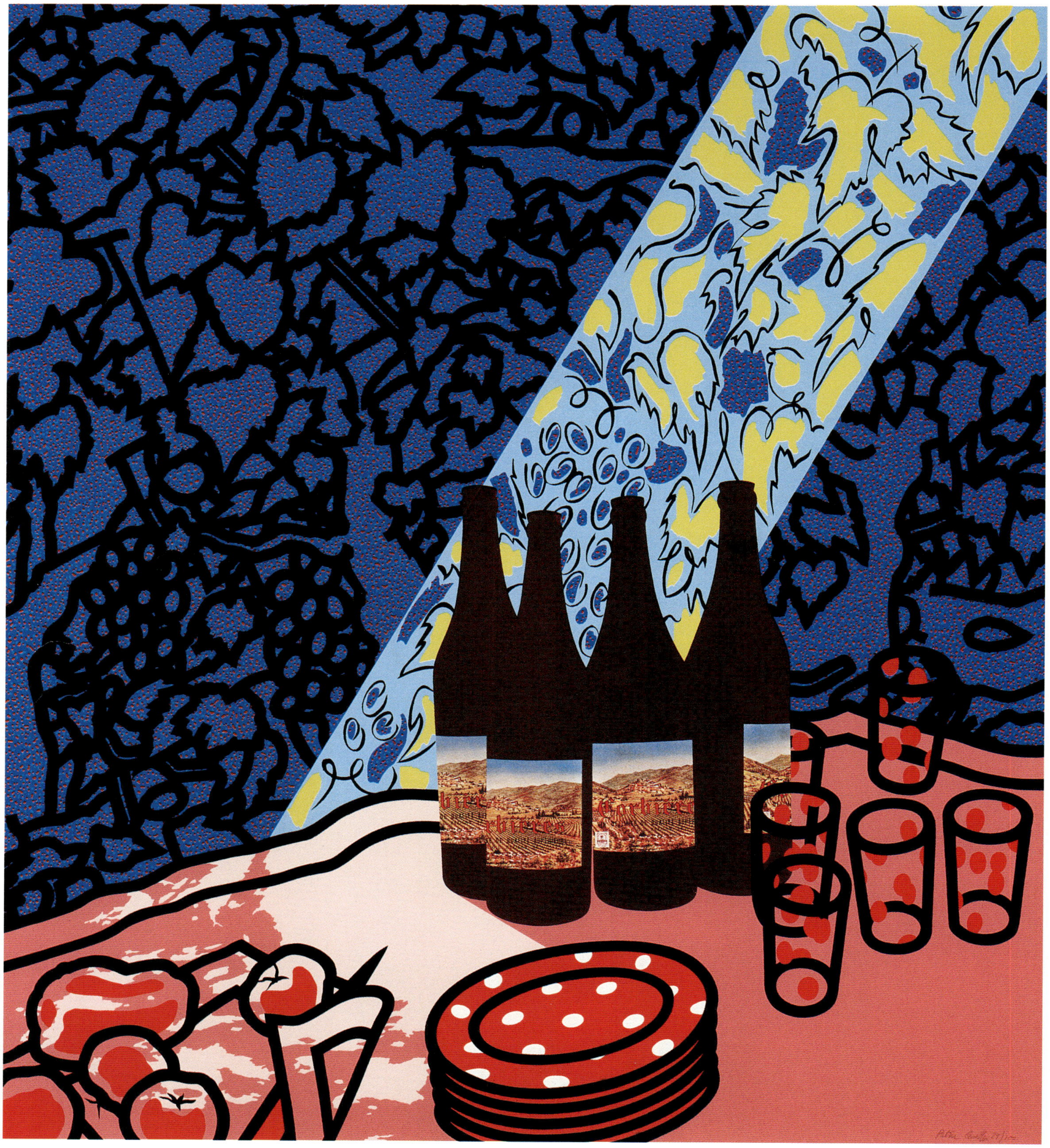

56. **Picnic Set** 1978

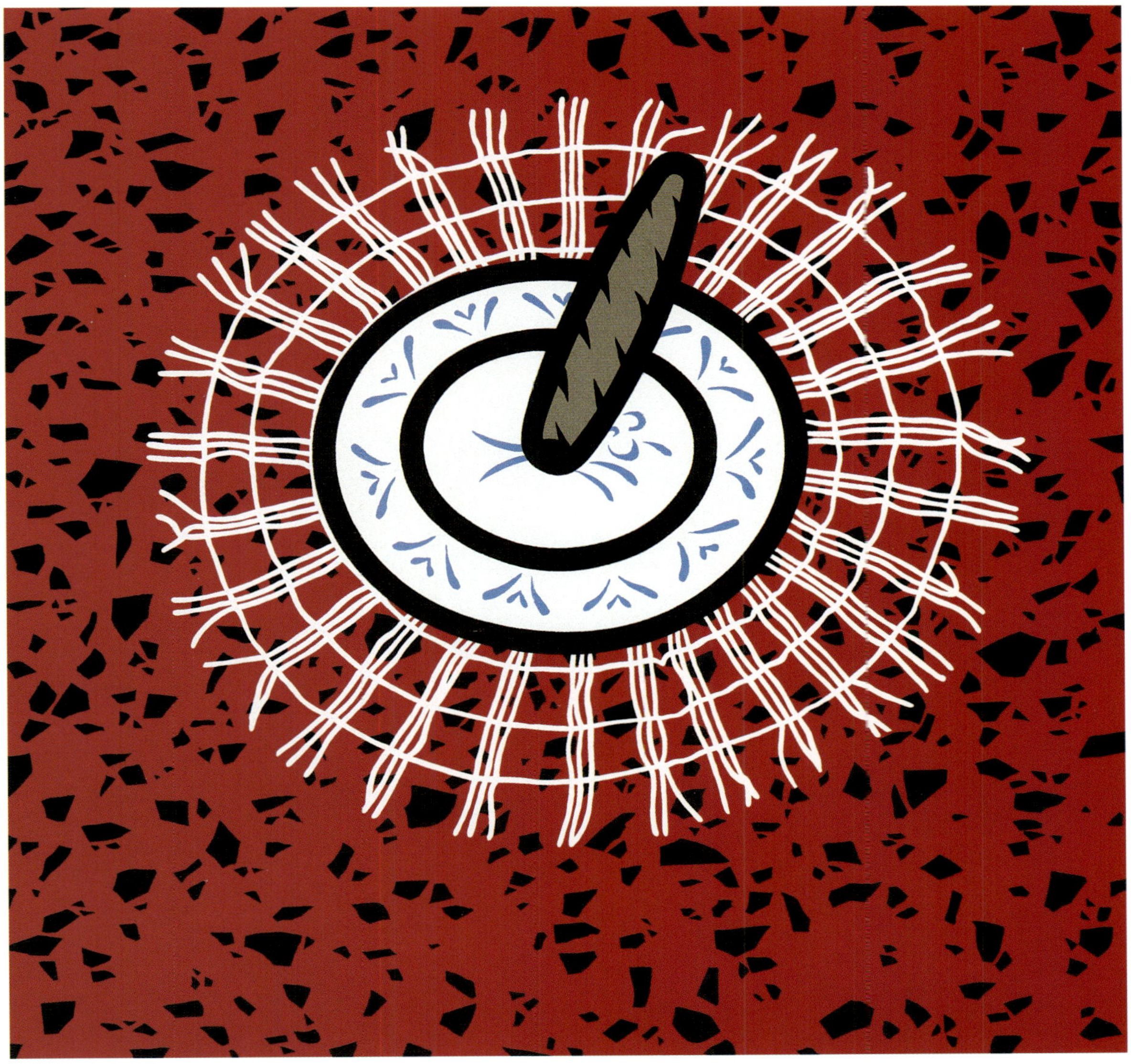

57. **Cigar** 1978

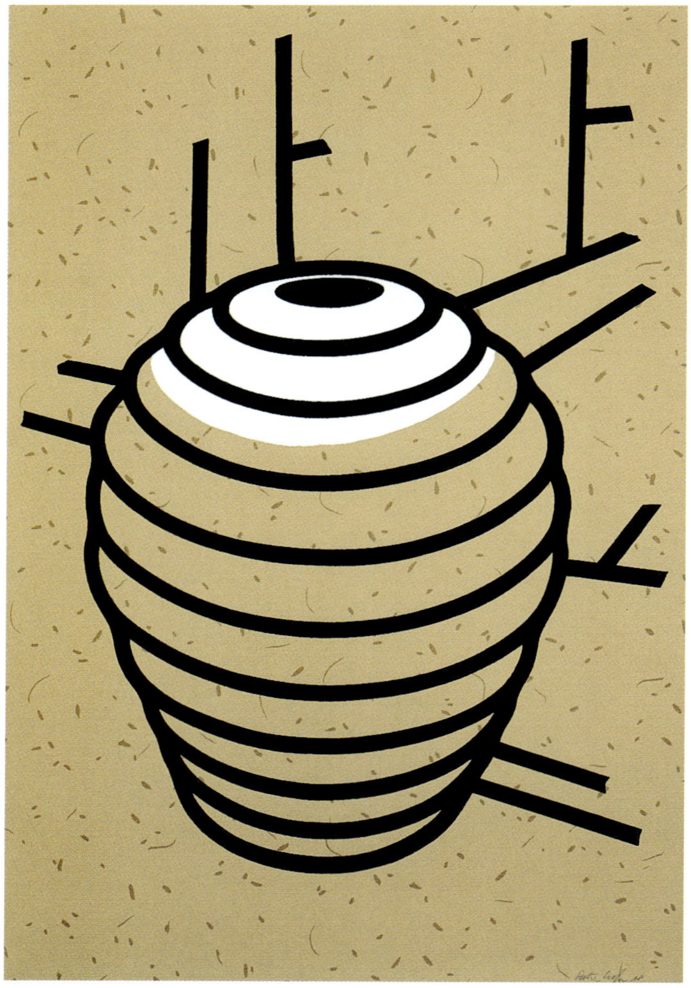

58. **Ridged Jar** 1979-80

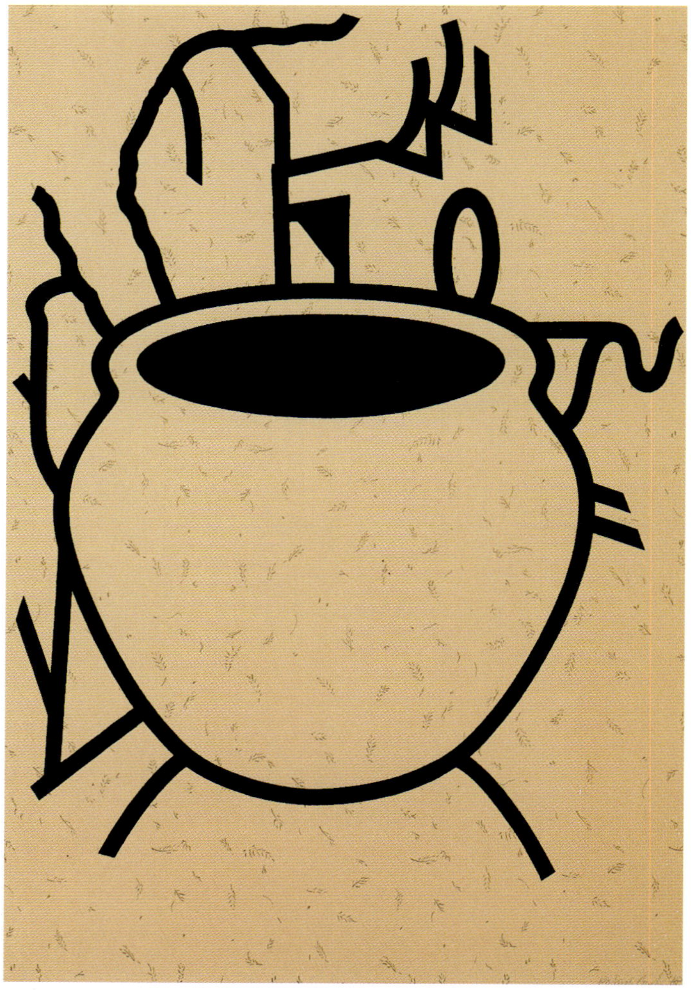

59. **Fern Pot** 1979-80

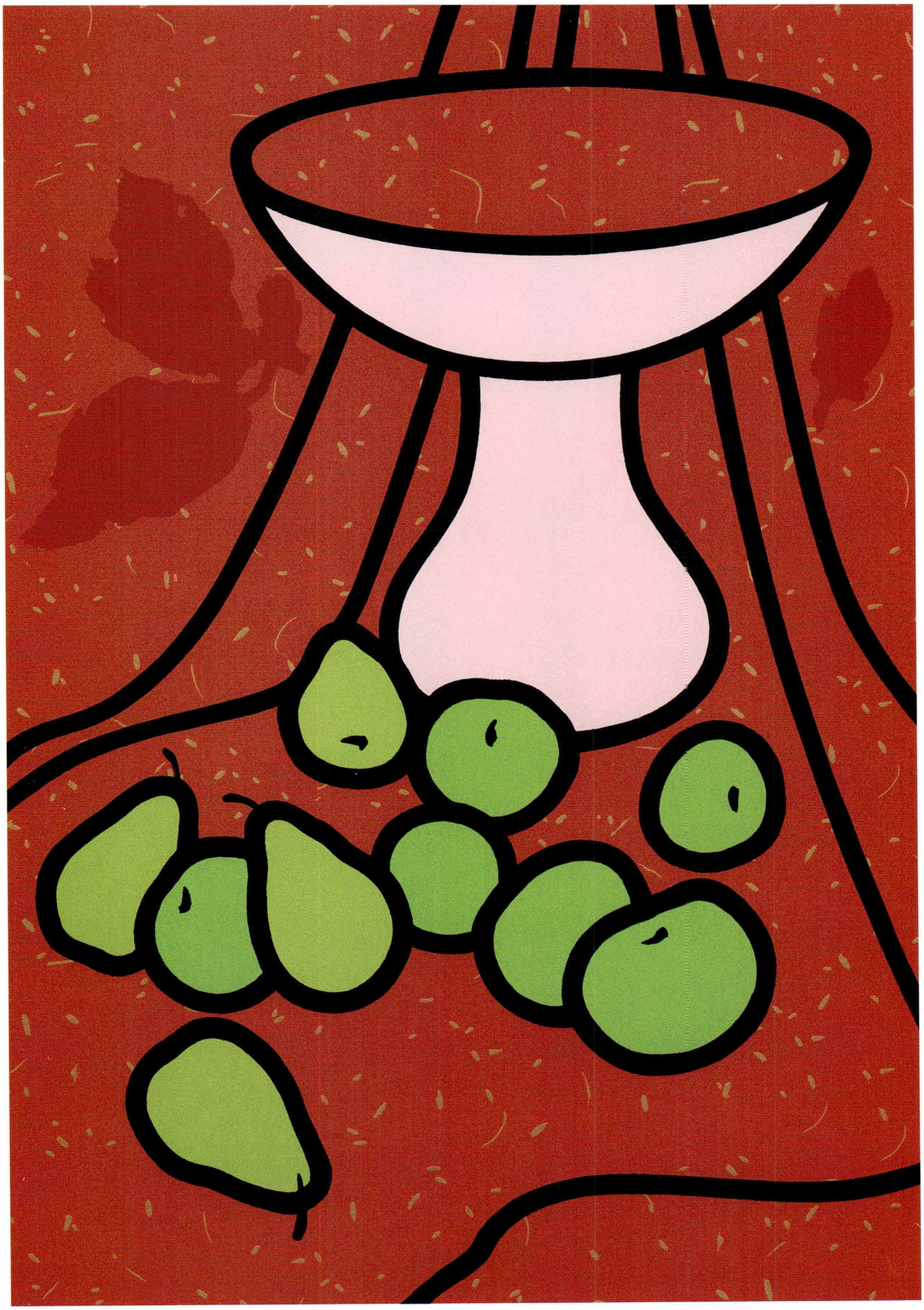

60. **Fruit and Bowl** 1979-80

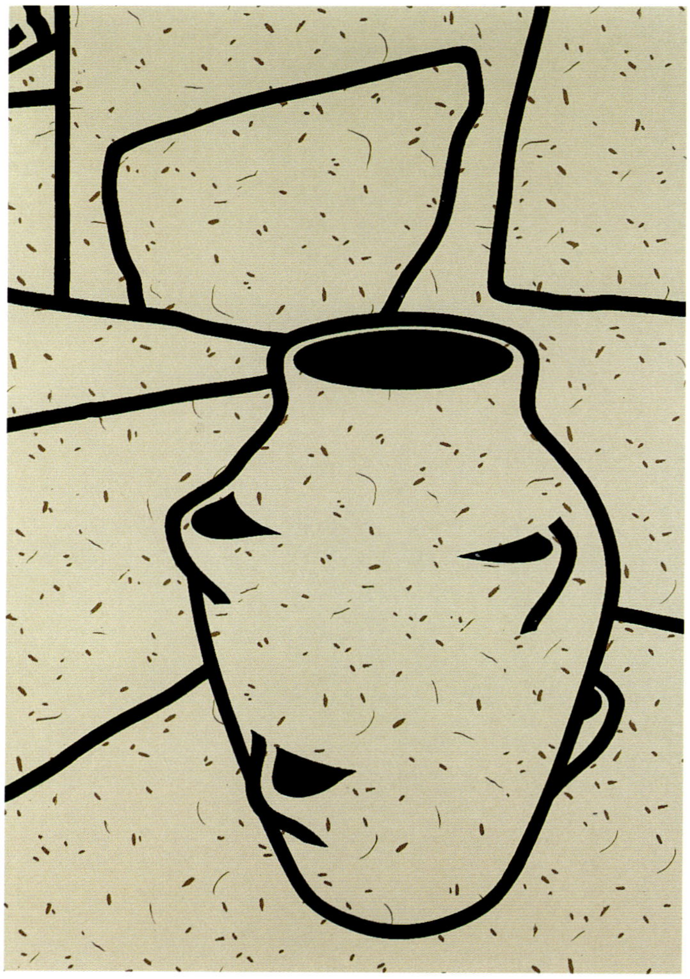

61. **Plant Pot** 1979-80

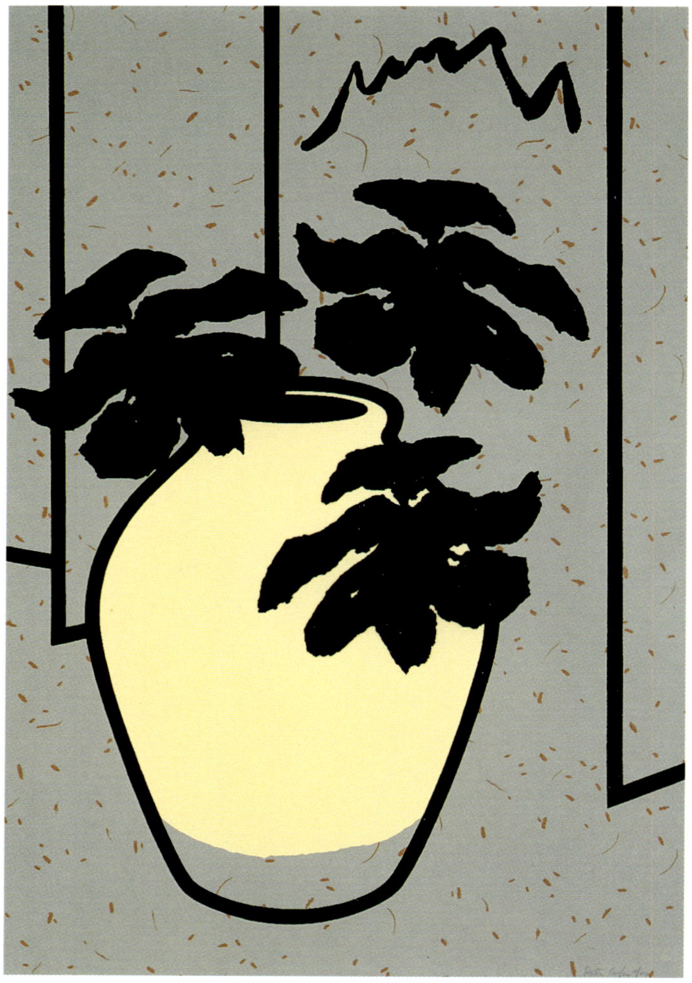

62. **Cream Glazed Pot** 1979-80

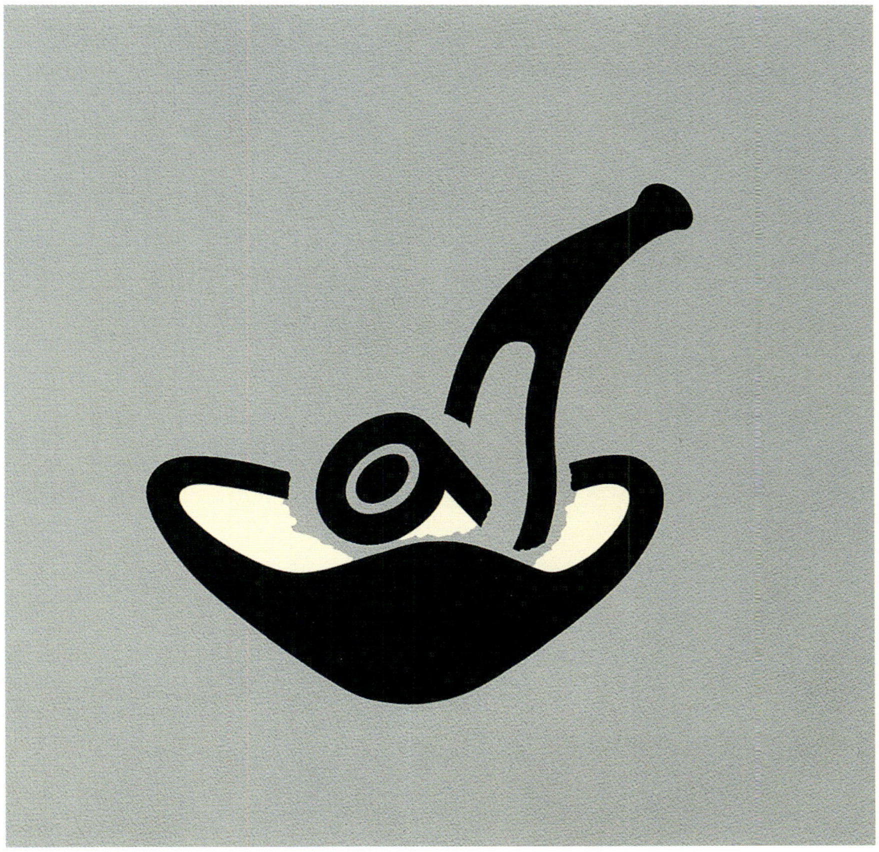

64. **Grey Pipe** 1981

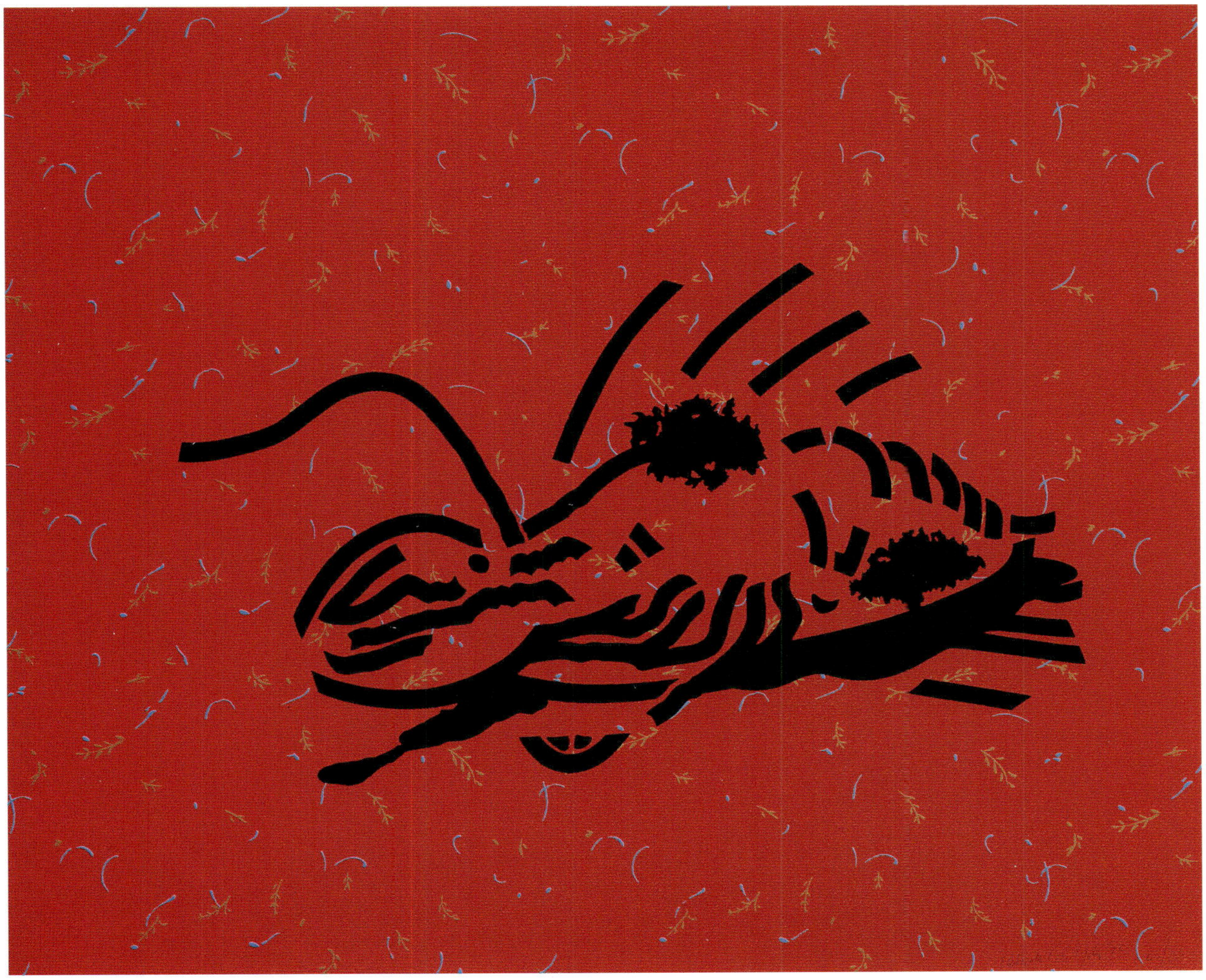

63. **Dressed Lobster** 1980

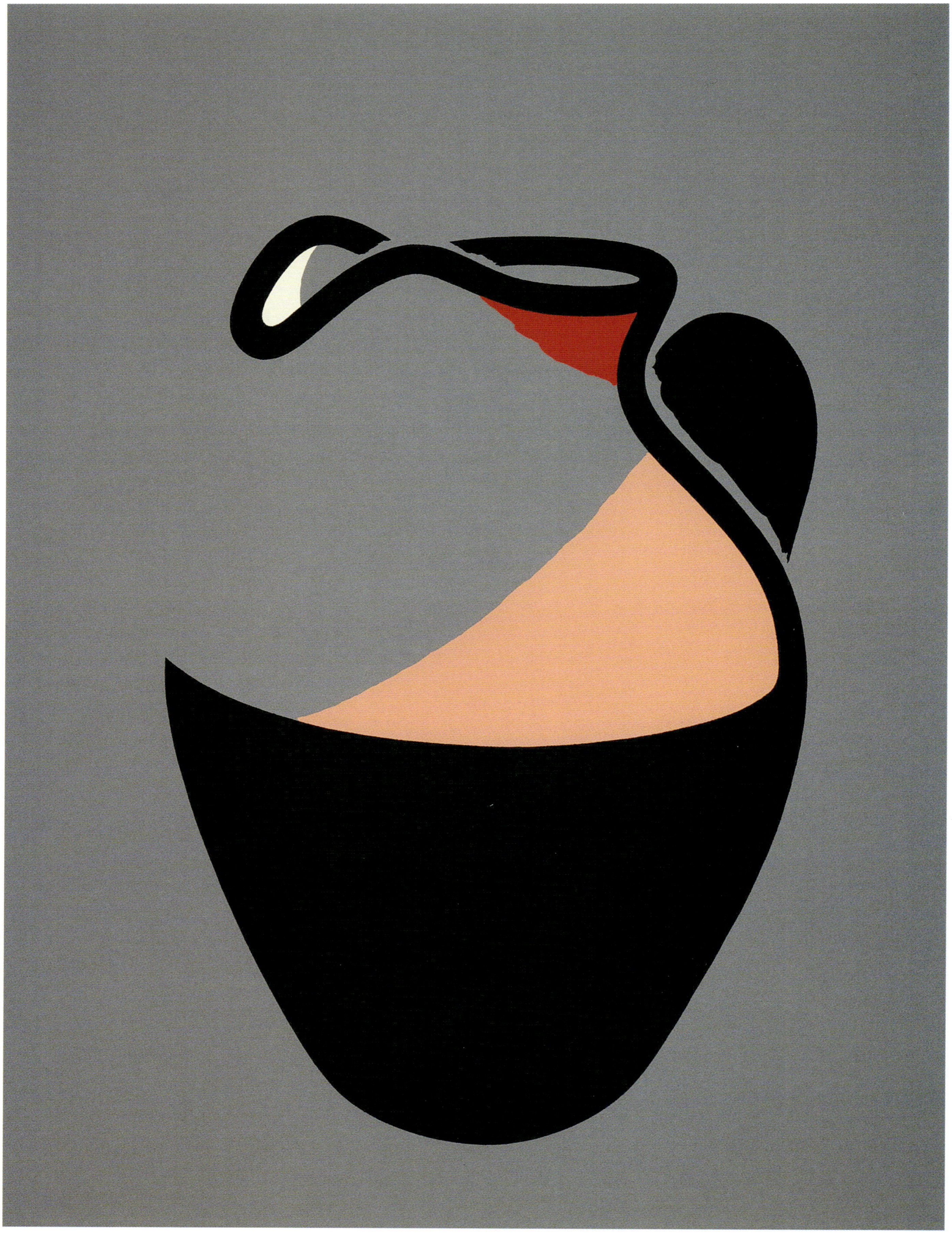

65. **Pink Jug** 1981-82

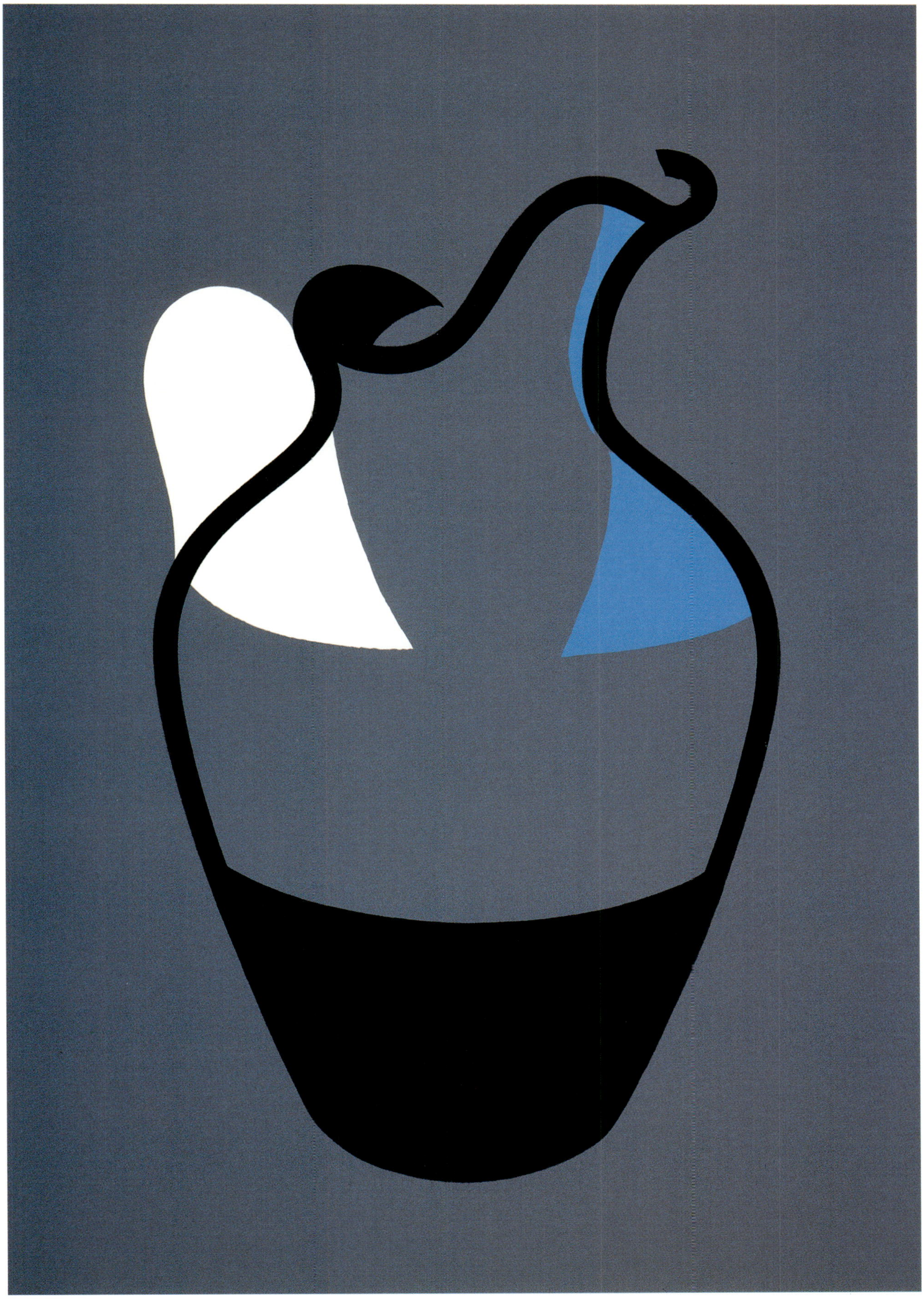

66. **Water Jug** 1981-82

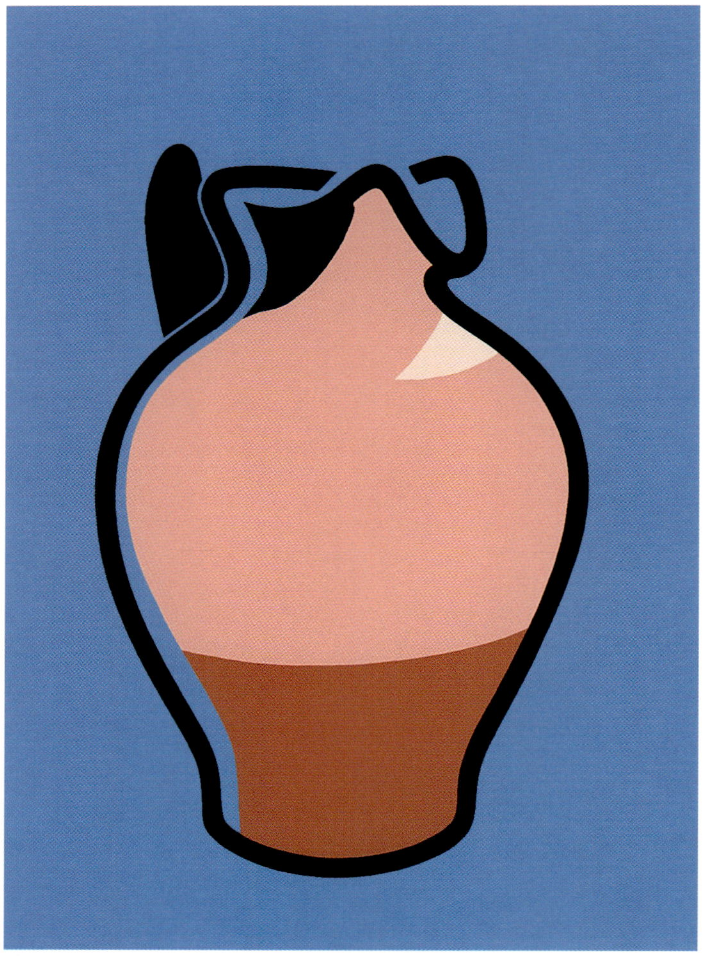

67. **Brown Jug** 1981-82

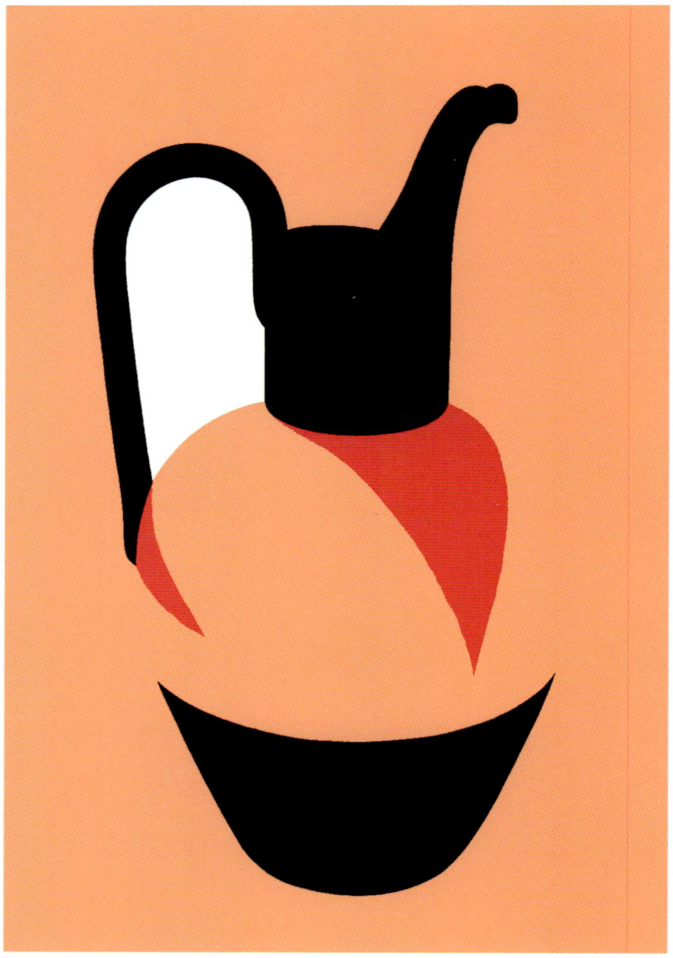

68. **Pitcher** 1981-82

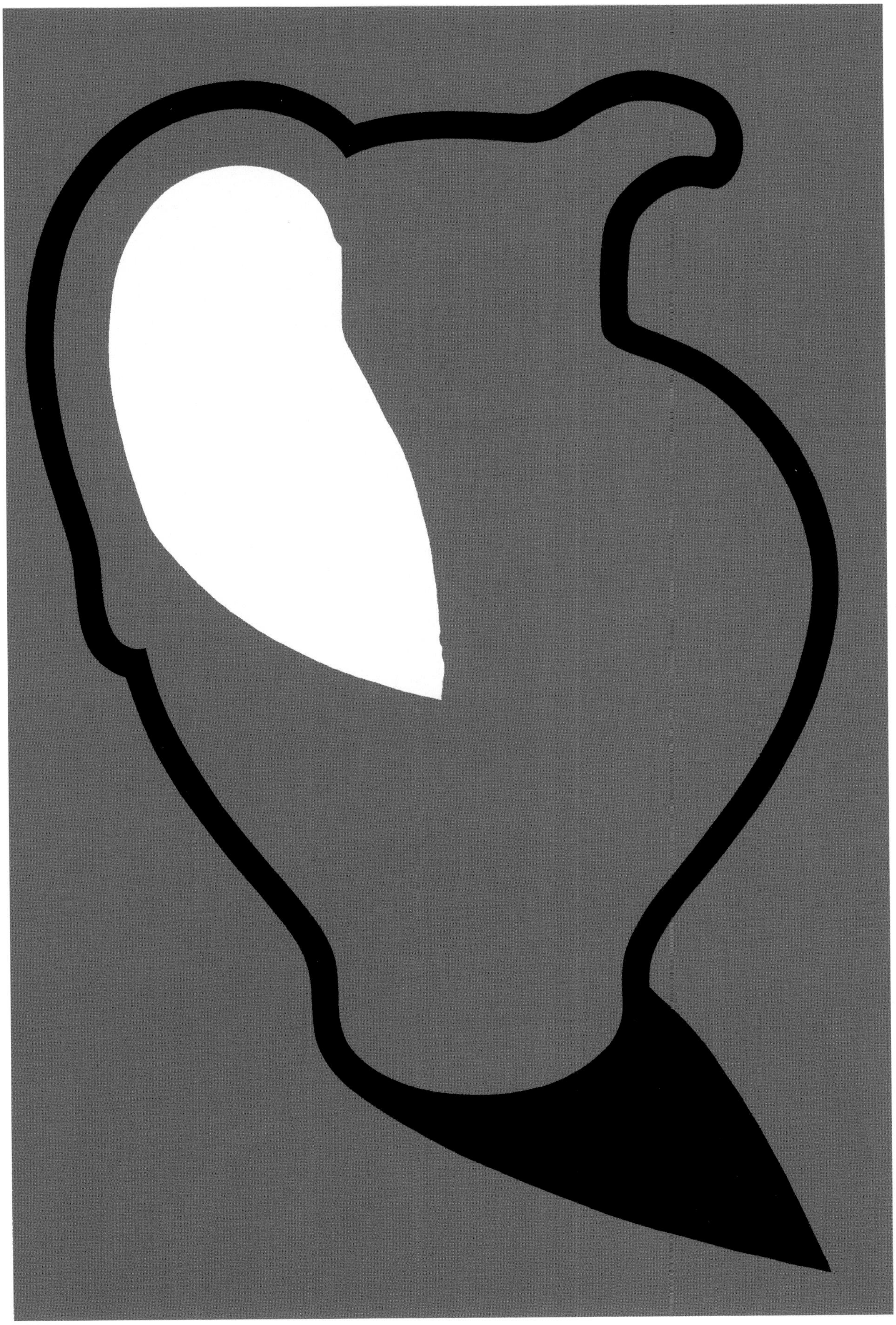

69. **Large Jug** 1983

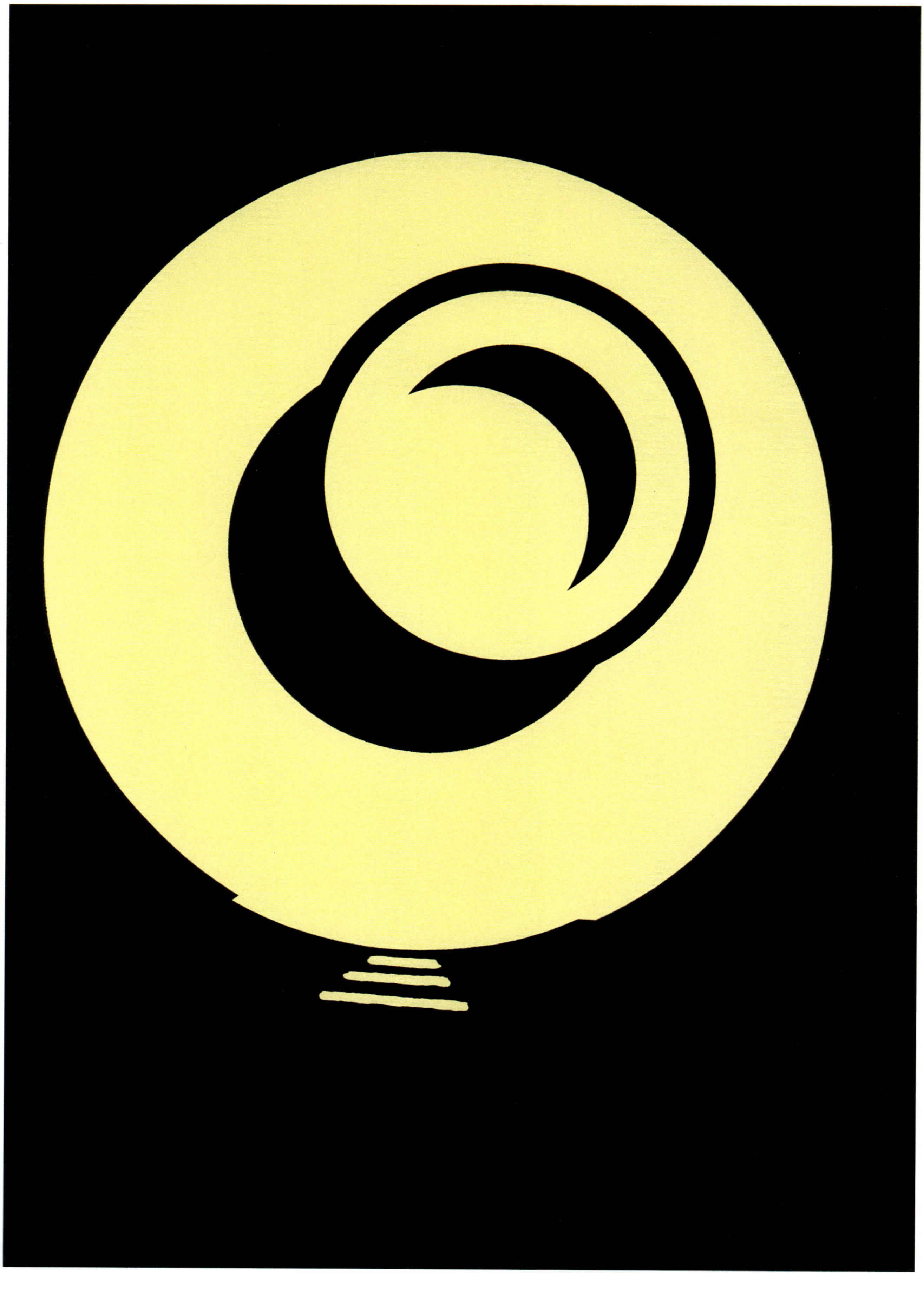

70. **Wall Plate: Highlights** 1987

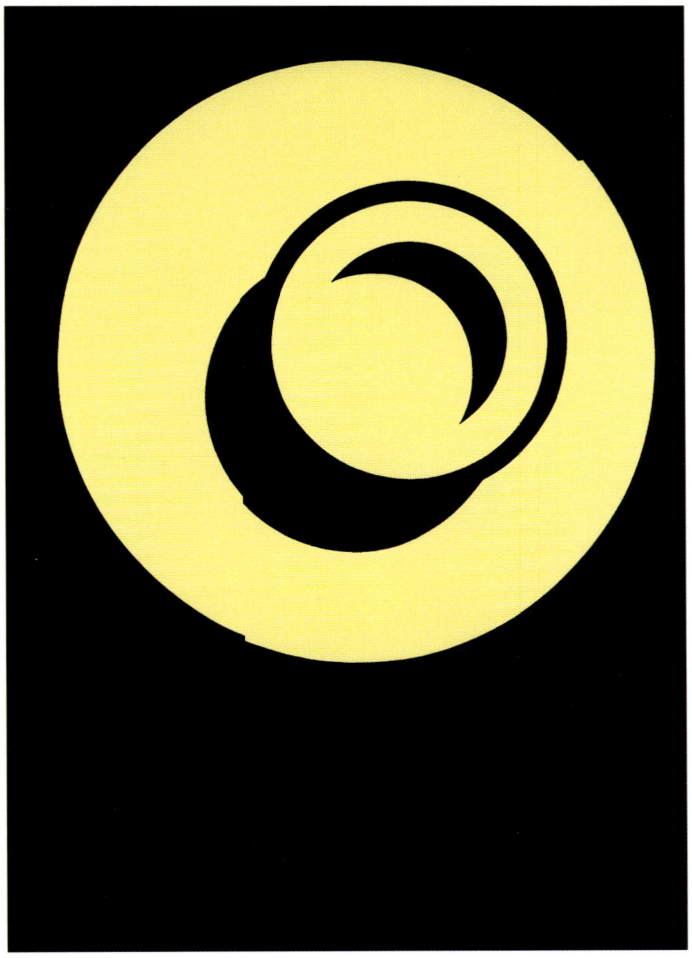

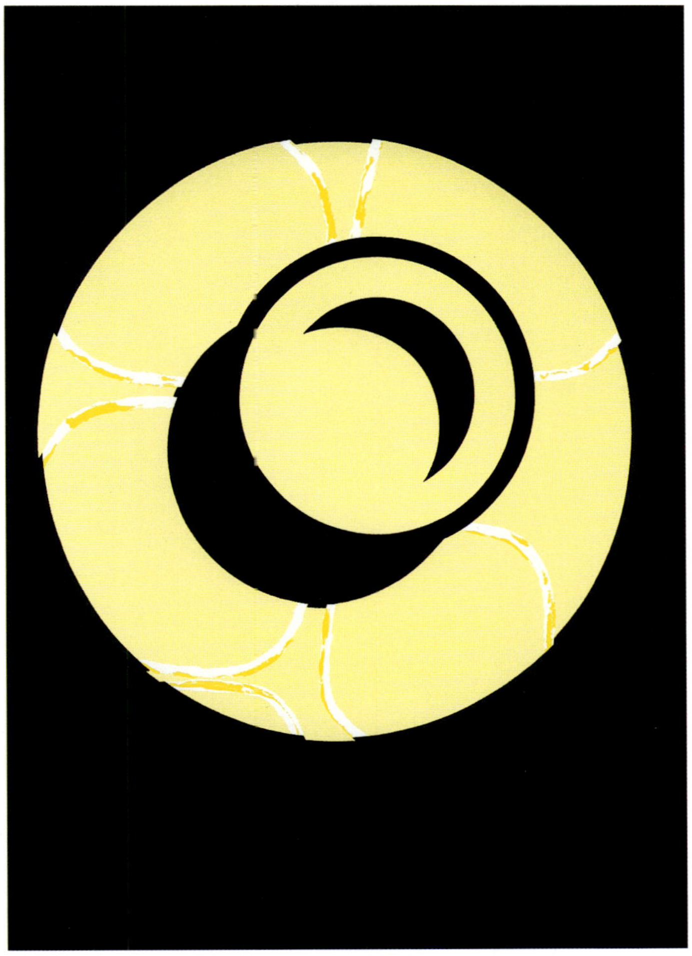

71. **Wall Plate: Stucco** 1987

72. **Wall Plate: Stones** 1987

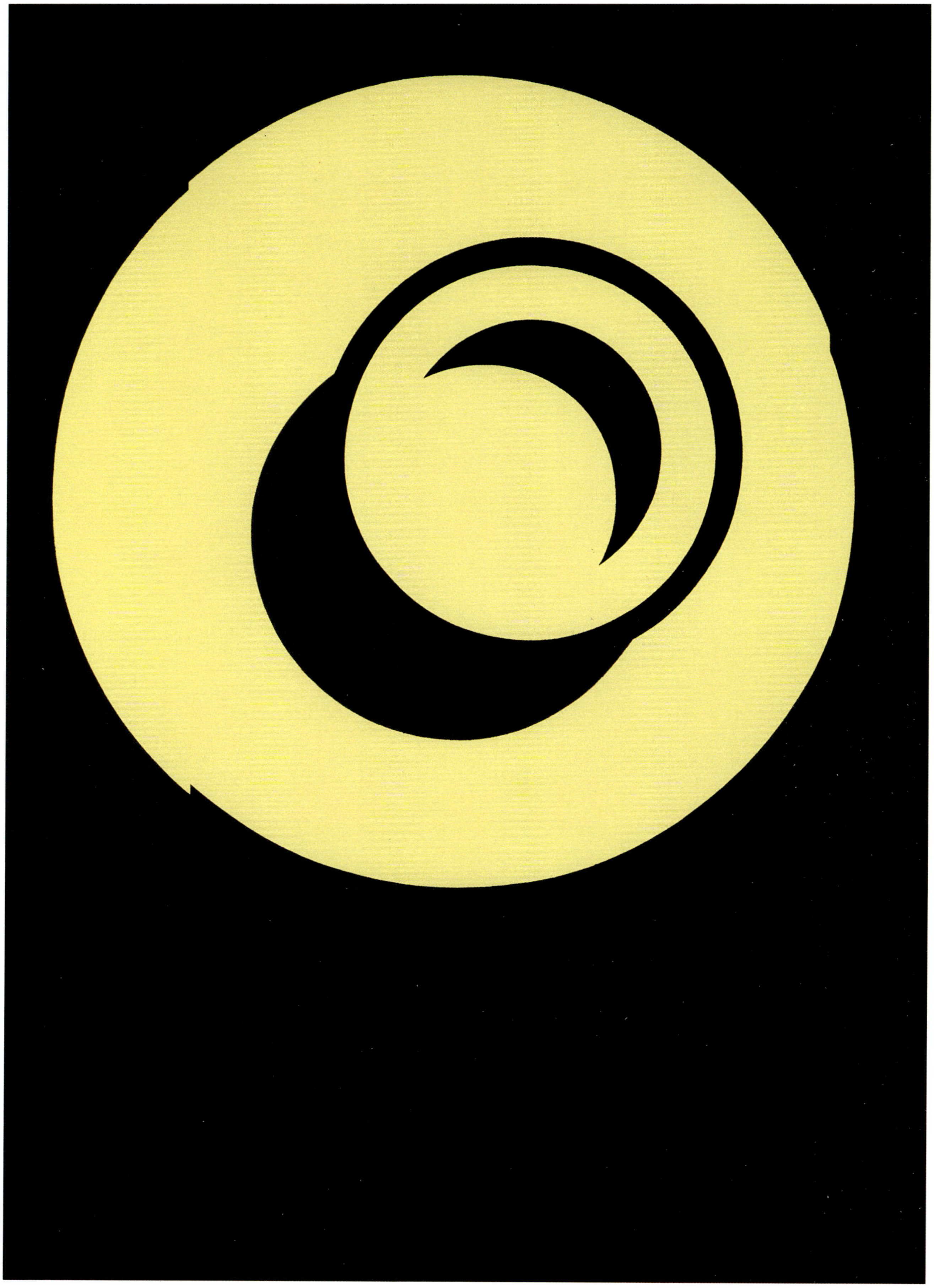

73. **Wall Plate: Screen** 1987

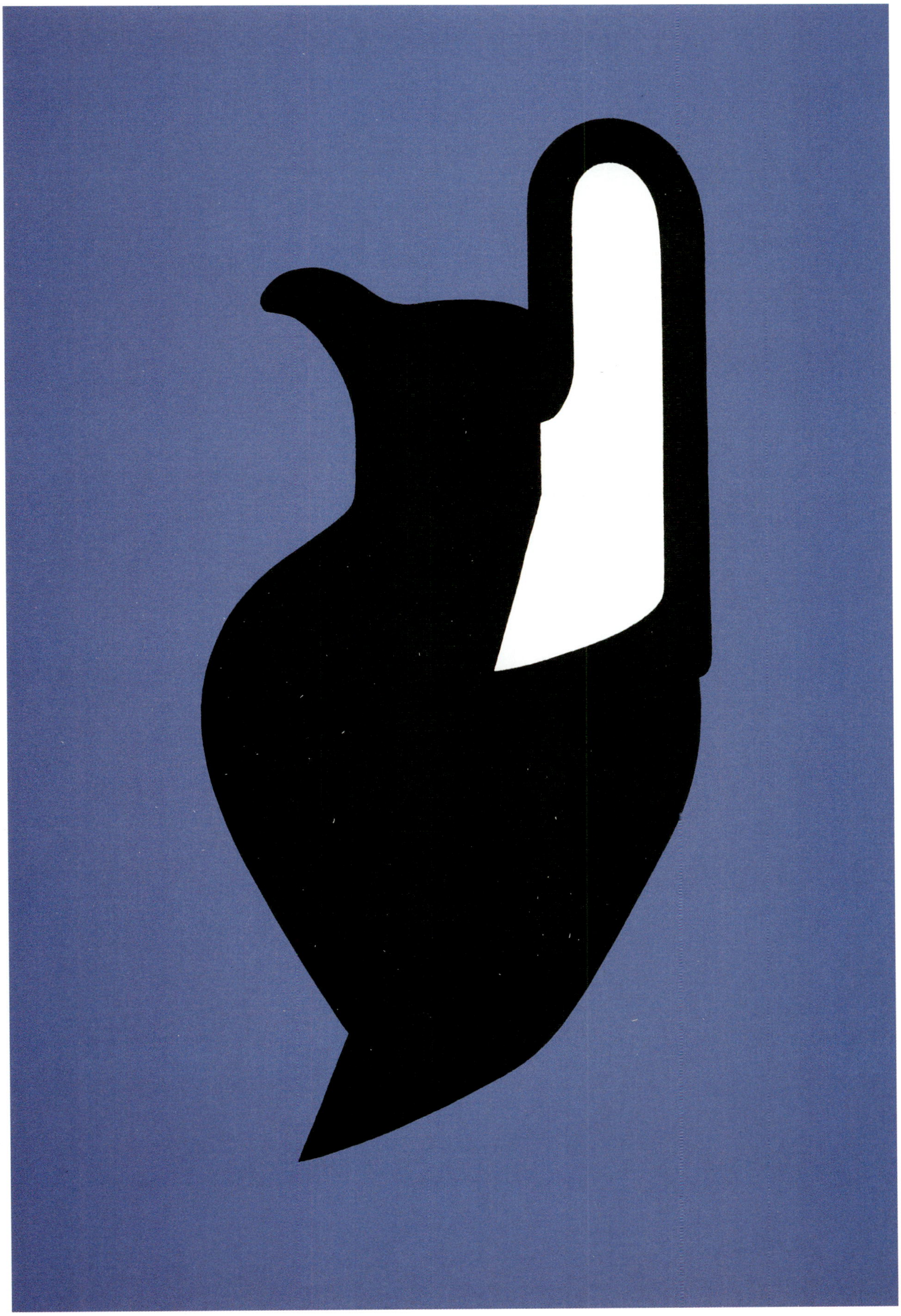

74. **Vessel** 1987

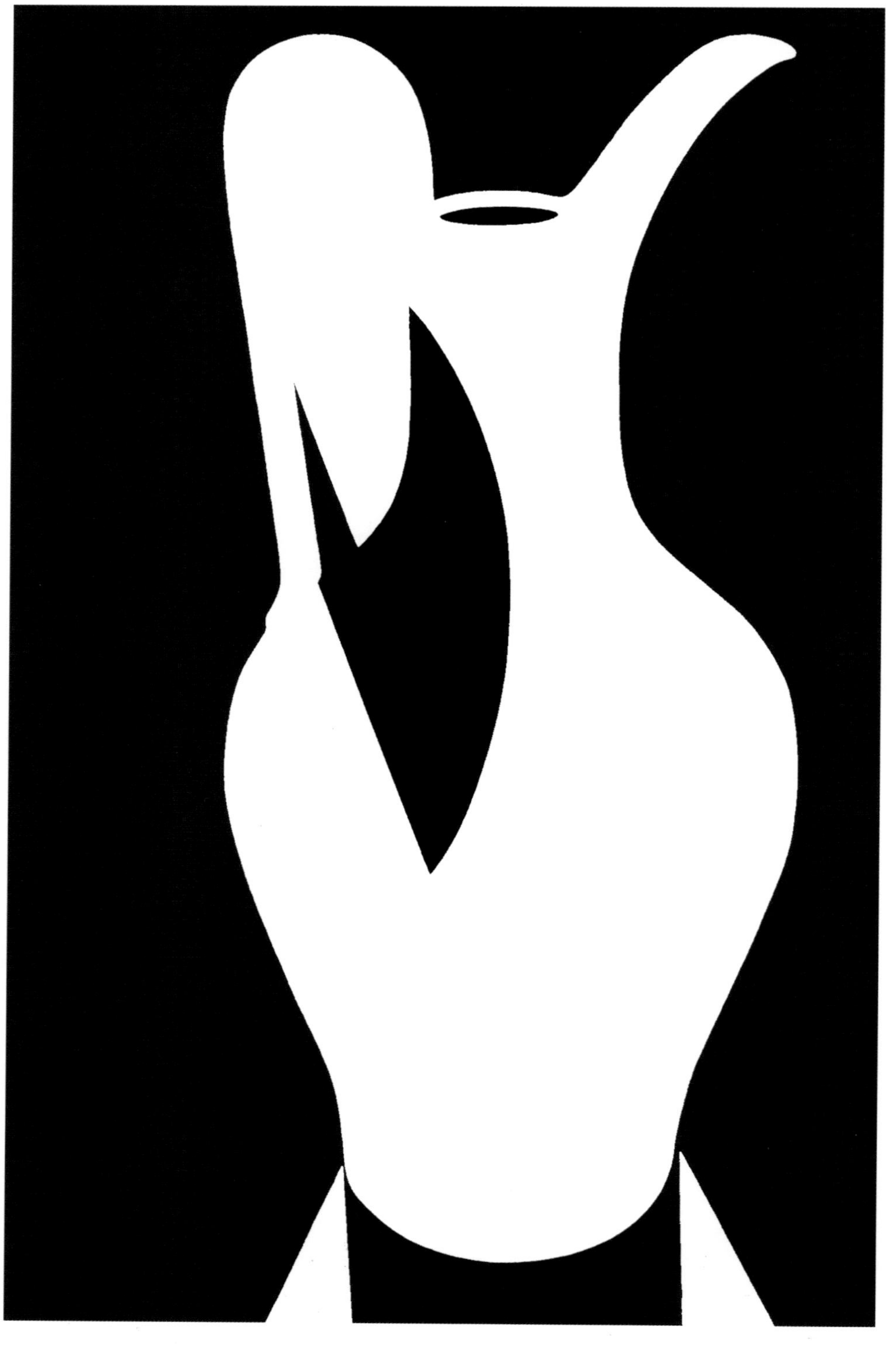

75. **Large White Jug** 1990

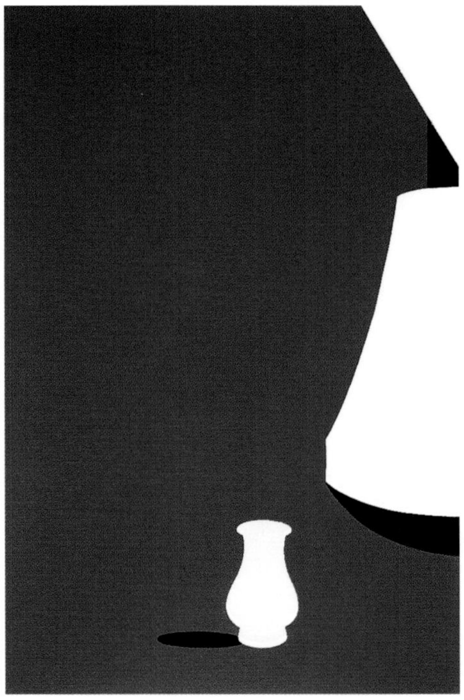

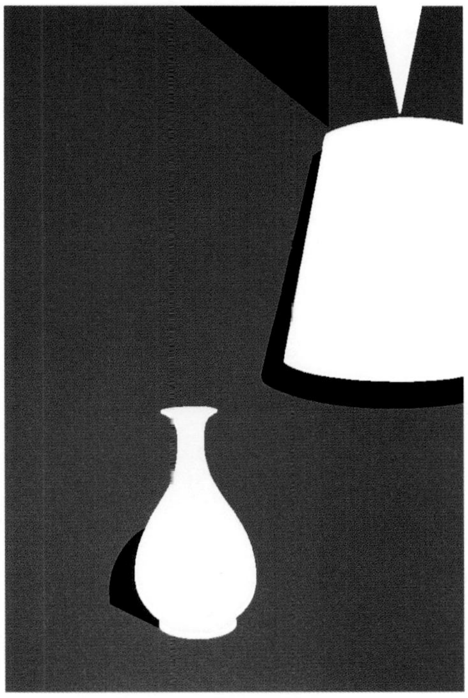

80. **Lamp and Kuan Ware** 1990

78. **Lamp and Lung Ch'uan Ware** 1990

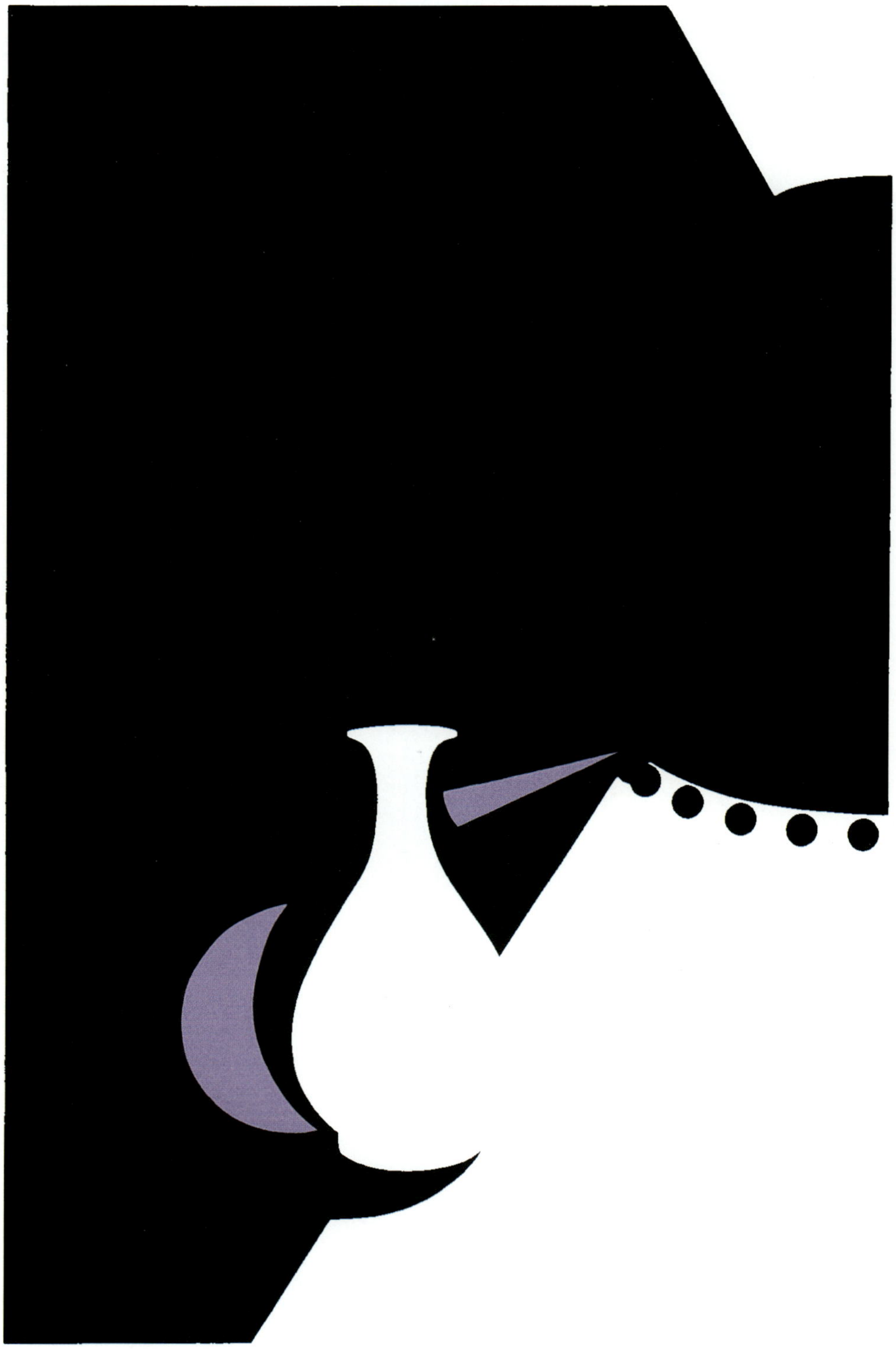

79. **Lung Ch'uan Ware and Black Lamp** 1990

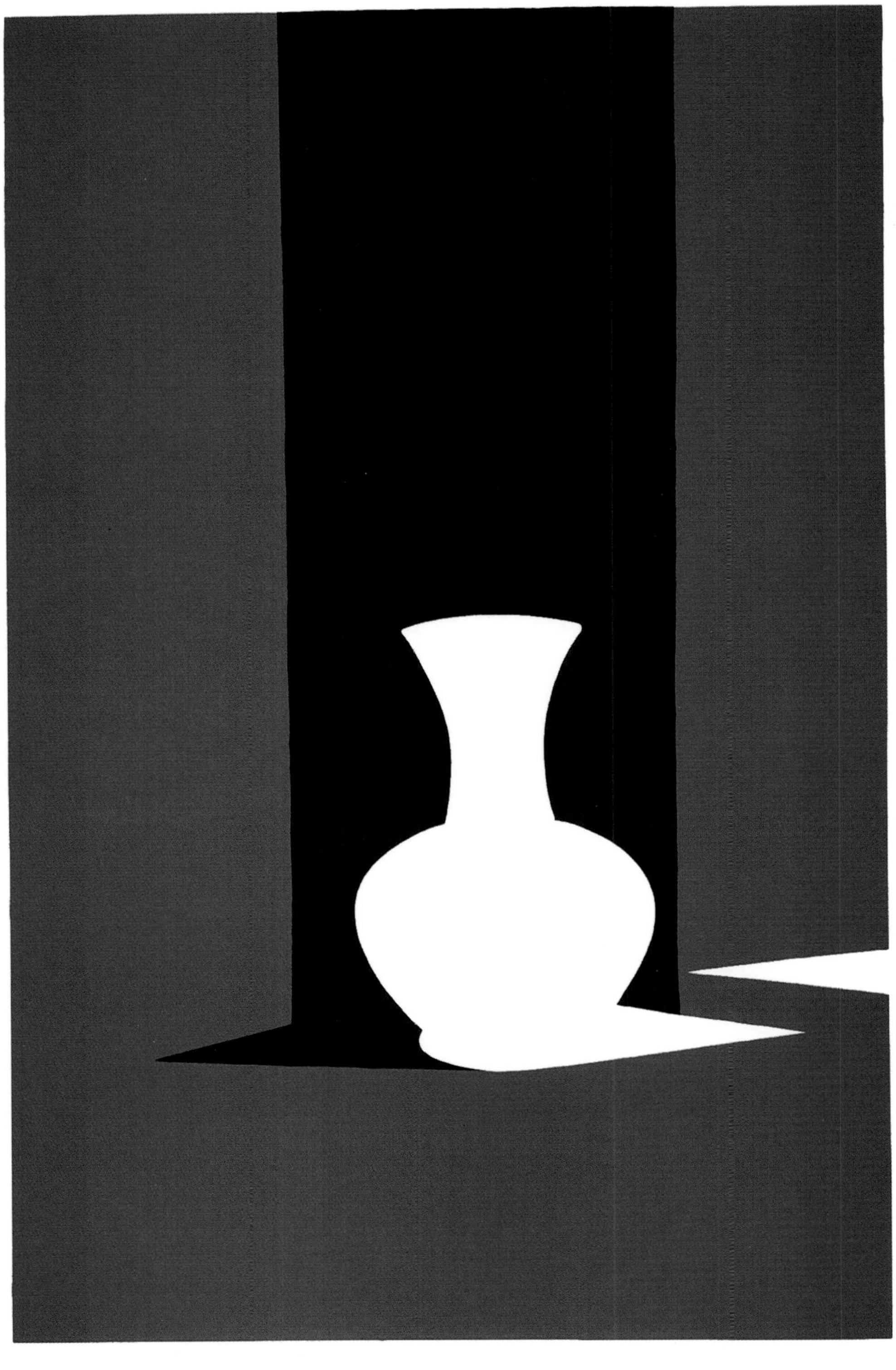

81. **Sue Ware Jar** 1990

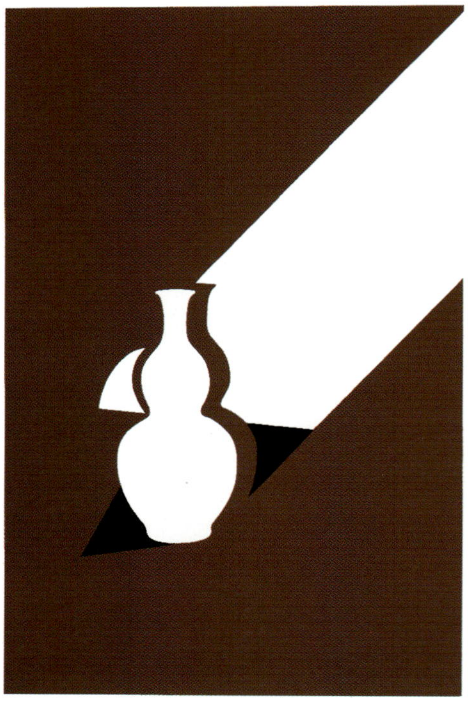

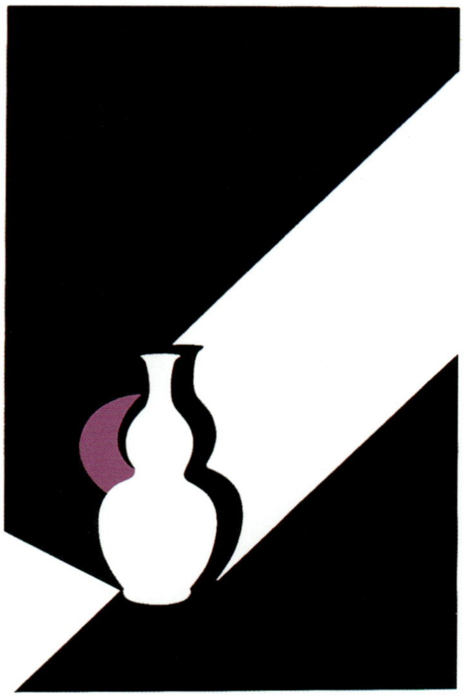

76. **Arita Flask** 1990

82. **Arita Flask-black** 1990

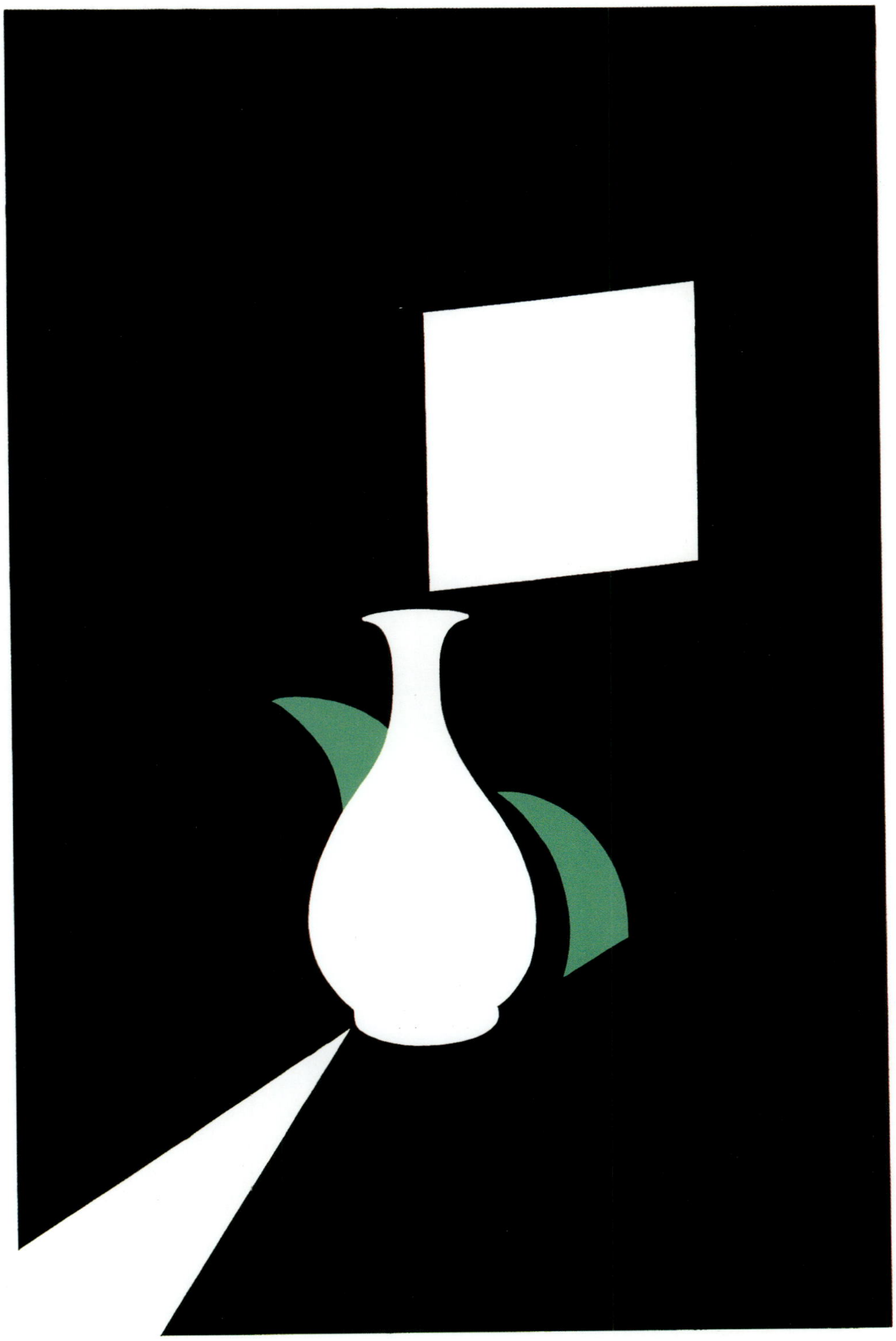

77. **Lung Ch'uan Ware and Window** 1990

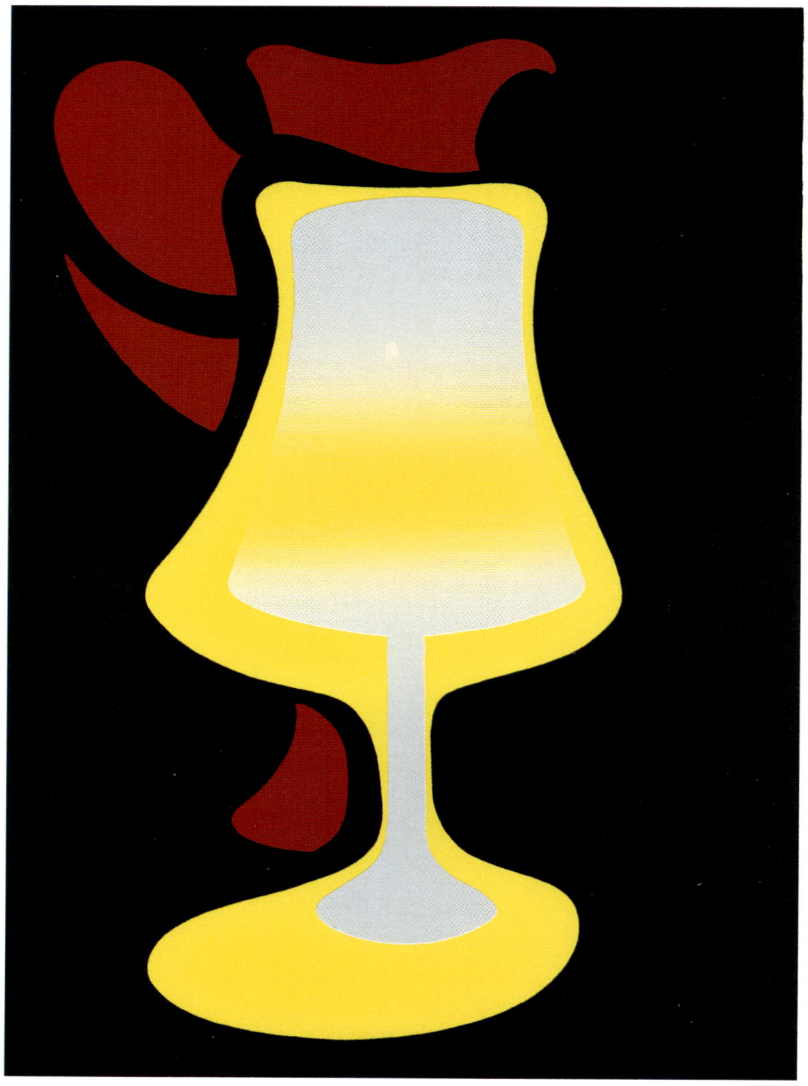

83. **Red Jug and Lamp** 1992

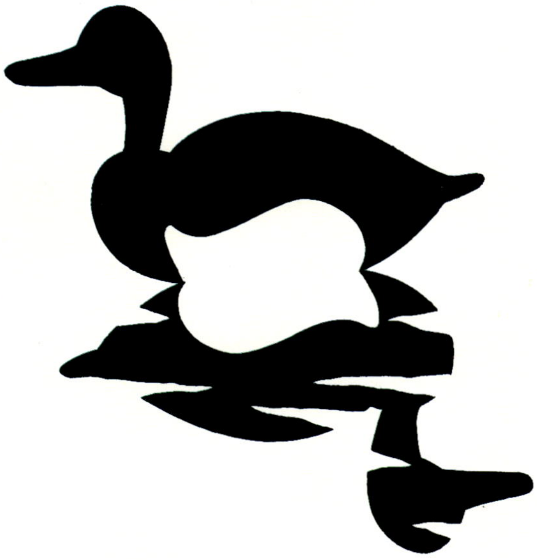

84. **Duck** 1994

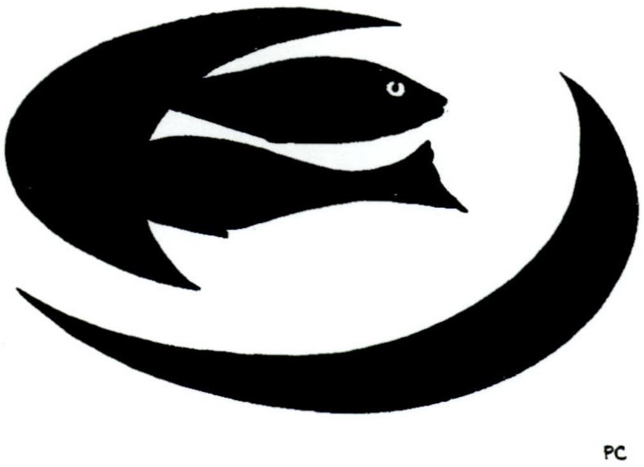

89. **Two Fish on a Plate** 1999

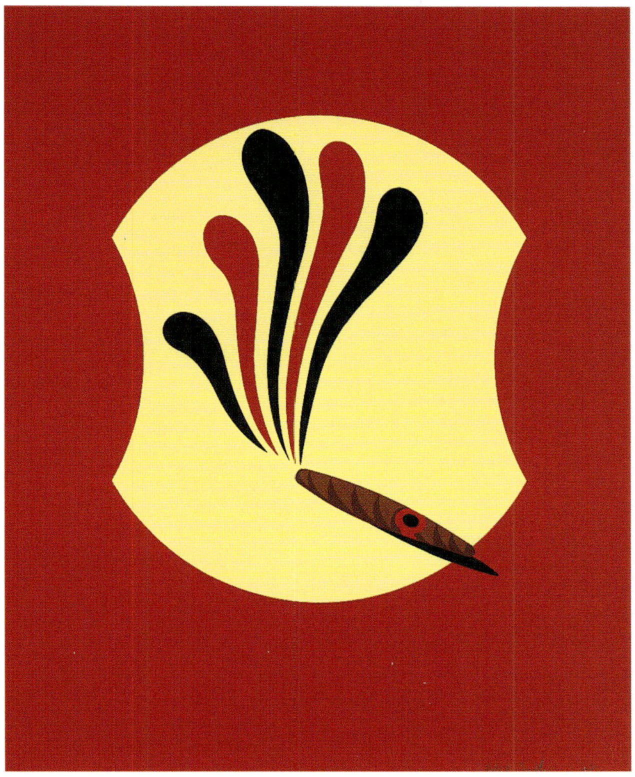

88. **Freud's Smoke** 1997

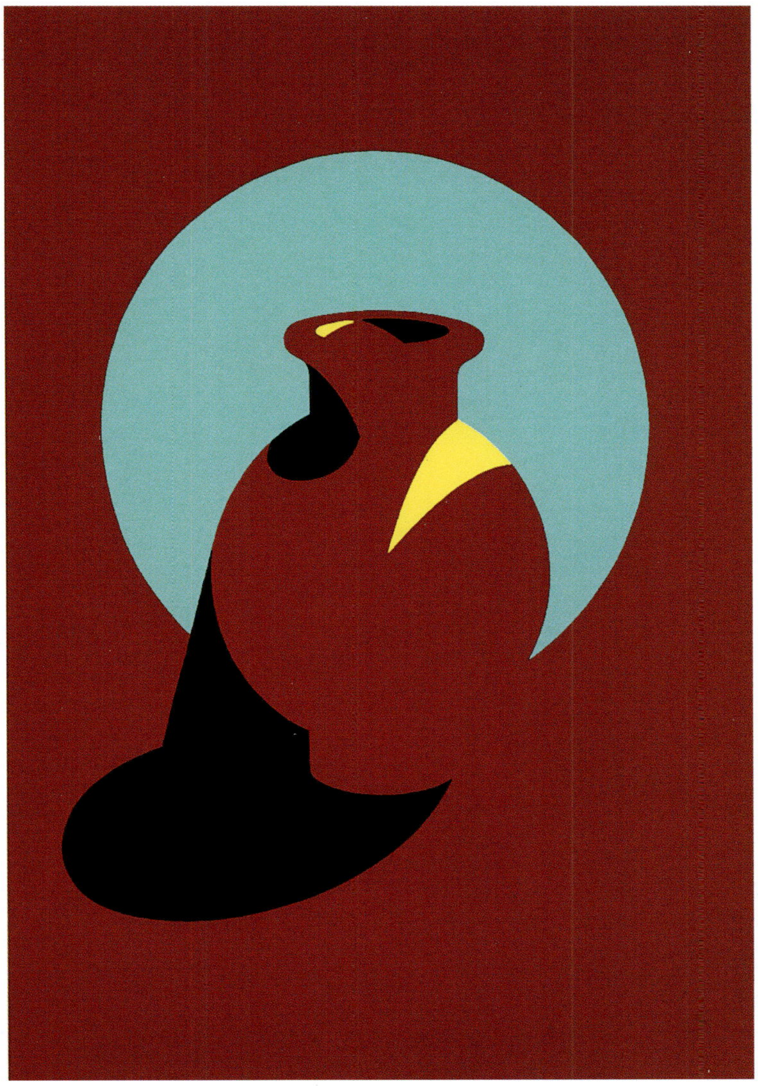

85. **Brown Pot** 1994

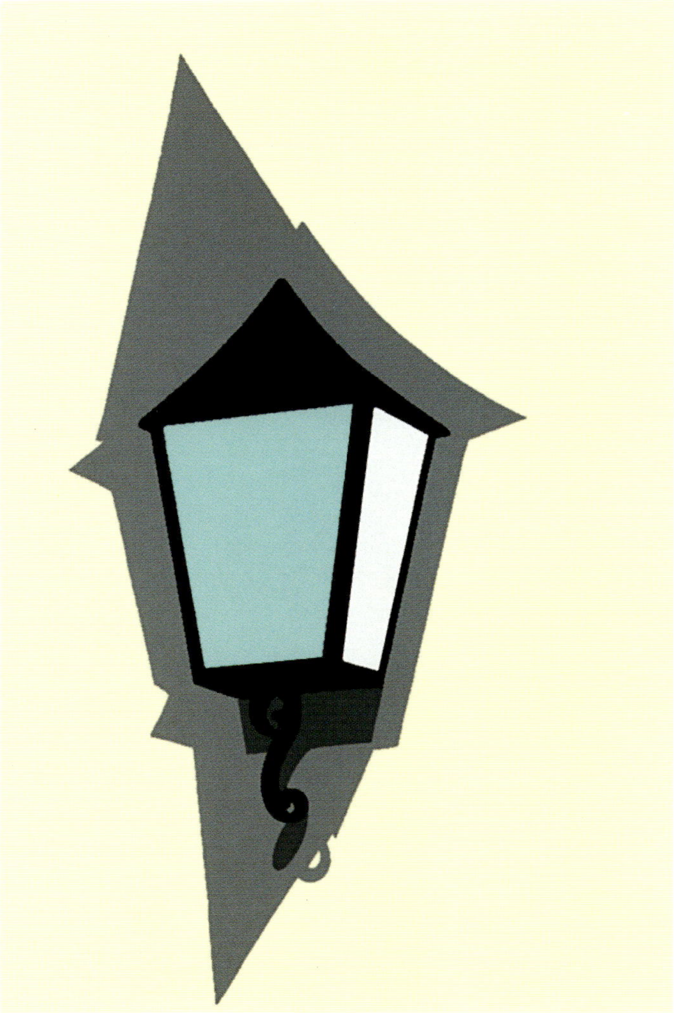

87. **Coach Lamp** 1994

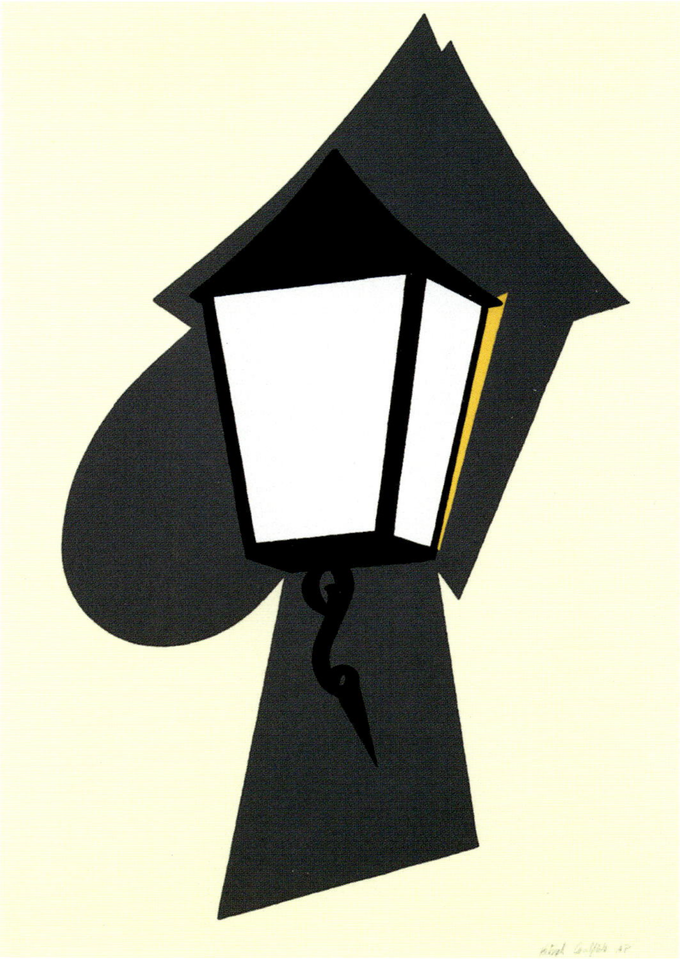

86. **Wall Lamp** 1994

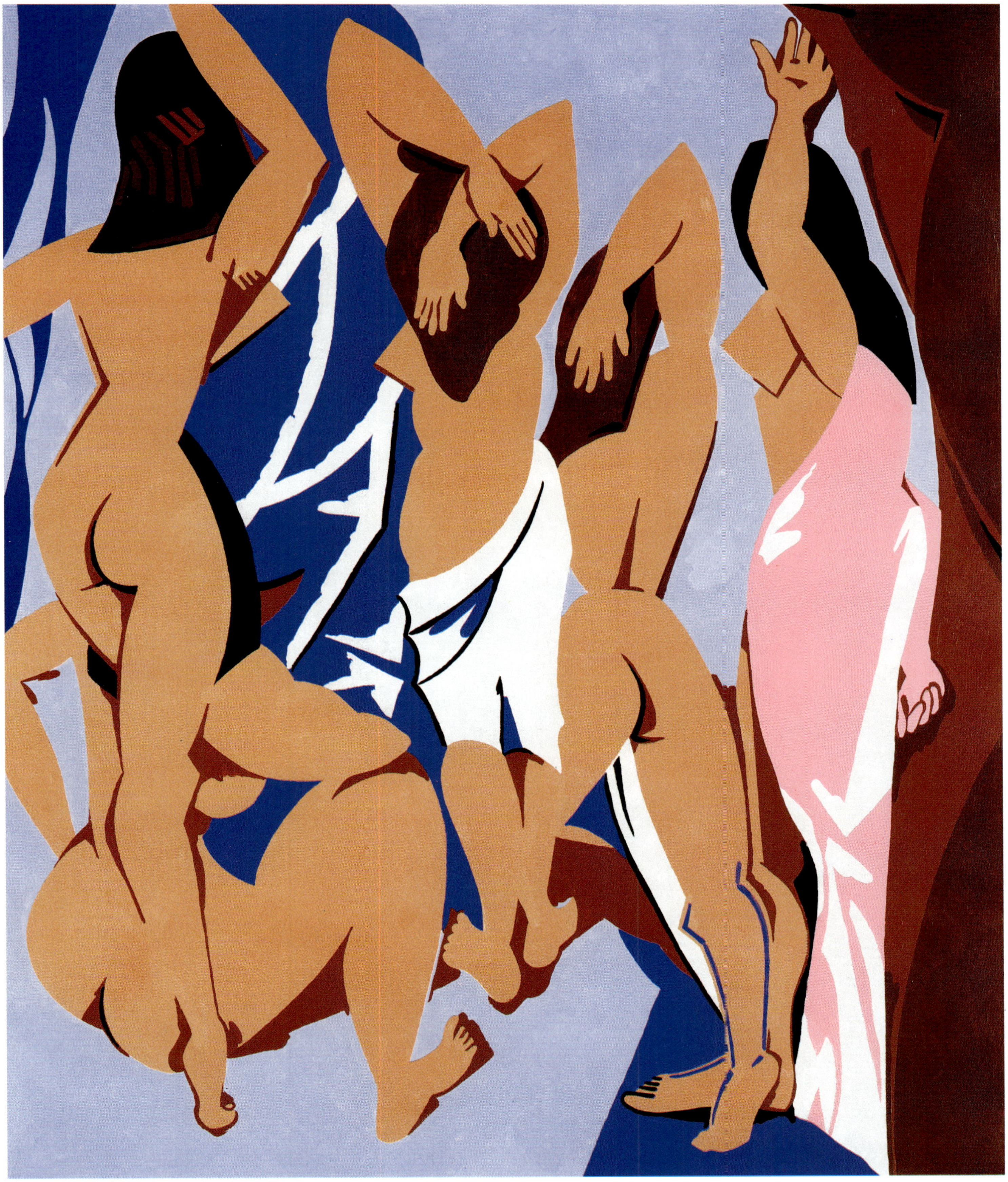

90. **Les Demoiselles d'Avignon vues de Derrière** 1999
Illustration taken from Patrick Caulfield's design for the print

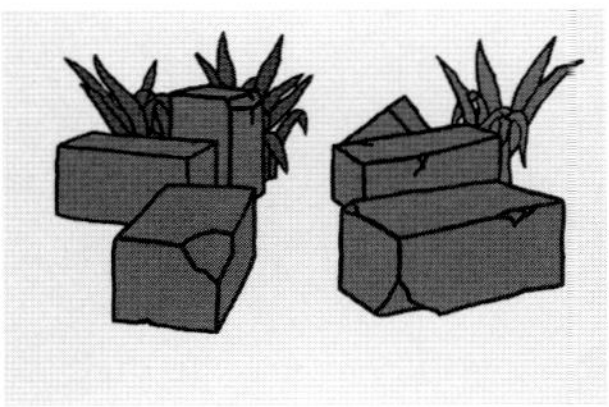

1

Print Documentation

The number preceding each entry indicates the catalogue raisonné reference

All measurements are given in centimetres with height preceding width

1964

1 **Ruins**
Screenprint
Paper and image 50.8 × 76.3 cm
Edition of 40 with 10 proofs
Printed at Kelpra Studio, London
Published in the 'ICA Print Portfolio' by the Institute of Contemporary Arts, London

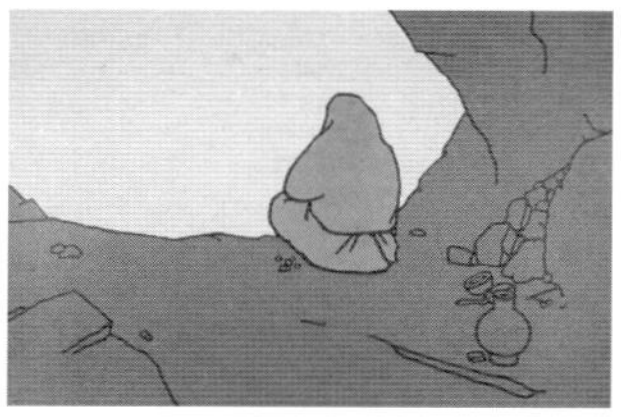
2

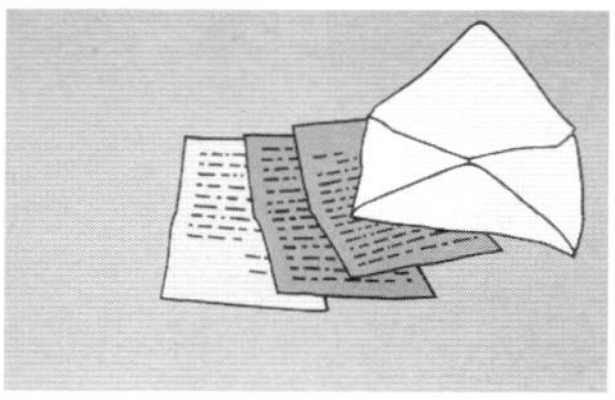
3

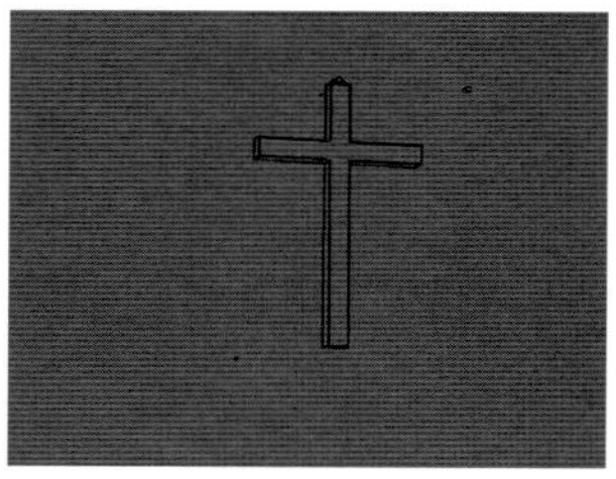
8

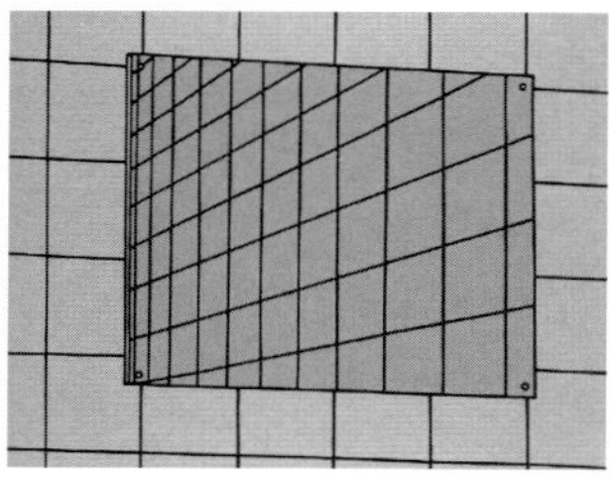
9

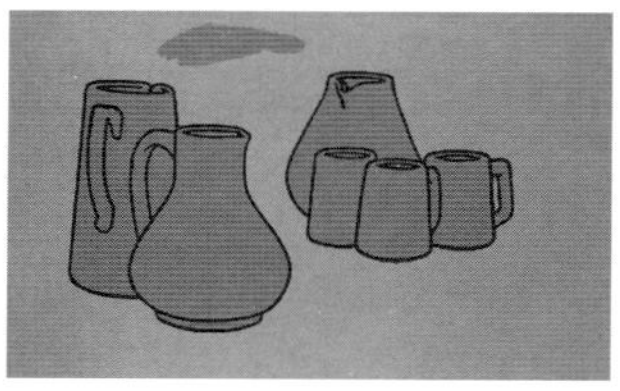
4

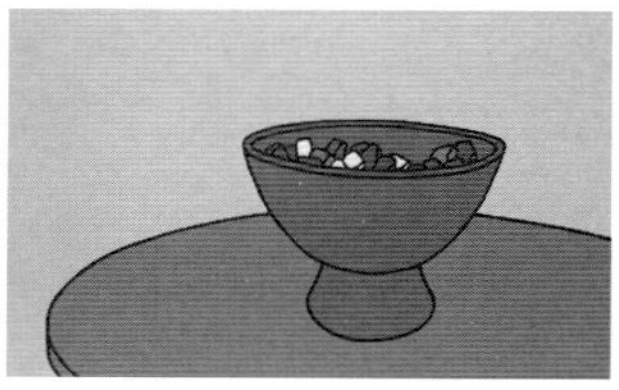
5

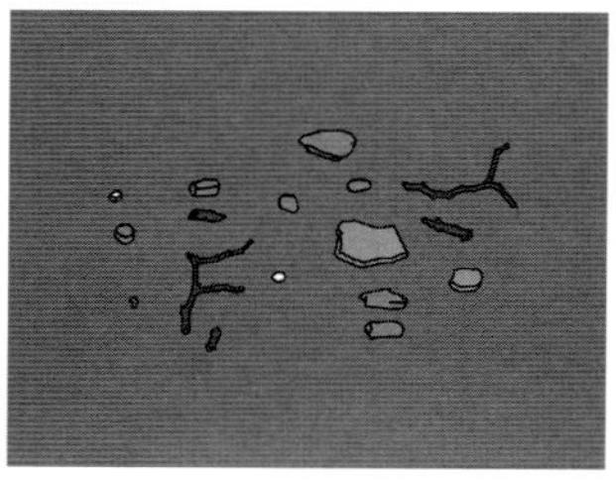
10

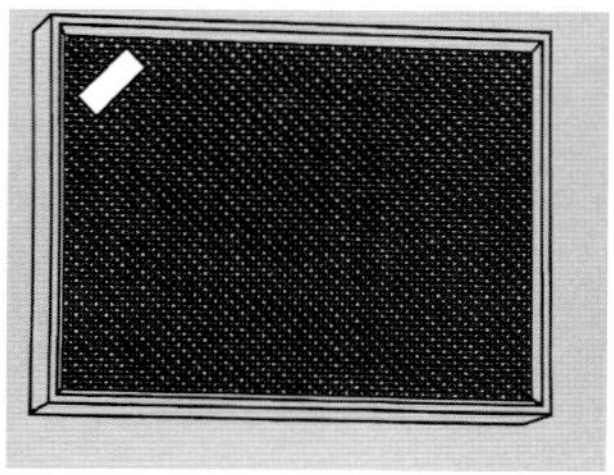
11

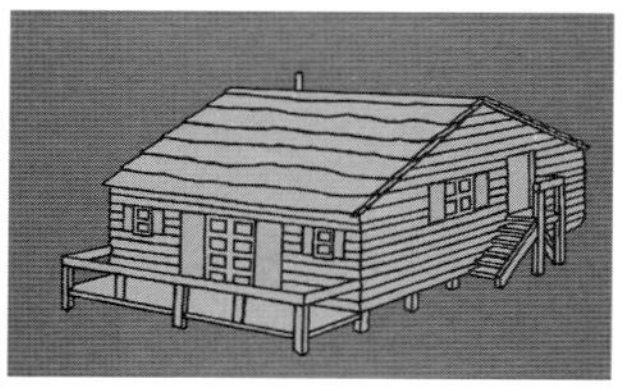
6

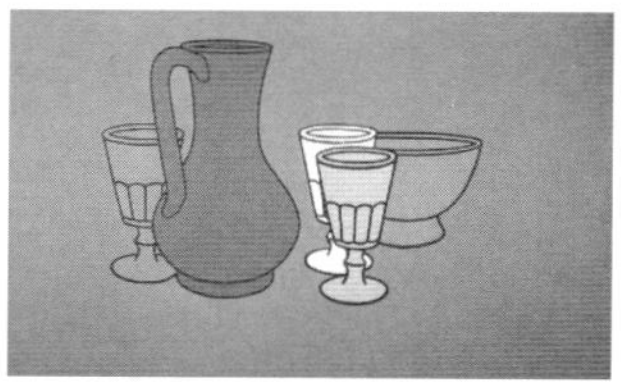
7

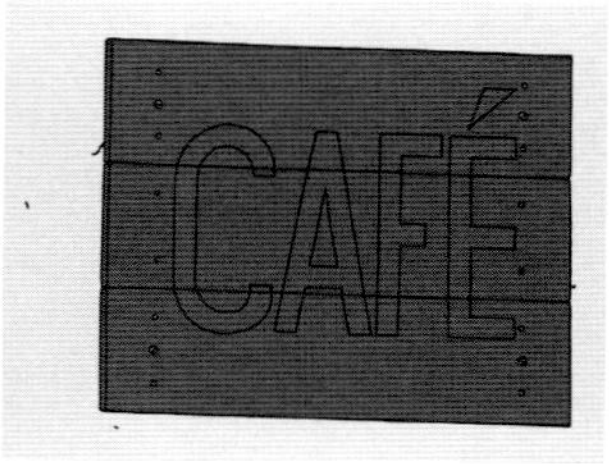

12

1967

2 **The Hermit**
Paper and image 55.9 × 83.8 cm
3 **The Letter**
Paper and image 48.0 × 76.0 cm
4 **Earthenware**
Paper and image 55.7 × 91.2 cm
5 **Sweet Bowl**
Paper and image 55.7 × 91.2 cm
6 **Weekend Cabin**
Paper and image 55.7 × 91.2 cm
7 **Coloured Still Life**
Paper and image 55.7 × 91.2 cm
A series of six screenprints
Edition of 75 with 10 proofs (of each)
Printed at Kelpra Studio, London
Published by Editions Alecto, London

1968

8 **Crucifix**
9 **Bathroom Mirror**
10 **Found Objects**
11 **Loudspeaker**
12 **Café Sign**
A series of five screenprints
Paper and image 71.0 × 93.2 cm
Edition of 75 with 10 proofs (of each)
Printed at Kelpra Studio, London
Published by Leslie Waddington Prints, London

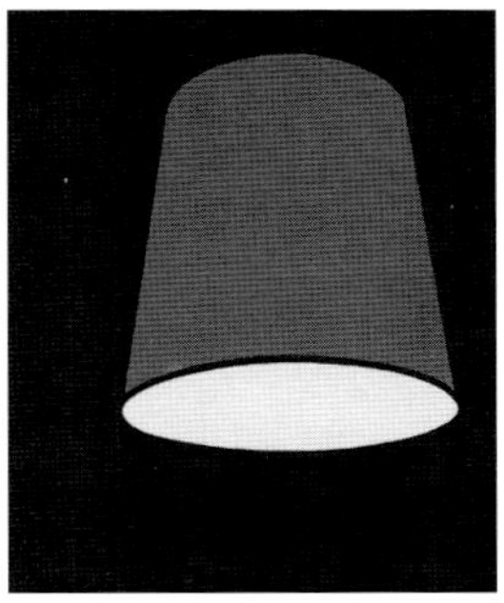

13

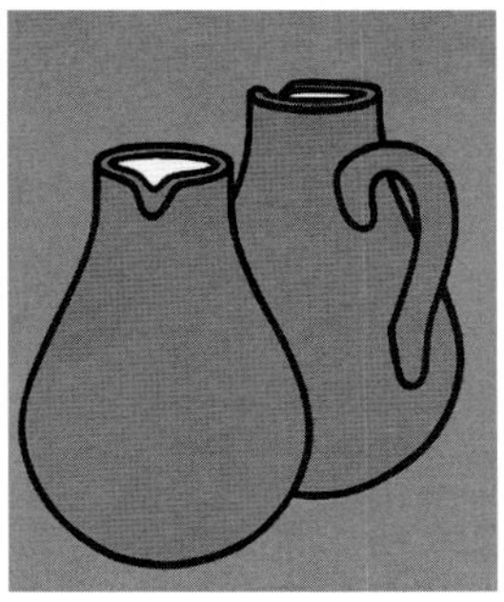

14

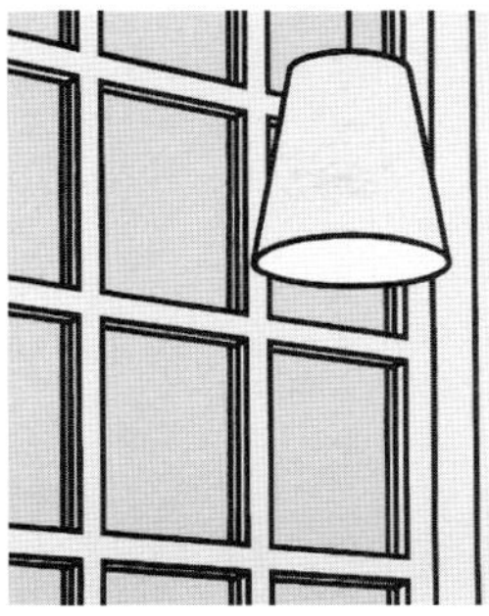

18

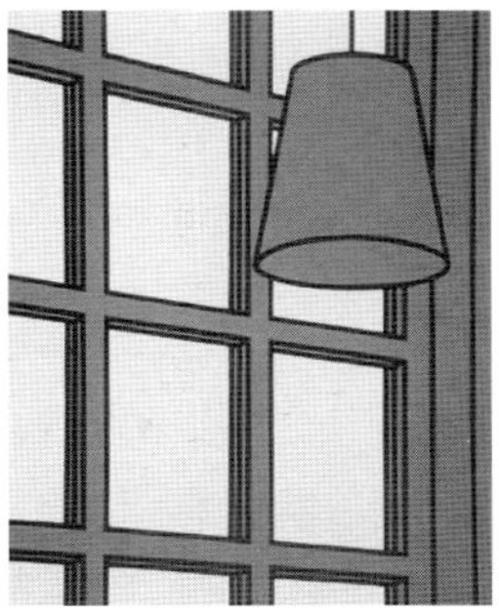

19

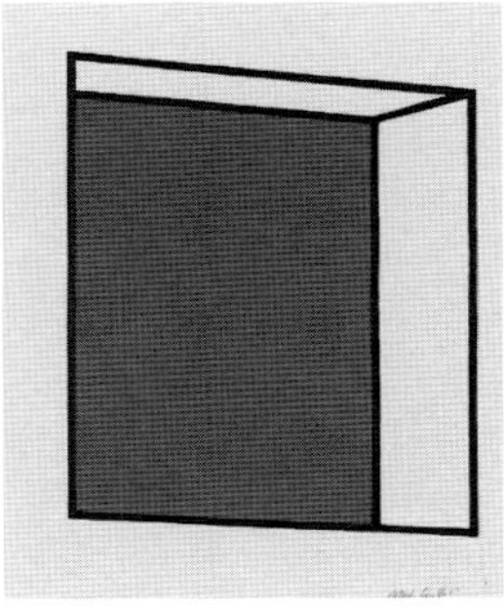

15

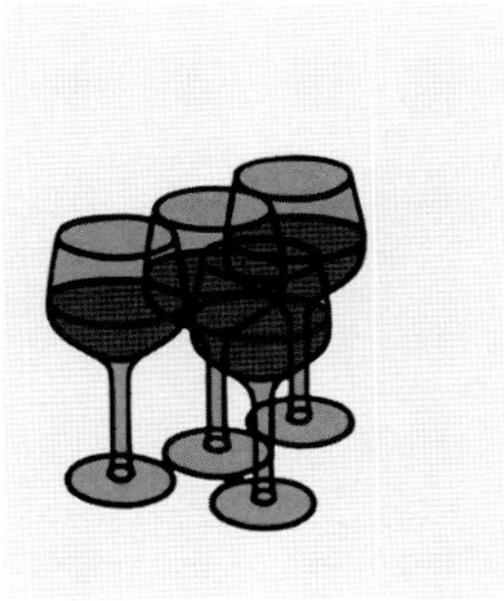

16

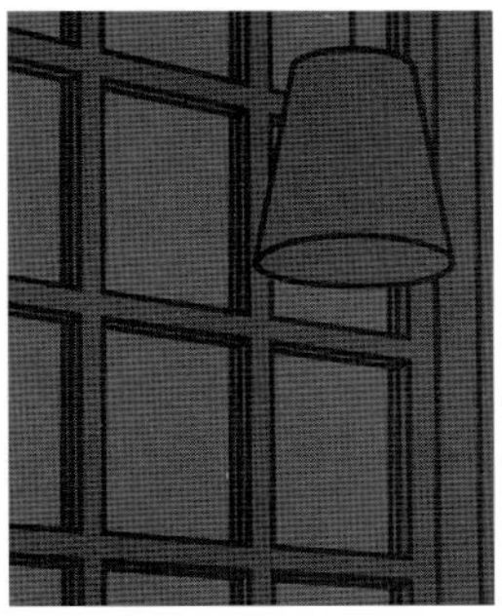

20

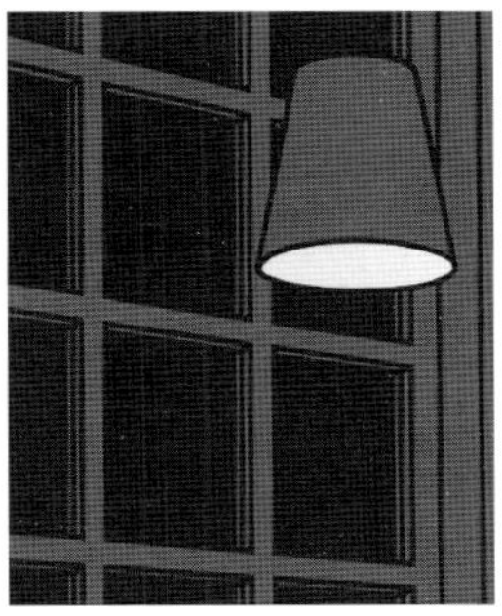

21

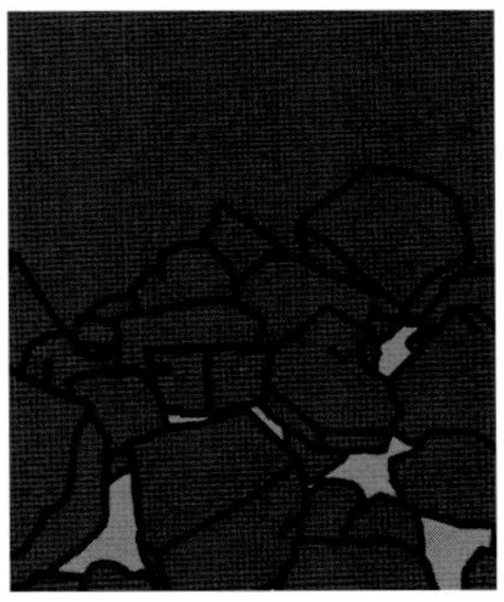

17

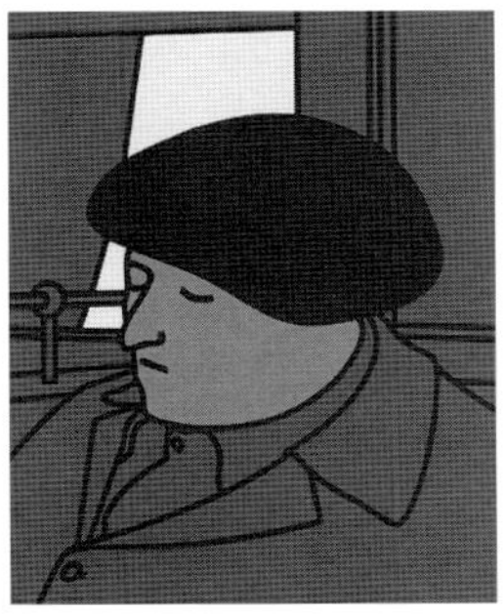

22

1969

13 **Lampshade**
14 **Two Jugs**
15 **Small Window**
16 **Wine Glasses**
17 **Coal Fire**
A series of five screenprints
Paper and image 35.5 × 30.5 cm
Edition of 75 with 10 proofs (of each)
Printed at Kelpra Studio, London
Published by Leslie Waddington Prints, London

1971

Interiors
18 **Interior : Morning**
19 **Interior : Noon**
20 **Interior : Evening**
21 **Interior : Night**
A set of four screenprints
Paper and image 71.0 × 58.4 cm
Edition of 100 with 10 proofs (of each)
Printed at Kelpra Studio, London
Published by Leslie Waddington Prints, London

22 **Portrait of a Frenchman**
Screenprint
Paper and image 63.5 × 53.3 cm
Edition of 75 with 10 proofs
Printed at Kelpra Studio, London
Published by Leslie Waddington Prints, London

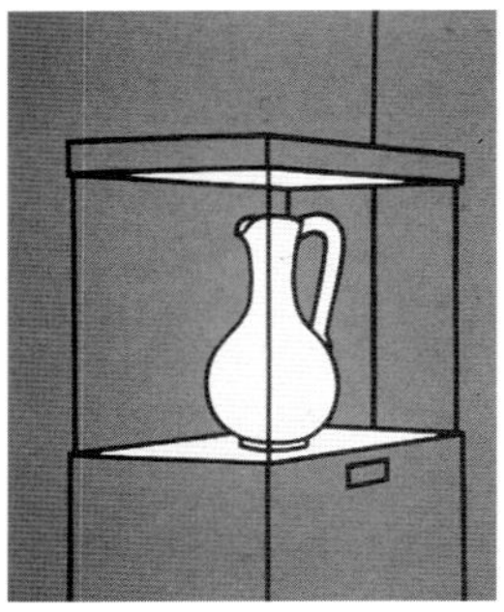

23

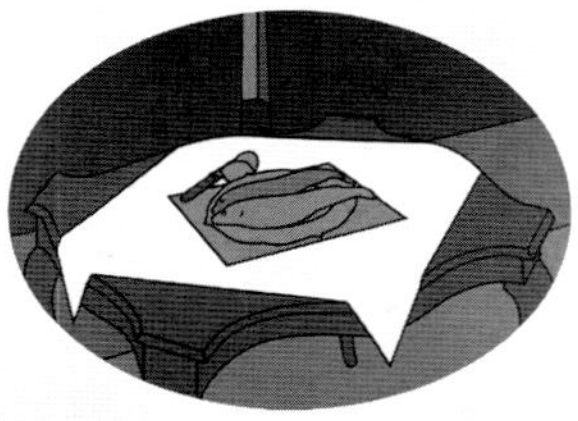

24

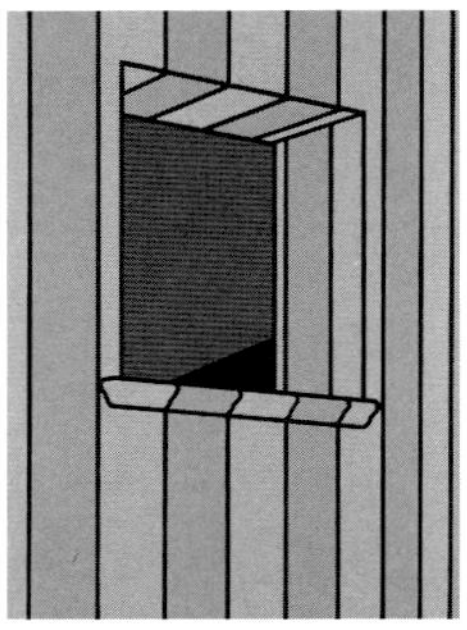

25

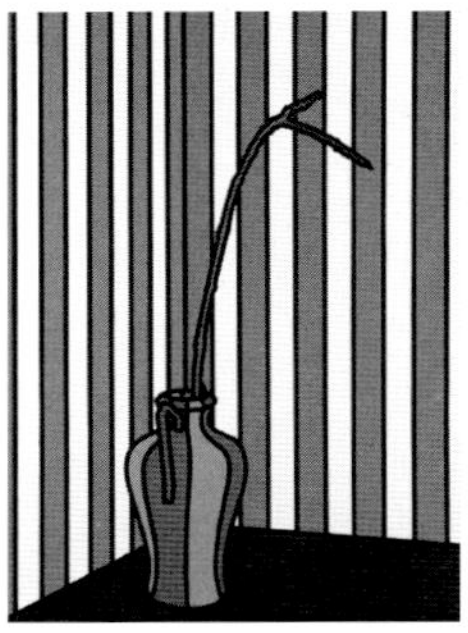

26

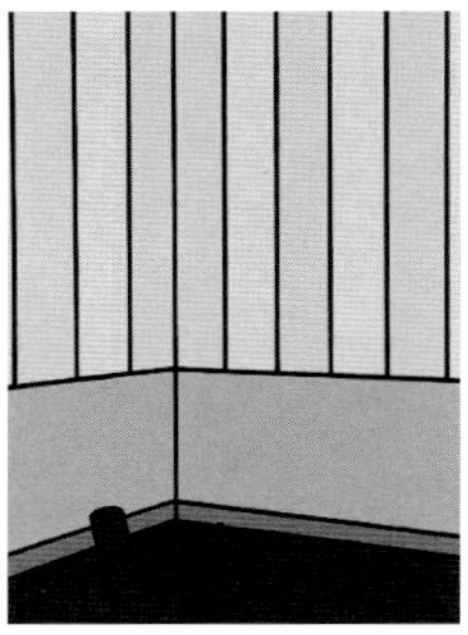

27

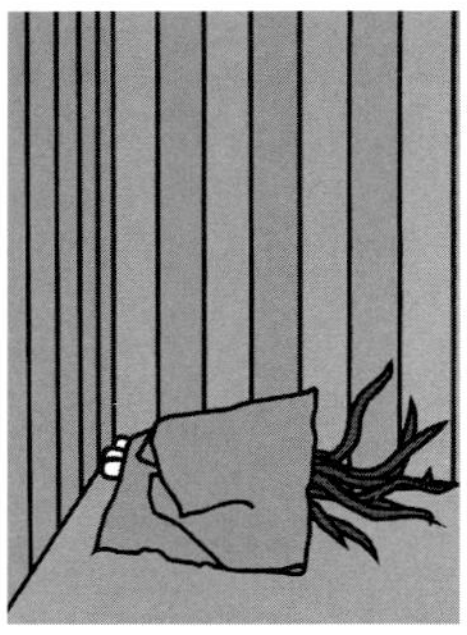

28

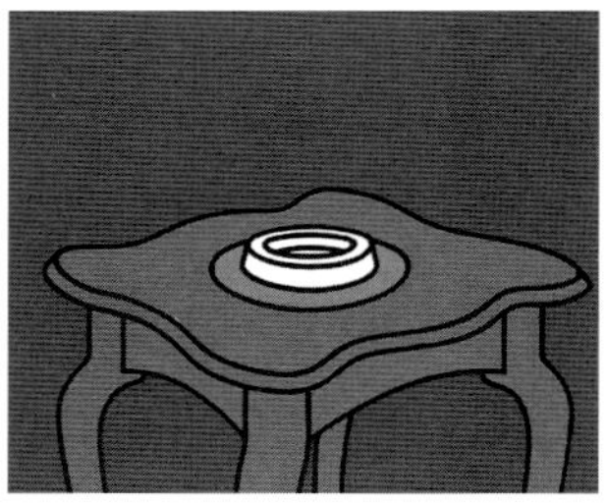

29

23 **Vase on Display**
Screenprint
Paper and image 66.0 × 55.9 cm
Edition of 100 with 10 proofs
Printed at Kelpra Studio, London
Published by Leslie Waddington Prints, London

1972

24 **Two Whiting**
Screenprint
Paper 110.5 × 153.0 cm / Image 100.5 × 142.2 cm
Edition of 100 with 15 proofs
Printed at Advanced Graphics, London
Published in the '14 BIG Prints' portfolio
by Bernard Jacobson, London

25 **Window at Night**
26 **Fig Branch**
27 **Pipe**
28 **Napkin and Onions**
A series of four screenprints
Paper 100.3 × 74.5 cm / Image 86.8 × 66.2 cm
Edition of 72 with 15 proofs (of each)
Printed at Kelpra Studio, London
Published by Leslie Waddington Prints, London

29 **Occasional Table**
Screenprint
Paper and image 58.3 × 71.4 cm
Edition of 500 with 25 proofs
Printed at Kelpra Studio, London
Published by Observer Art, London

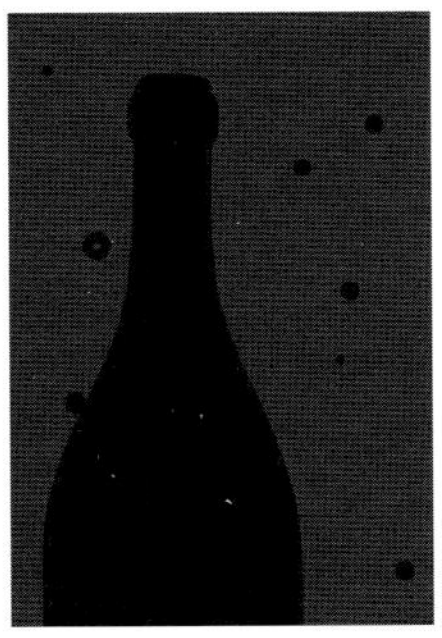

30

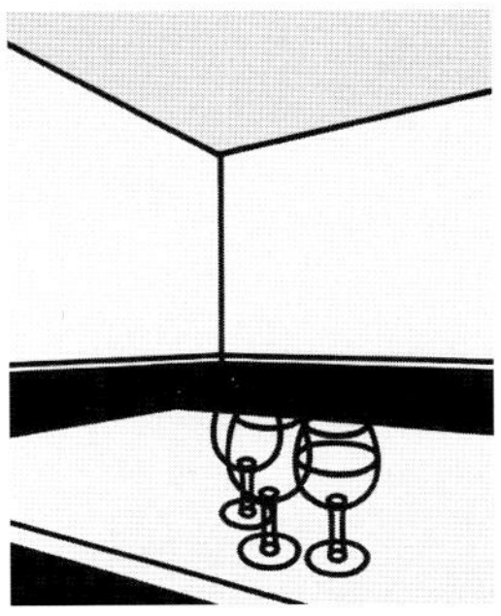

31

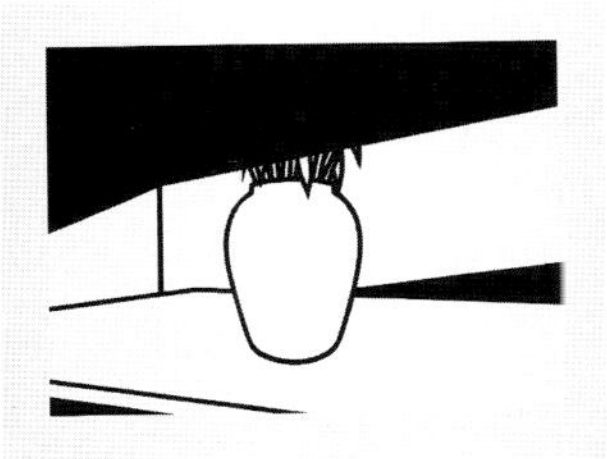

32

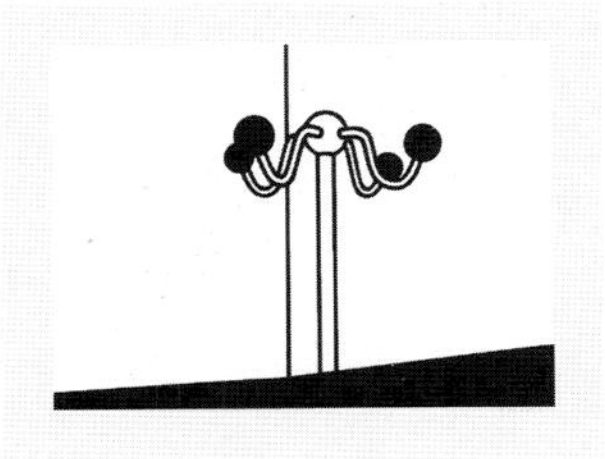

33

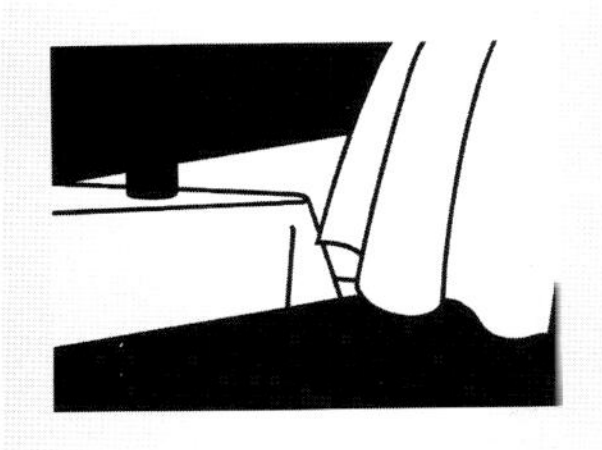

34

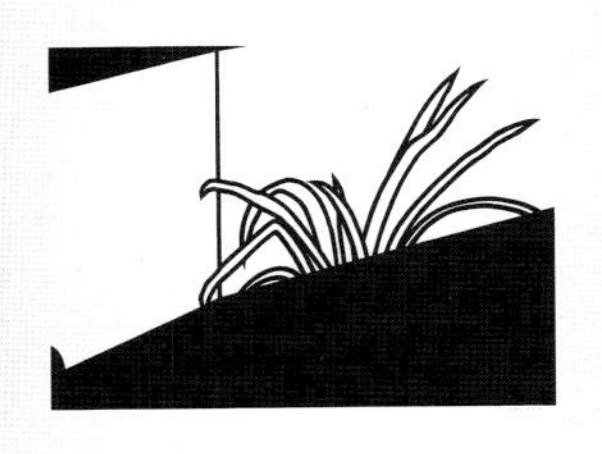

35

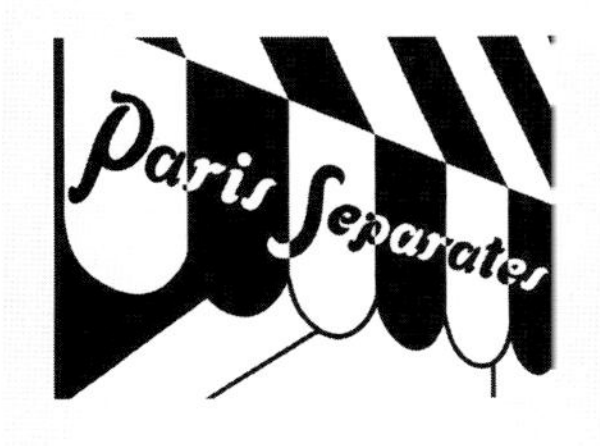

36

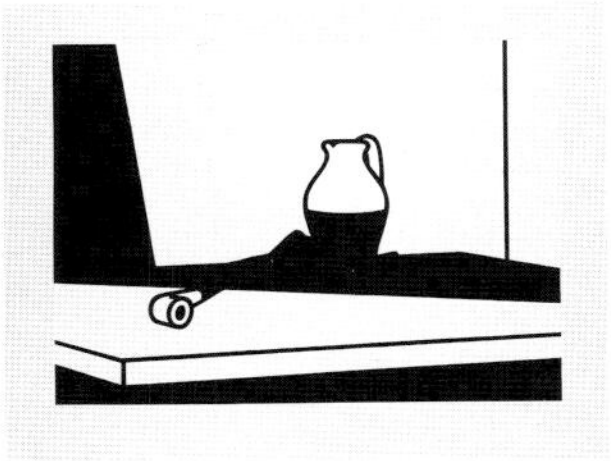

37

1973

30 **Night Sky**
Screenprint
Paper and image 20.8 × 14.8 cm
Edition of 100 with 15 proofs
Printed at Advanced Graphics, London
Published in the 'Eighteen Small Prints' portfolio by Bernard Jacobson, London

31 **Black and White Café**
Screenprint
Paper and image 91.2 × 71.0 cm
Edition of 75 with 15 proofs
Printed at Kelpra Studio, London
Published in 'The Rothko Memorial Portfolio' by Matthews, Miller & Dunbar, for the Mark Rothko Memorial Fund

32 **Tulips**
33 **Coat Stand**
34 **Curtain and Bottle**
35 **Spider Plant**
36 **Paris Separates**
37 **Pipe and Jug**
A series of six screenprints
Paper and image 72.8 × 95.0 cm
Edition of 72 with 15 proofs (of each)
Printed at Kelpra Studio, London
Published by Waddington Graphics, London

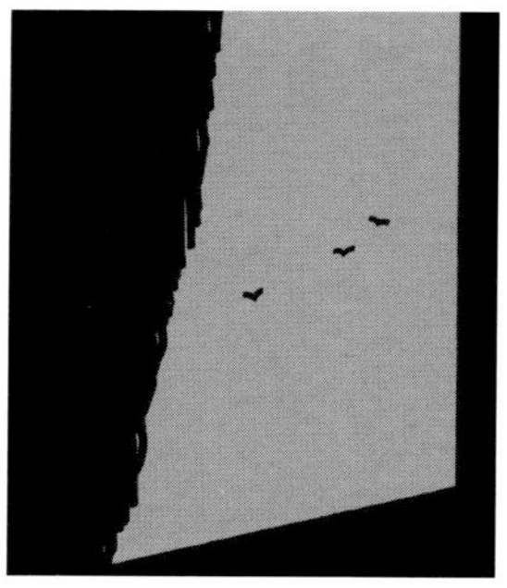
38a

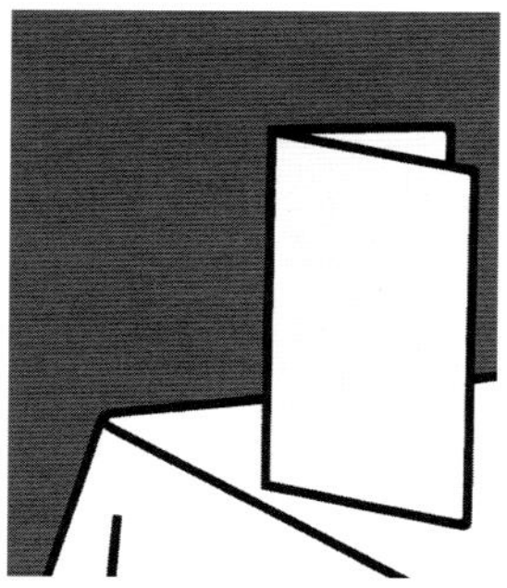
38b

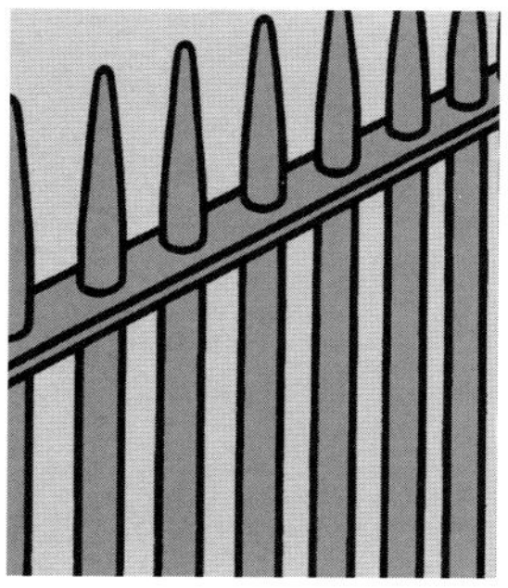
38c

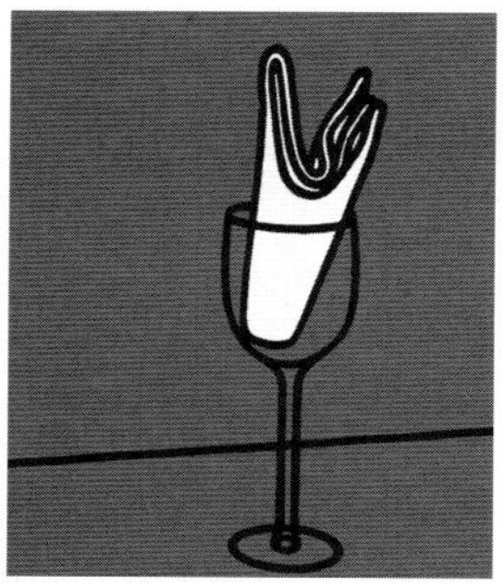
38d

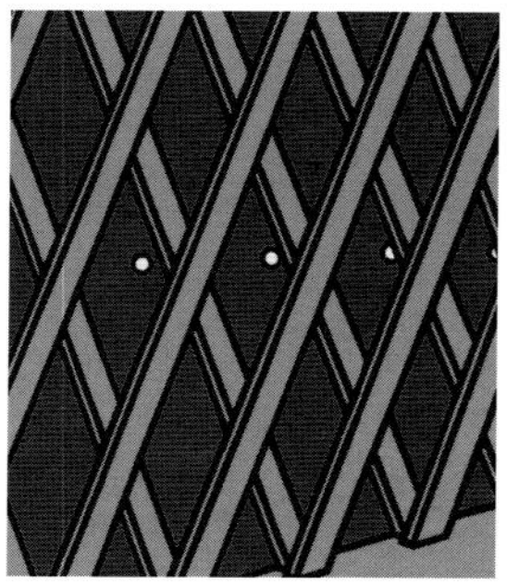
38e

38f

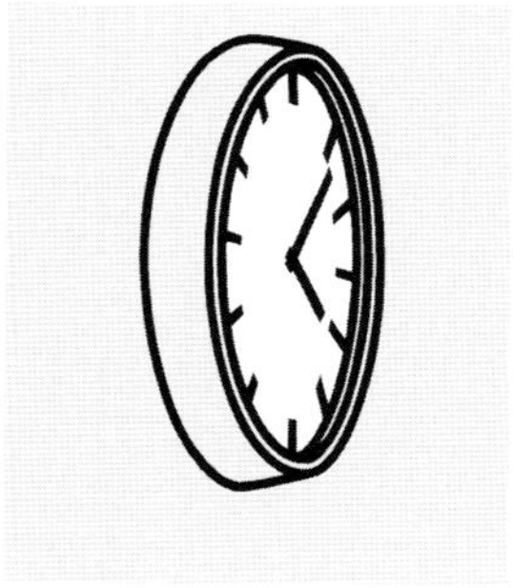
38g

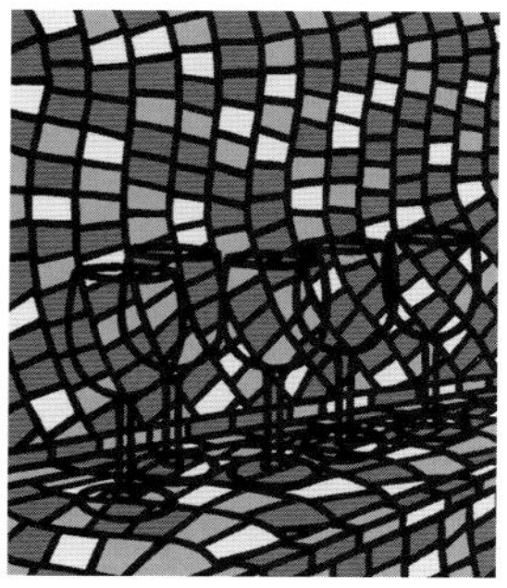
38h

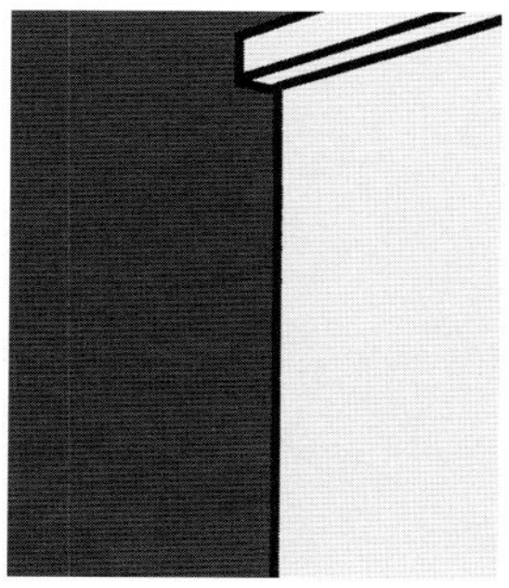
38i

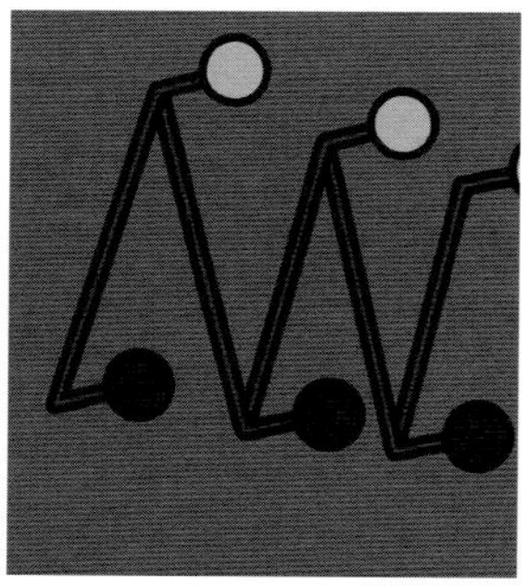
38j

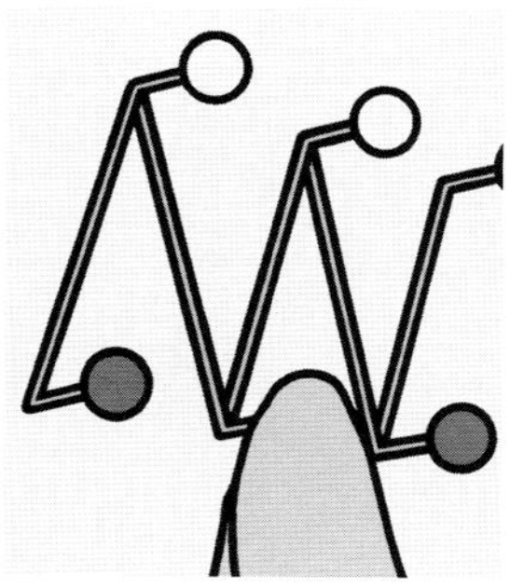
38k

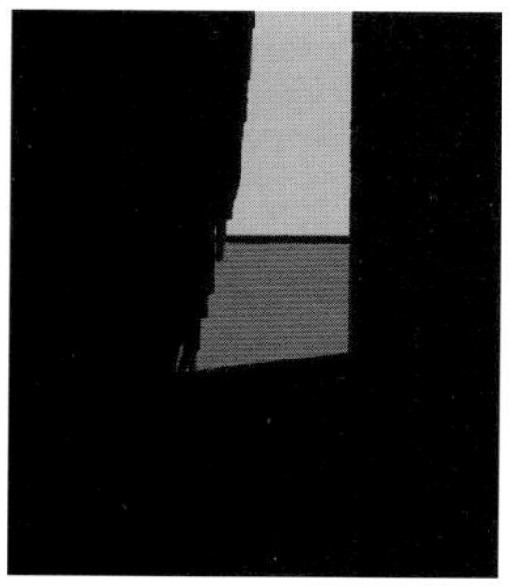
38l

38 **Some Poems of Jules Laforgue**
A book of twenty-two screenprinted illustrations for twelve poems in three varying editions
Proofed by Advanced Graphics, London, and editioned by Frank Kicherer, Stuttgart
Books, sleeves, slipcases, and portfolios bound in full leather by Rudolph Rieser, Cologne
Published by Petersburg Press in association with Waddington Galleries, London

38a **1 Ah! this Life is so everyday**
38b **2 Watch me eat, without appetite, à la carte**
38c **3 She fled along the avenue**
38d **4 Her handkerchief swept me along the Rhine**
38e **5 I'll take my life monotonous**
38f **6 You'll be sick if you spend all your time indoors**
38g **7 Crying to the walls: My God! My God! will she relent?**
38h **8 All these confessions . . .**
38i **9 Making circles on park lagoons**
38j **10 Oh! if one of Them, some fine evening, would try**
38k **11 Thus she would come, escaped, half-dead to my door**
38l **12 And, with my eyes bolting toward the Unconscious**
38m **13 We wanted to bleed the Silence**
38n **14 Along a twilighted sky**
38o **15 Oh Helen, I roam my room**
38p **16 I've only the friendship of hotel rooms**

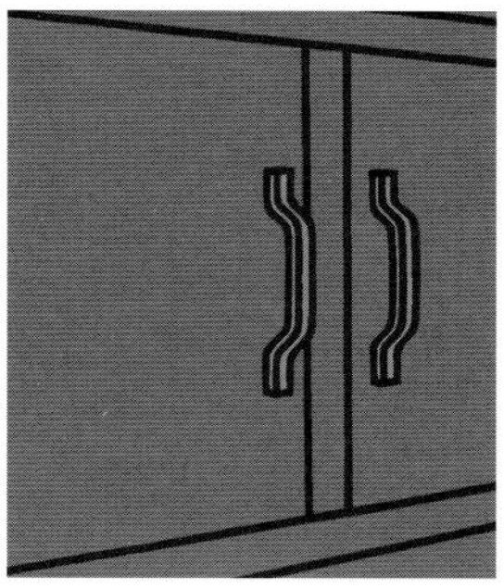
38m

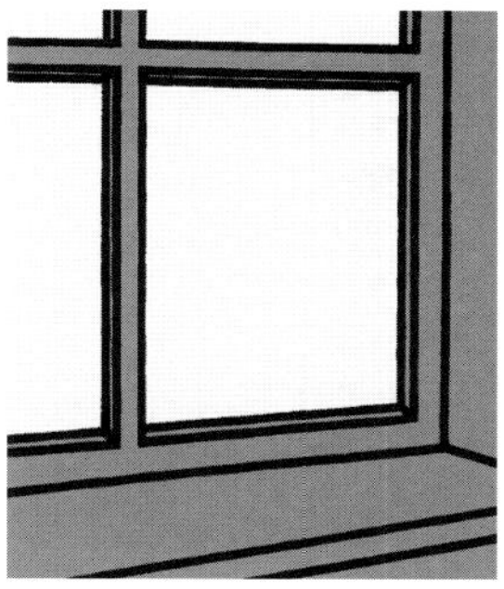
38n

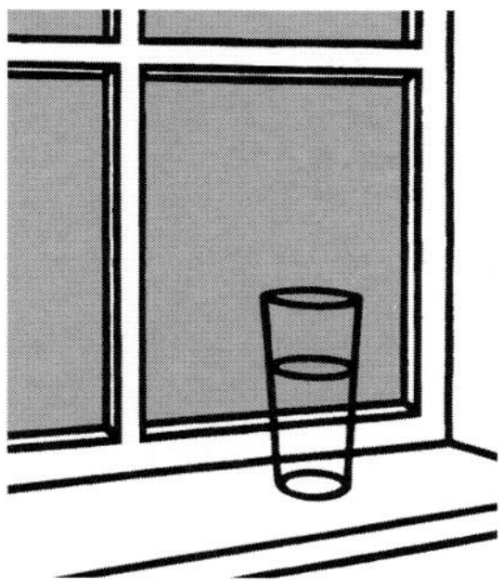
38o

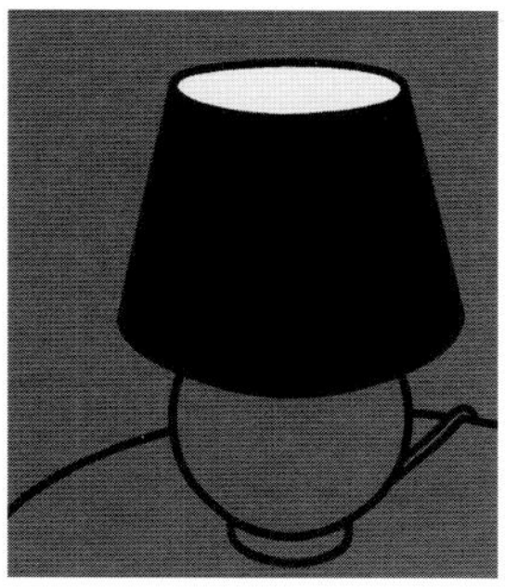
38p

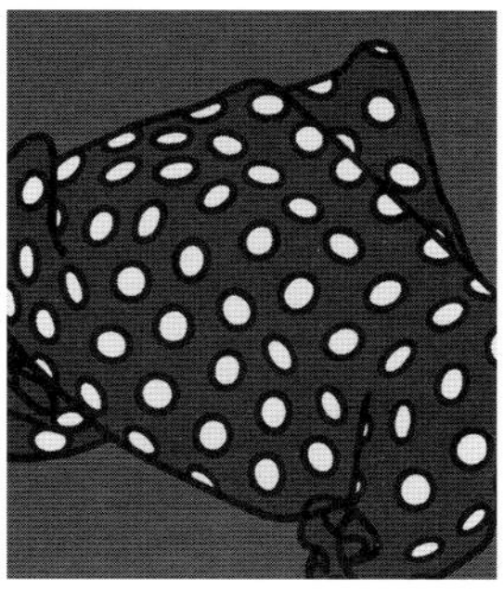
38q

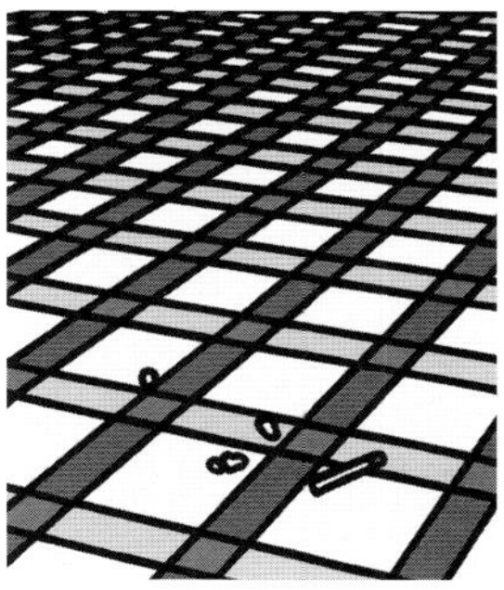
38r

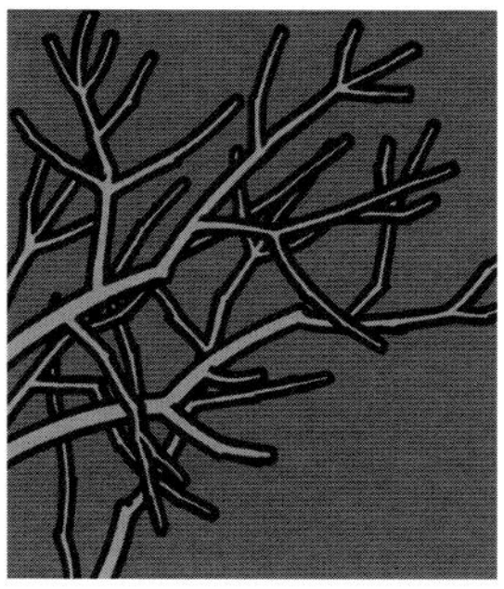
38s

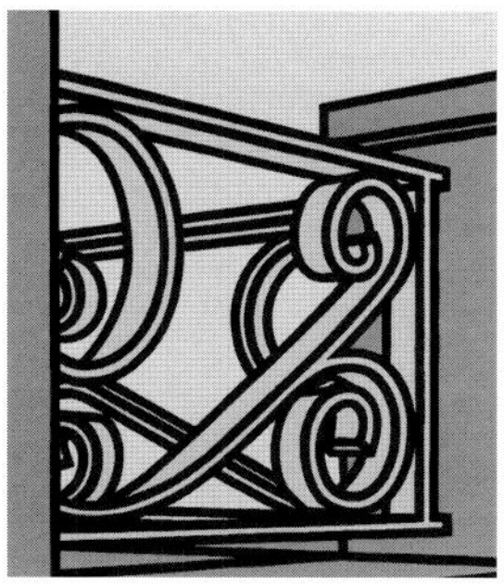
38t

38u

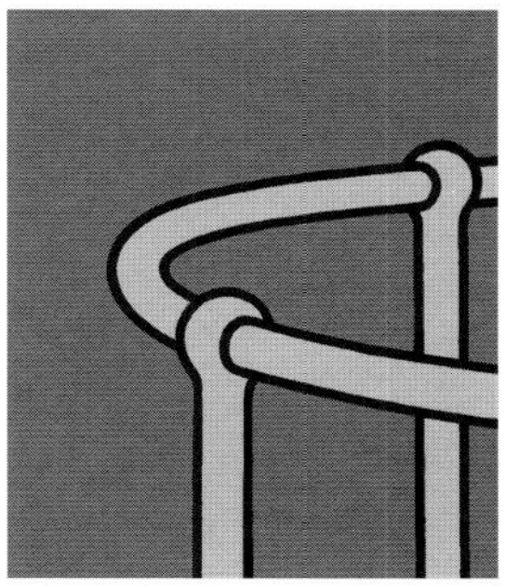
38v

38q **17 She'll have forgotten her scarf**
38r **18 And I am alone in my house**
38s **19 All the benches are wet, the woods are so rusty**
38t **20 Ah! storm clouds rushed from the Channel coasts**
38u **21 Curtains drawn back from balconies of shores**
38v **22 My life inspires so many desires!**

Edition A
The book in English together with a slip case containing six signed loose prints **(1, 3, 6, 8, 15, 17)**
Paper and image 40.5 × 35.5 cm
Edition of 200 with 20 proofs

Edition B
The book with the original French text together with a slip case containing six signed loose prints **(4, 5, 16, 18, 20, 22)**
Paper and image 40.5 × 35.5 cm
Edition of 200 with 20 proofs

Edition C
The book in English together with a portfolio of all twenty-two signed images printed on paper with wide margins
Paper 61.0 × 56.0 cm / Image 40.5 × 35.5 cm
Edition of 100 with 20 proofs

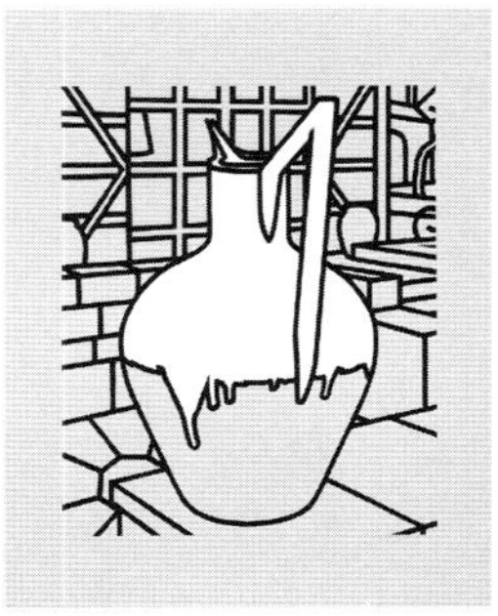
39

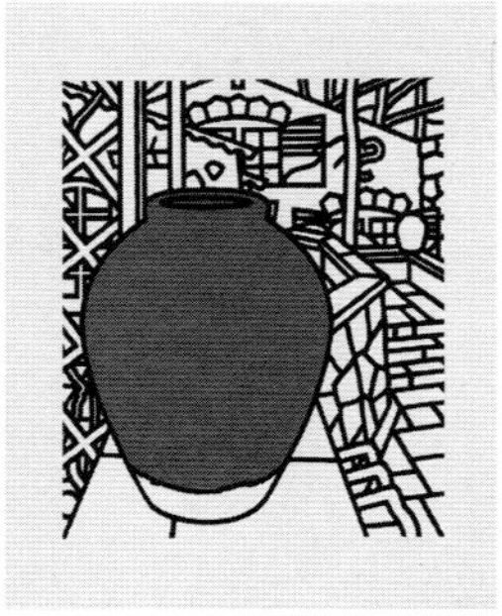
40

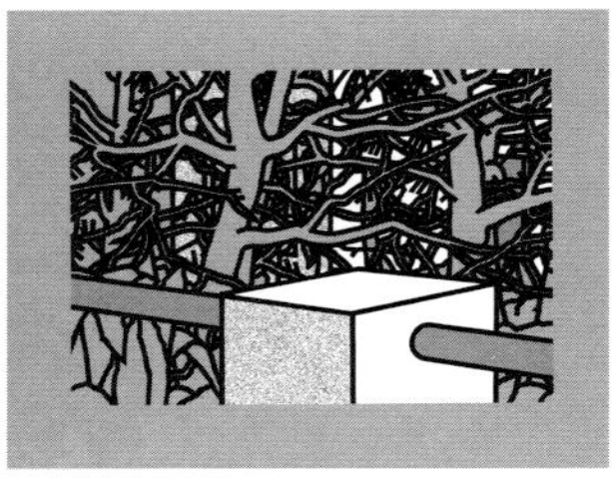
41

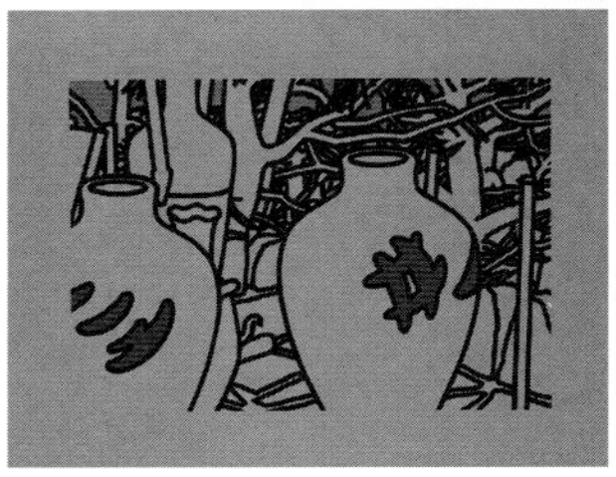
42

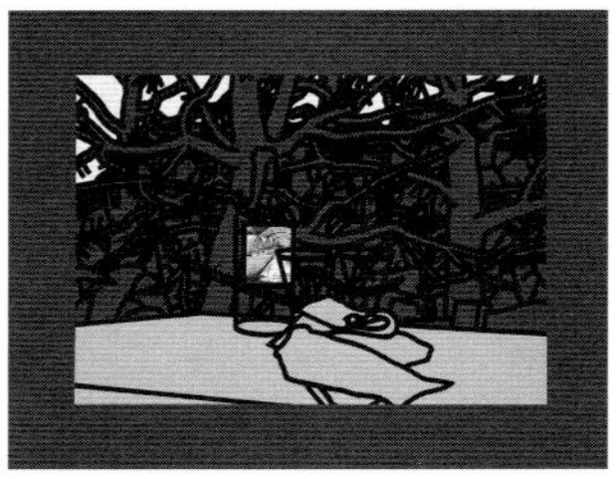
43

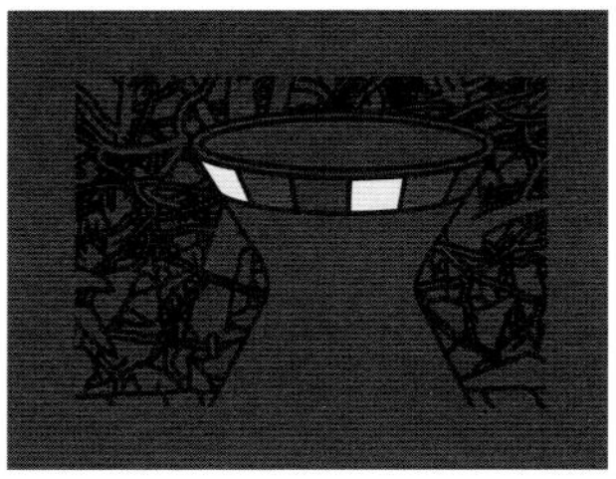
44

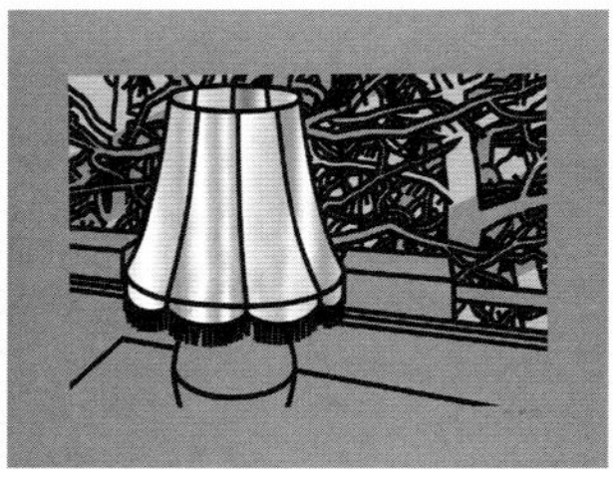
45

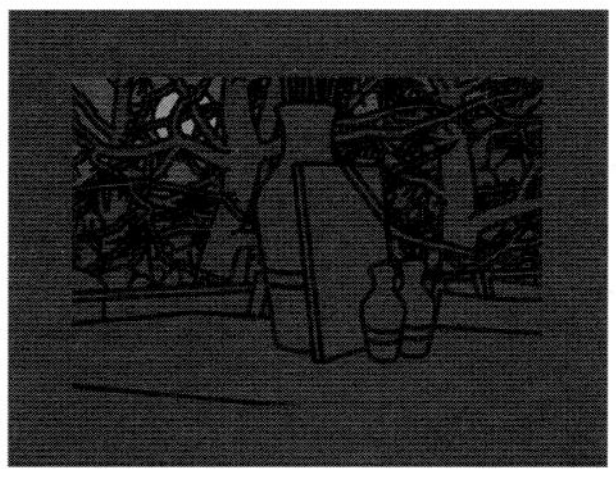
46

1974

39 **Jug**
40 **Jar**
A pair of screenprints
Paper and image 87.6 × 71.1 cm
Edition of 70 with 15 proofs (of each)
Printed at Kelpra Studio, London
Published by Waddington Graphics, London

1975

41 **Garden with Pines**
42 **Signature Pots**
43 **Rosé Bottle**
44 **Terracotta Vase**
45 **Lamp and Pines**
46 **Evening Menu**
A series of six screenprints
Paper and image 77.3 × 102.6 cm
Edition of 70 with 15 proofs (of each)
Printed at Kelpra Studio, London
Published by Waddington Graphics, London

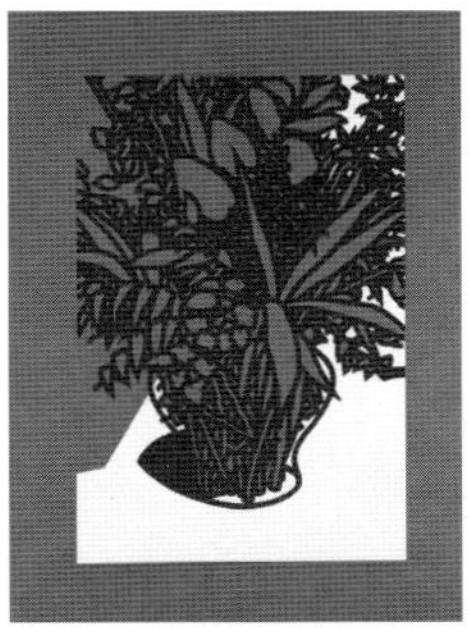

47

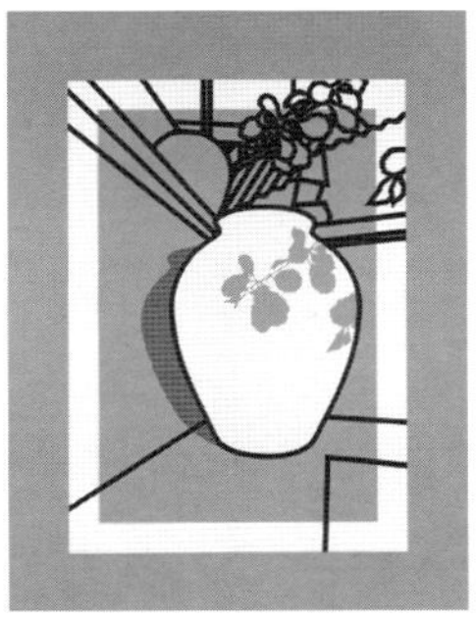

48

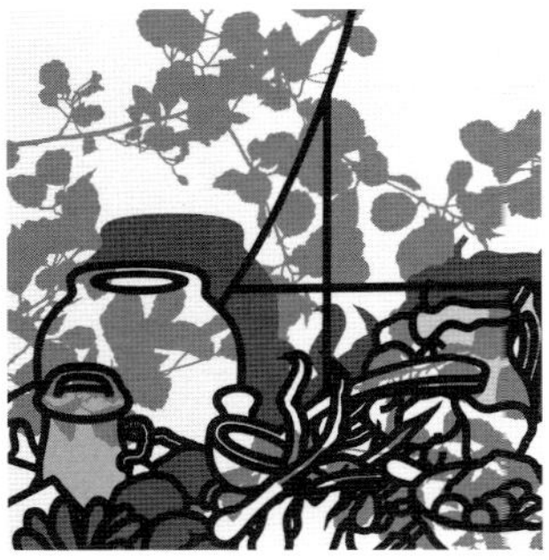

49

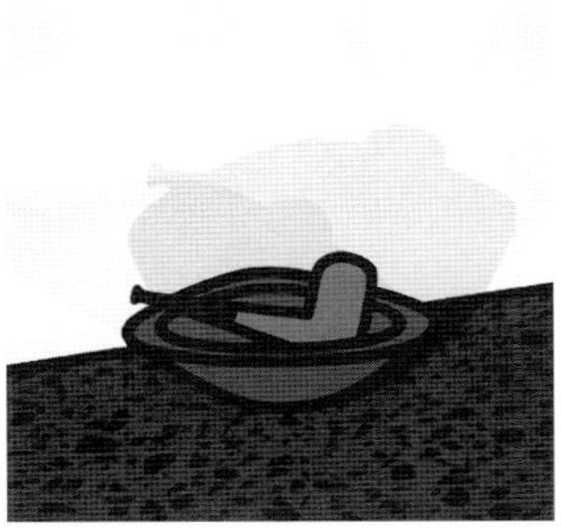

50

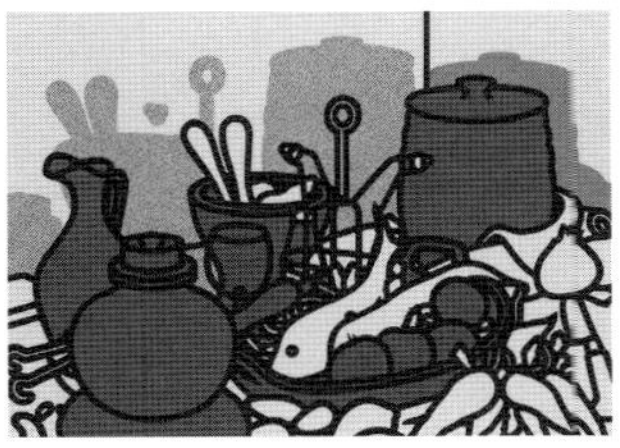

51

1976

47 **For John Constable**
Screenprint
Paper and image 102.5 × 77.2 cm
Edition of 100 with 15 proofs
Printed at Advanced Graphics, London
Published in the 'For John Constable' portfolio
by Bernard Jacobson, London

48 **White Pot**
Screenprint
Paper and image 98.2 × 77.3 cm
Edition of 76 with 15 proofs
Printed at Kelpra Studio, London
Published by Waddington Graphics, London

49 **Still Life Ingredients**
Screenprint
Paper 71.1 × 71.1 cm / Image 53.2 × 53.4 cm
Edition of 76 with 15 proofs
Printed at Kelpra Studio, London
Published by Waddington Graphics, London

50 **Pipe in Bowl**
Screenprint
Paper 58.4 × 58.4 cm / Image 40.6 × 40.6 cm
Edition of 76 with 15 proofs
Printed at Kelpra Studio, London
Published by Waddington Graphics, London

51 **Glazed Earthenware**
Screenprint
Paper 77.2 × 99.3 cm / Image 54.4 × 76.6 cm
Edition of 76 with 15 proofs
Printed at Kelpra Studio, London
Published by Waddington Graphics, London

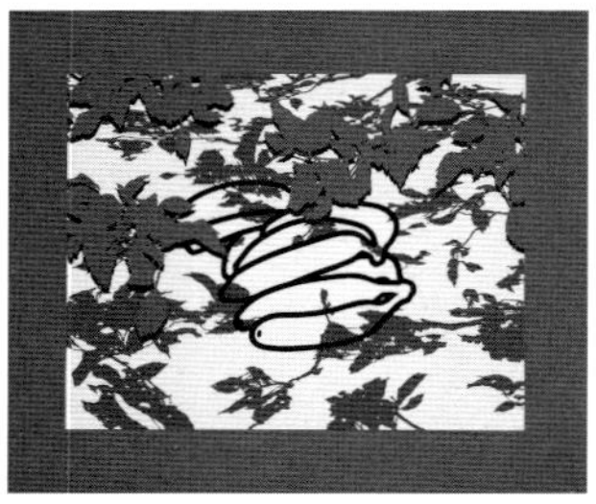

52

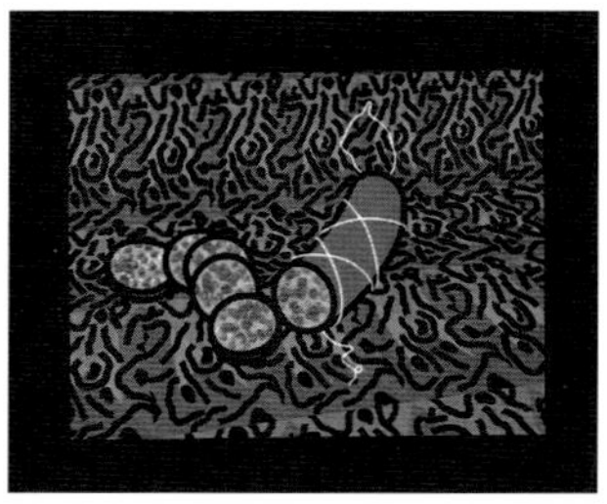

53

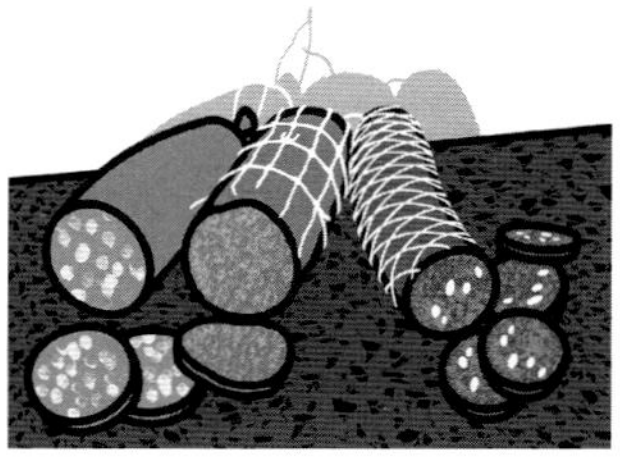

54

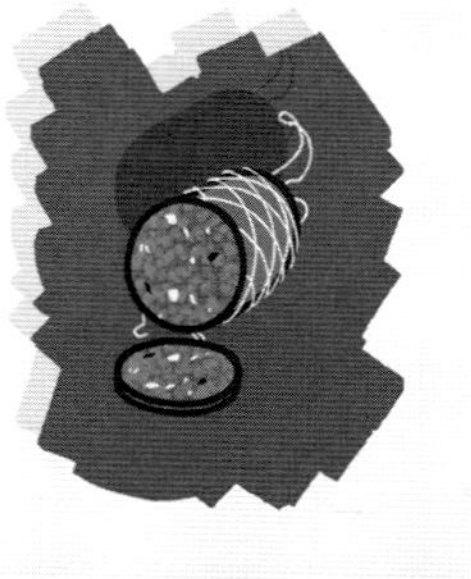

55

1977

52 **Bananas with Leaves**
Screenprint
Paper and image 74.5 × 91.0 cm
Edition of 75 with 15 proofs
Printed at Kelpra Studio, London
Published by Waddington Graphics, London

1978

53 **Sausage**
Screenprint
Paper and image 74.4 × 91.2 cm
Edition of 75 with 15 proofs
Printed at Kelpra Studio, London
Published by Waddington Graphics, London

54 **Three Sausages**
Screenprint
Paper 74.5 × 91.3 cm / Image 54.4 × 70.8 cm
Edition of 75 with 15 proofs
Printed at Kelpra Studio, London
Published by Waddington Graphics, London

55 **Big Sausage**
Screenprint
Paper and image 89.7 × 74.4 cm
Edition of 75 with 15 proofs
Printed at Kelpra Studio, London
Published by Waddington Graphics, London

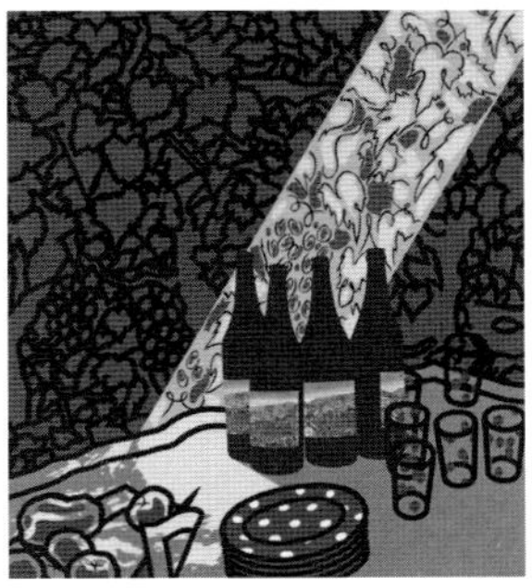

56

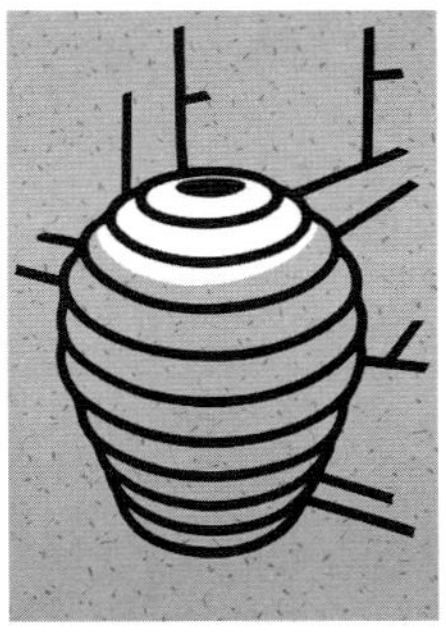

58

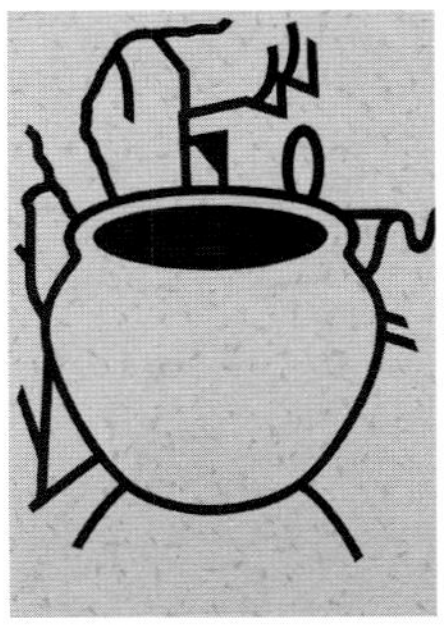

59

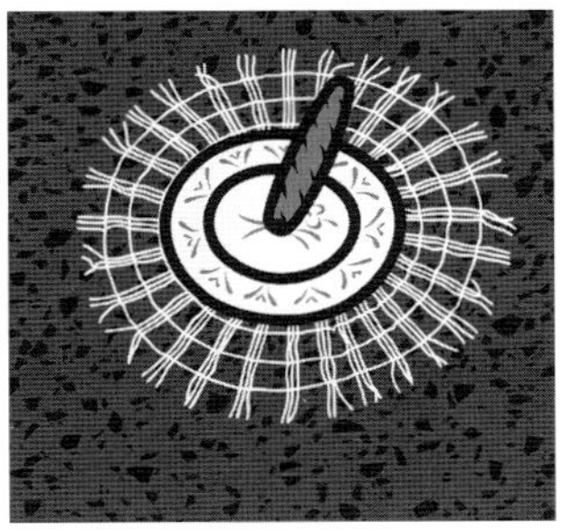

57

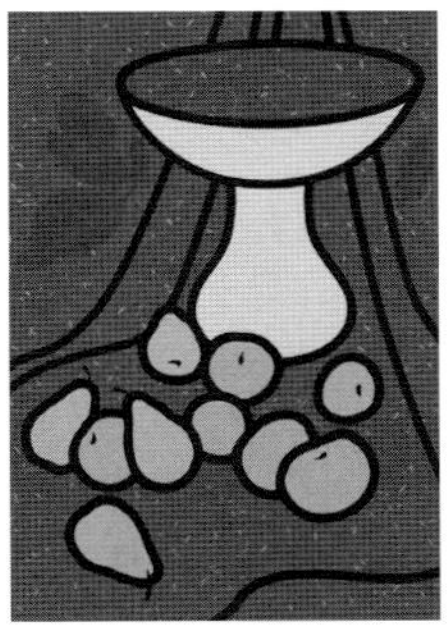

60

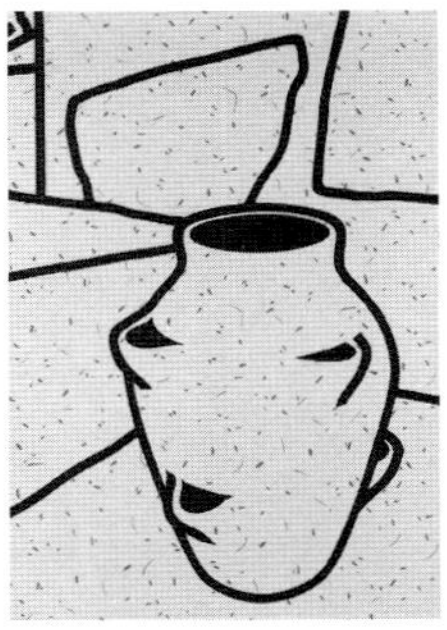

61

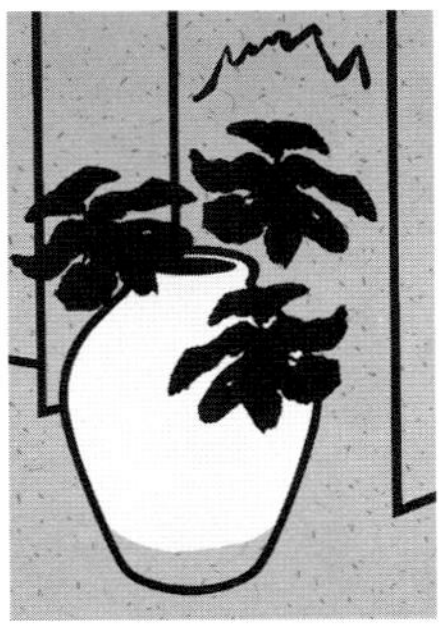

62

56 **Picnic Set**
Screenprint
Paper and image 91.2 × 86.0 cm
Edition of 100 with 15 proofs
Printed at Kelpra Studio, London
Published by Waddington Graphics, London

57 **Cigar**
Screenprint
Paper 57.5 × 60.8 cm / Image 44.8 × 48.0 cm
Edition of 75 with 15 proofs
Printed at Kelpra Studio, London
Published by Waddington Graphics, London

1979-80

58 **Ridged Jar**
Edition of 40 with 10 proofs

59 **Fern Pot**
Edition of 65 with 10 proofs

60 **Fruit and Bowl**
Edition of 100 with 15 proofs

61 **Plant Pot**
Edition of 100 with 15 proofs

62 **Cream Glazed Pot**
Edition of 100 with 15 proofs
A series of five screenprints
Paper and image 83.8 × 59.6 cm
Printed at Kelpra Studio, London
Published by Waddington Graphics, London

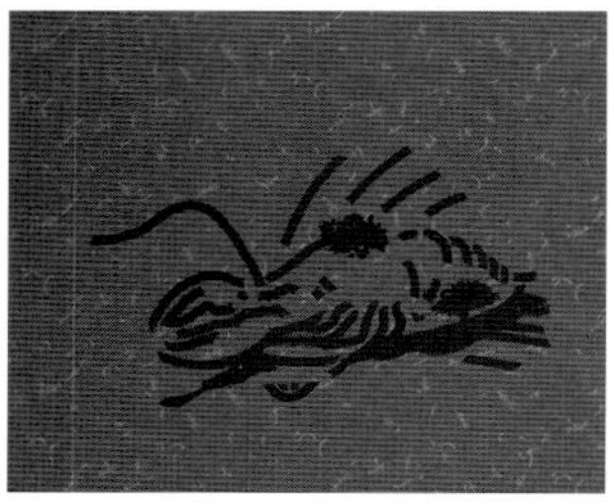

63

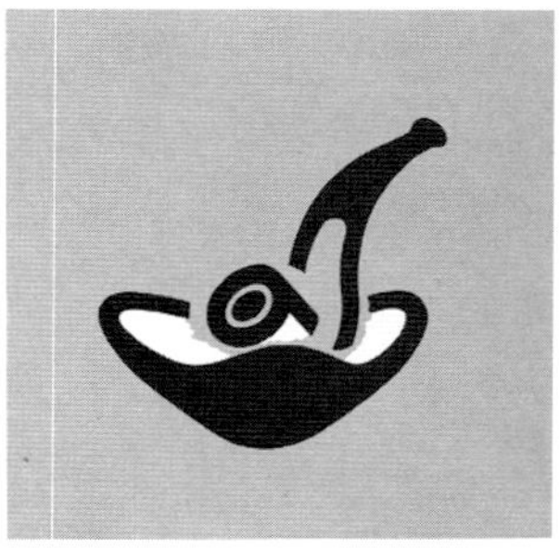

64

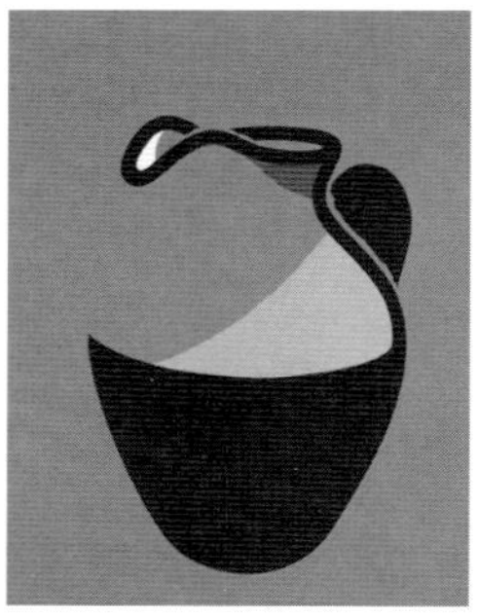

65

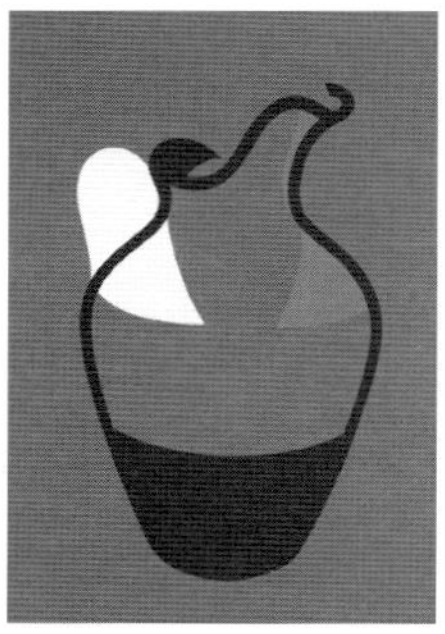

66

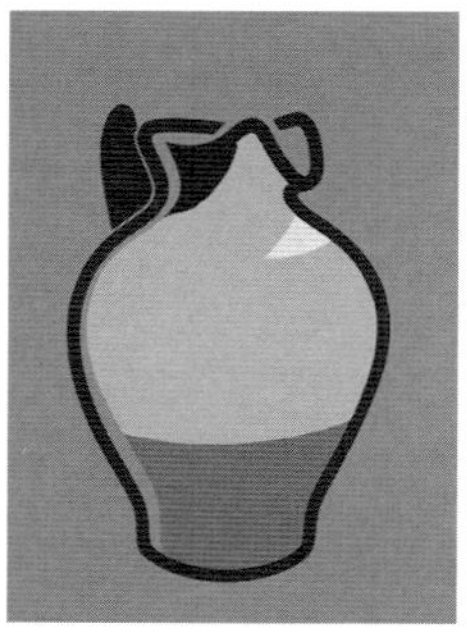

67

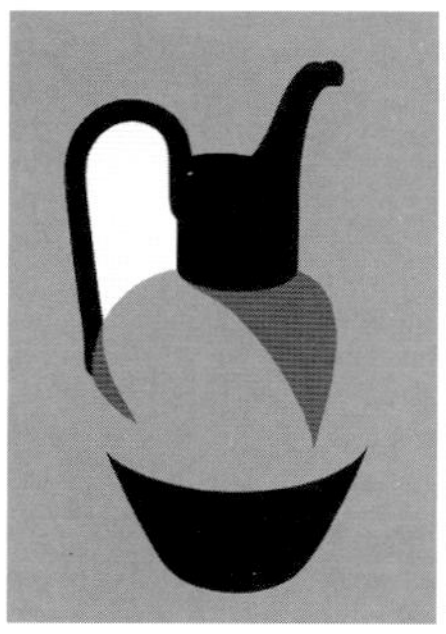

68

1980

63 **Dressed Lobster**
Screenprint
Paper and image 60.0 × 75.0 cm
Edition of 150 with 15 proofs
Printed at Kelpra Studio, London
Published in the 'Kelpra/Tate Gallery Portfolio' by Kelpra Studio in collaboration with the Tate Gallery and Waddington Graphics, London

1981

64 **Grey Pipe**
Screenprint
Paper 71.8 × 74.3 cm / Image 48.8 × 51.3 cm
Edition of 75 with 15 proofs
Printed at Kelpra Studio, London
Published by Waddington Graphics, London

1981-82

65 **Pink Jug**
Paper 98.6 × 80.3 cm / Image 76.1 × 59.7 cm
66 **Water Jug**
Paper 102.3 × 77.5 cm / Image 79.3 × 57.1 cm
67 **Brown Jug**
Paper 99.8 × 77.6 cm / Image 76.8 × 57.1 cm
68 **Pitcher**
Paper 102.0 × 77.6 cm / Image 79.2 × 57.1 cm
A series of four screenprints
Edition of 80 with 14 proofs (of each)
Printed at Kelpra Studio, London
Published by Waddington Graphics, London

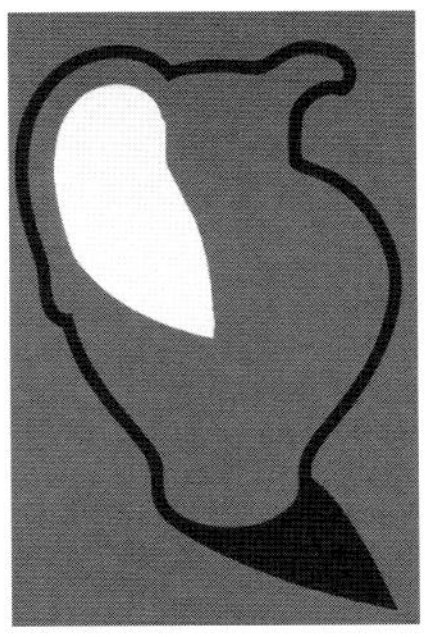

69

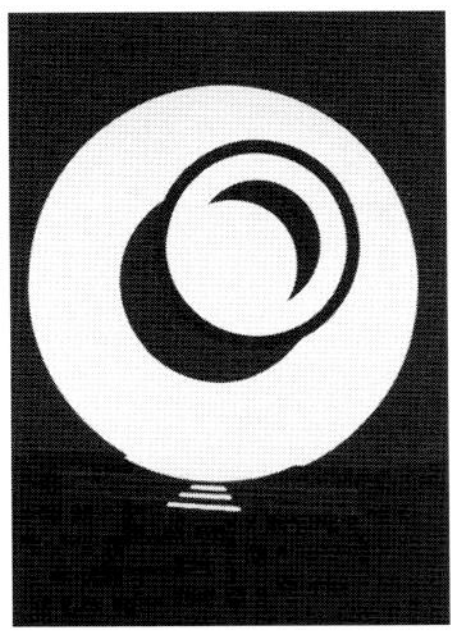

70

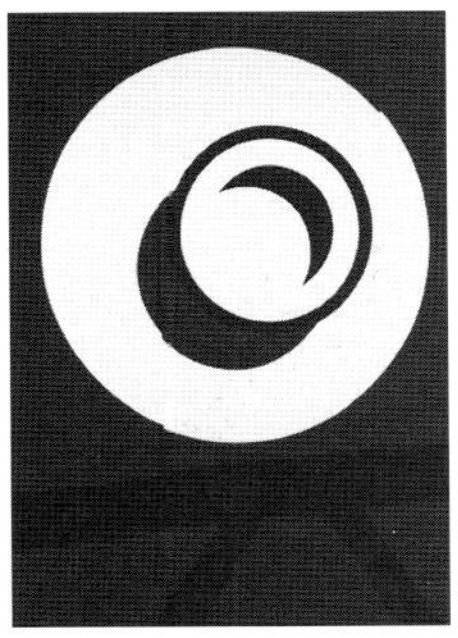

71

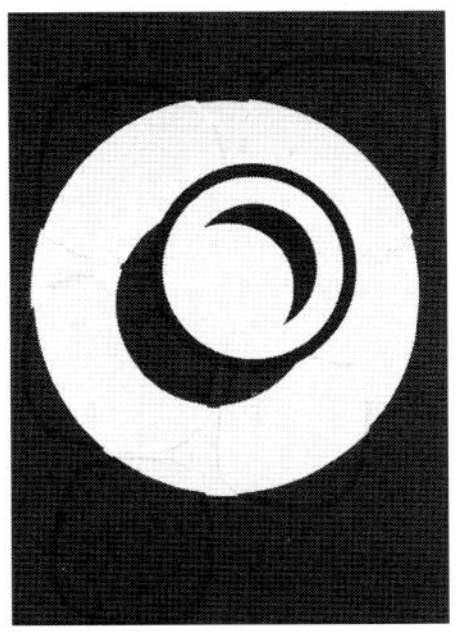

72

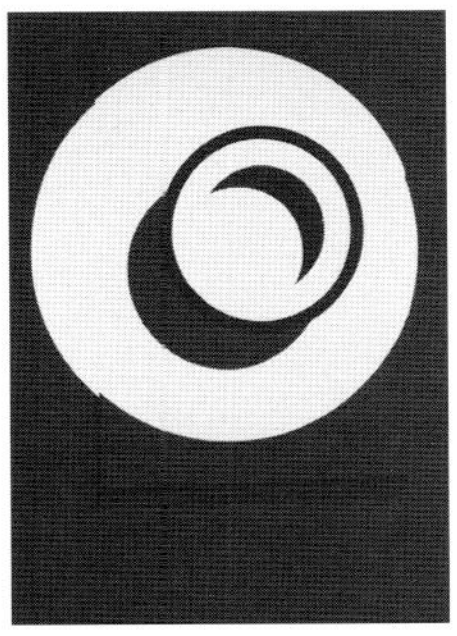

73

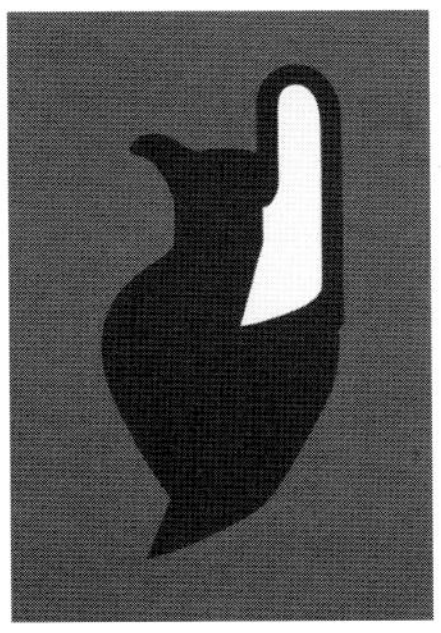

74

1983

69 **Large Jug**
Screenprint
Paper 116.5 × 83.8 cm / Image 93.3 × 63.3 cm
Edition of 80 with 14 proofs
Printed at Kelpra Studio, London
Published by Waddington Graphics, London

1987

Wall Plates
70 **Wall Plate: Highlights**
71 **Wall Plate: Stucco**
72 **Wall Plate: Stones**
73 **Wall Plate: Screen**
A set of four screenprints
Paper 129.4 × 101.5 cm / Image 104.0 × 76.0 cm
Edition of 50 with 10 proofs (of each)
Printed at Kelpra Studio, London
Published by Waddington Graphics, London

74 **Vessel**
Screenprint
Paper 116.0 × 87.2 cm / Image 94.2 × 65.5 cm
Edition of 35 with 15 proofs
Printed at Kelpra Studio, London
Published by Waddington Graphics, London

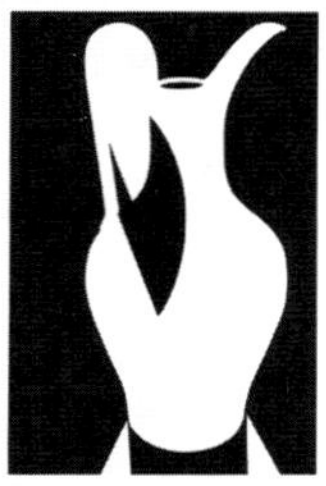

75

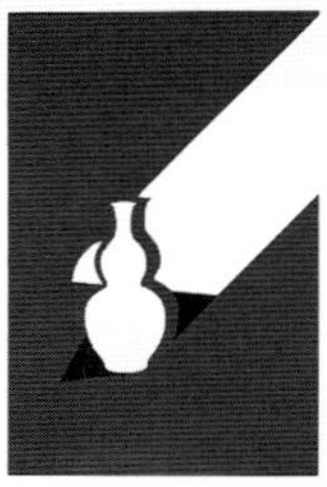

76

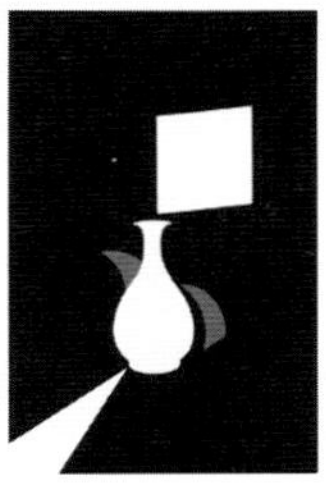

77

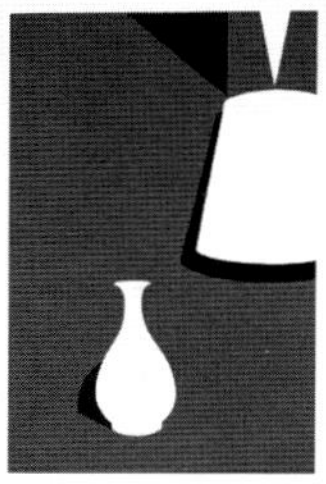

78

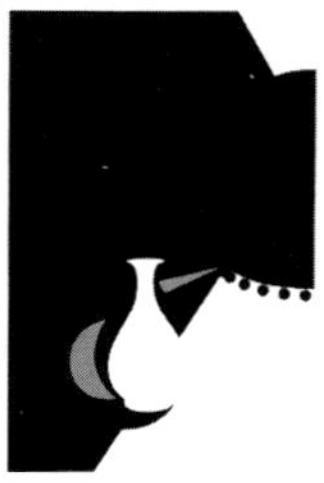

79

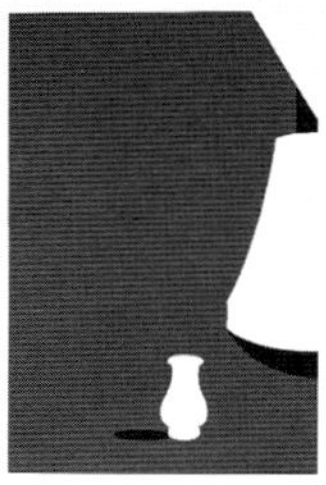

80

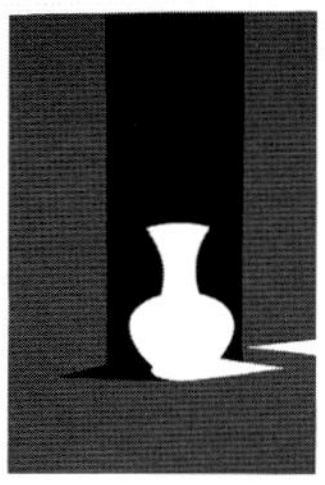

81

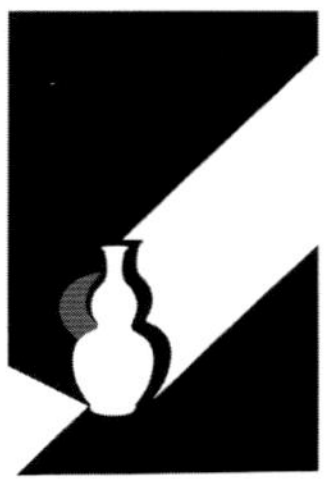

82

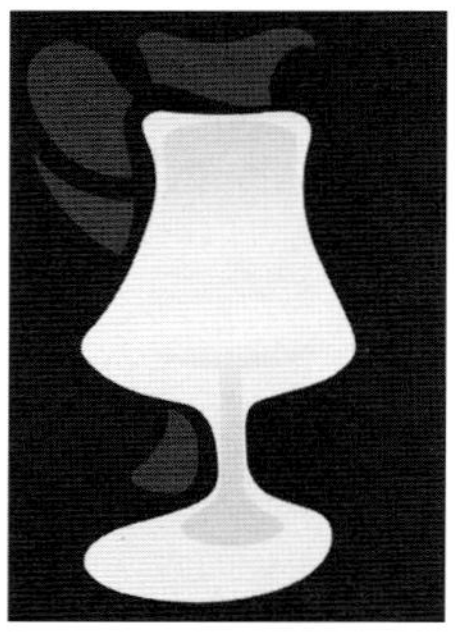

83

1990

White Ware Prints
75 **Large White Jug**
76 **Arita Flask**
77 **Lung Ch'uan Ware and Window**
78 **Lamp and Lung Ch'uan Ware**
79 **Lung Ch'uan Ware and Black Lamp**
80 **Lamp and Kuan Ware**
81 **Sue Ware Jar**
82 **Arita Flask-black**
A set of eight screenprints
Paper and image 107.2 × 81.1 cm
Edition of 45 with 13 proofs (of each)
Printed at Advanced Graphics, London
Published by Waddington Graphics, London

1992

83 **Red Jug and Lamp**
Screenprint
Paper 77.3 × 59.2 cm / Image 59.5 × 44.5 cm
Edition of 150 with 15 proofs
Printed at Advanced Graphics, London
Published by Waddington Graphics for The Serpentine Gallery, London

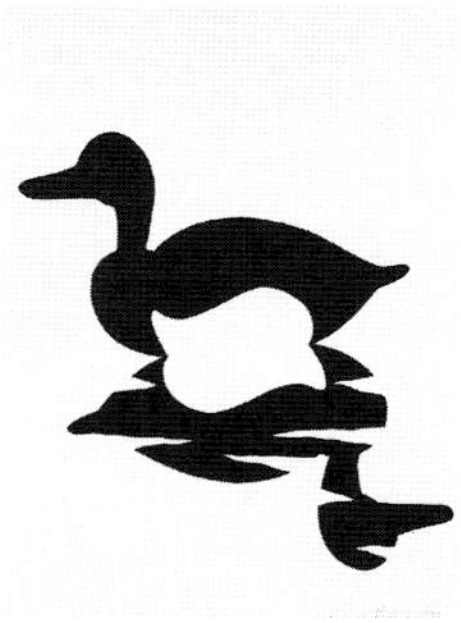

84

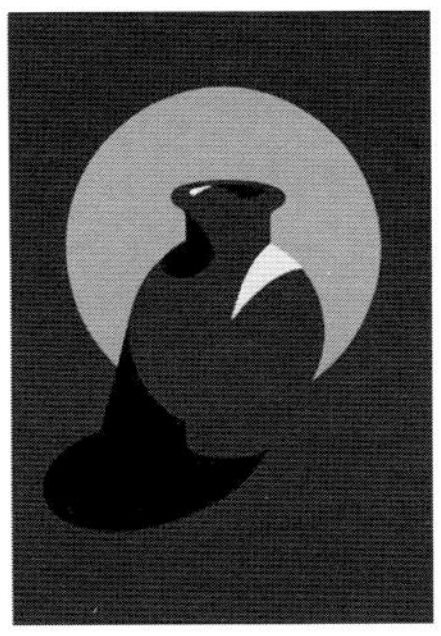

85

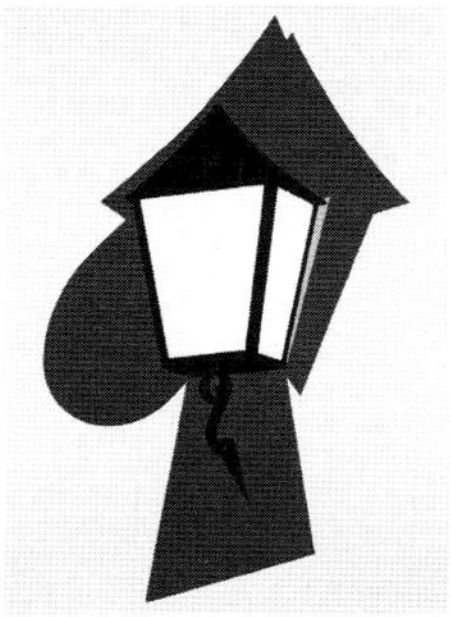

86

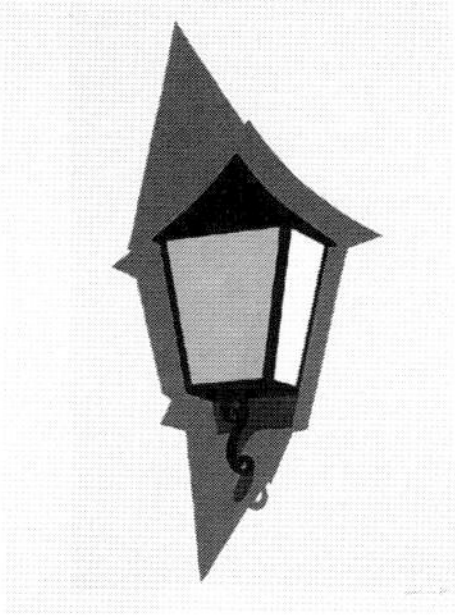

87

1994

84 **Duck**
Screenprint
Paper and image 40.3 × 30.3 cm
Edition of 80 with XX proofs
Printed at Byam Shaw School of Art, London
Published in the 'Nine London Birds' portfolio by Byam Shaw School of Art, London

85 **Brown Pot**
Screenprint
Paper 94.0 × 69.8 cm / Image 73.5 × 52.0 cm
Edition of 80 with 10 proofs
Printed at Advanced Graphics, London
Published by Advanced Graphics and Waddington Graphics, London

86 **Wall Lamp**
Screenprint
Paper and image 76.0 × 56.0 cm
Edition of 50 with 20 proofs
Printed at the Printmaking Workshop of The Royal College of Art, London
Published in 'Six Artists, The 1994 Royal College of Art Portfolio of Prints' by The Royal College of Art Printmaking Course, London

87 **Coach Lamp**
Screenprint
Paper 103.6 × 76.0 cm / Image 81.0 × 55.6 cm
Edition of 50 with 15 proofs
Printed at the Printmaking Workshop of The Royal College of Art, London
Published by Waddington Graphics, London

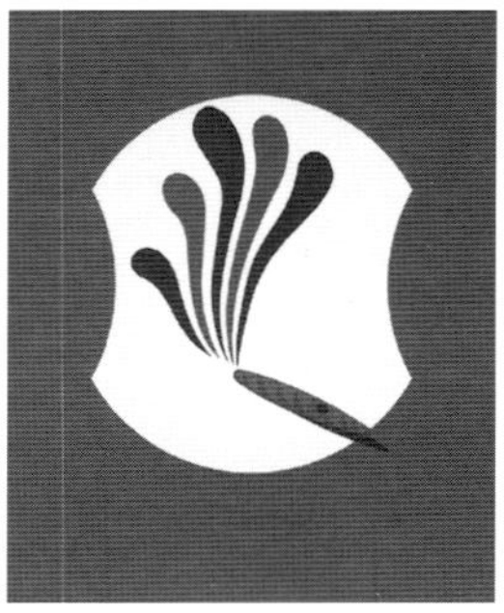

88

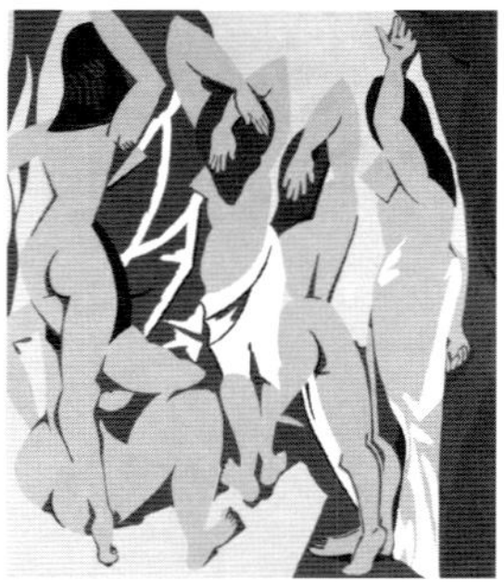

90

89

1997

88 **Freud's Smoke**
Screenprint
Paper and image 61.0 × 50.8 cm
Edition of 100 with 29 proofs
Printed at Gresham Studio, Cambridge
Published in 'The Freud Museum Tenth Anniversary Portfolio' by The Freud Museum, London

1999

89 **Two Fish on a Plate**
Lithograph
Paper and image 20.0 × 25.0 cm
Edition of 50
Printed by Alan Cox at Sky Editions, London
Published by Alan Cristea Gallery, London

An additional unsigned and unlimited quantity printed on different paper are to be distributed to subscribers of Contemporary Visual Arts Magazine with the April 1999 issue

90 **Les Demoiselles d'Avignon vues de Derrière**
Screenprint
Paper 132.1 × 111.7 cm / Image 106.2 × 92.2 cm
Edition of 65 with 14 proofs
Printed by Advanced Graphics, London
Published by Alan Cristea Gallery, London

Illustration taken from Patrick Caulfield's design for the print